ANTHROPOLOGICAL PAPERS
MUSEUM OF ANTHROPOLOGY, THE UNIVERSITY OF MICHIGAN
No. 19

MISCELLANEOUS STUDIES IN TYPOLOGY AND CLASSIFICATION

by
ANTA M. WHITE
LEWIS R. BINFORD
MARK L. PAPWORTH

ANN ARBOR
THE UNIVERSITY OF MICHIGAN, 1963

ISBN (print): 978-1-949098-26-6
ISBN (ebook): 978-1-951519-48-3

Browse all of our books at
sites.lsa.umich.edu/archaeology-books.

Order our books from the University of Michigan
Press at www.press.umich.edu.

For permissions, questions, or manuscript queries,
contact Museum publications by email at umma-pubs@umich.edu or visit the Museum website at
lsa.umich.edu/ummaa.

FOREWORD

The series of papers in this volume have a primary emphasis on the study of flint projectiles and other flint artfacts. Mrs. Anta White received her training in prehistory in France and in the Mediterranean basin. She began work in the Museum of Anthropology and was asked to study the Hopewell collection from the Snyders Site, Calhoun County, Illinois, applying her special training and experience. Her paper does not include the projectile points. These will be analysed in a future paper.

The paper, by Lewis H. Binford and Mark L. Papworth on the Eastport Site is the result of a detailed analysis of the available flint debris and artifacts, following a system developed by them under stimulus from Albert C. Spaulding. The Eastport Site was visited by J. B. Griffin and Papworth in the company of Edward Gillis and George Davis. Papworth, Gillis, and Davis excavated two pits, while Griffin excavated a smaller area, called, with some courtesy, Excavation Unit 3. Gillis and Davis very kindly turned over to the Museum of Anthropology their collection made at the site at an earlier date. Griffin and Papworth were intrigued by the Eastport site from the standpoint of the possible association with former lake beaches and then because of the indications that the cultural complex was deposited before the forest growth on the site. Binford's work on the identification and analysis of the techniques of flint work has benefited from his association with Joffre Coe at the University of North Carolina, from papers and studies by John Witthoft, and also from help provided by Mrs. White. David Taggart aided in the analysis of the material.

The Hodges site in Saginaw County has a predominant Late Woodland occupation which will be described at a later date. The special feature reported by Lewis Binford is a thousand years or so earlier, and seems to fit in rather well with the papers on the Eastport and Pomranky sites. The Pomranky site was called to our attention by Mr. Harold Moll, and we are indebted both to him and to the owner of the site for calling this find to our attention.

A portion of the support for the studies included in this volume was provided by the National Science Foundation and by the Wenner --Gren Foundation.

James B. Griffin
Museum of Anthropology

CONTENTS

ANALYTIC DESCRIPTION OF THE CHIPPED-STONE INDUSTRY FROM SNYDERS SITE CALHOUN COUNTY, ILLINOIS

Anta M. White

CONTENTS

Figures

Tables

INTRODUCTION

Cultural material presented in this paper is in the collections of the Museum of Anthropology, The University of Michigan. The largest part of the available assemblage was collected during two expeditions to the Snyders site, Calhoun County, Illinois. My thanks go to Lewis Binford for computing all of the statistical calculations for this paper. Part of the support for the analysis of this material was provided by the Wenner-Gren Foundation.

The following analysis will describe, from two standpoints, all of the flint artifacts collected at the Snyders site, with the exception of the projectile points. The two standpoints are: (*a*) the techniques of chipping and trimming selected raw materials, and (*b*) the different geometrical forms of the artifacts. Actually, the close interrelationship of technique and morphology gives an industry its characteristic features, since workmen attempt to produce flakes that can be modified easily into the eventual types of tools needed. On the other hand, the size and shape of a tool is related to the size and shape of the raw flake from which it is made. Consequently, waste or rejected flakes, which are the unfinished and broken pieces, furnish valuable information about chipping and retouching techniques. These have been included in the description and classification.

The word "industry" is applied here to the whole assemblage of chipped-stone artifacts which were found in one site and can be considered as a component.

Artifacts are segregated into groups on the basis of the descriptive attributes of the flakes used as raw materials, and of the type and placement of the retouching. Before going any further into a description of chipping and retouching techniques and an enumeration of the characteristics of each group, several terms will be defined. The following definitions deal with three different aspects of the chipped-stone industries. Nuclei and chipping rejects are considered first; second, the raw flakes and blades; and third, the utilized artifacts.

DEFINITIONS

A. Flaking

Raw materials applies to blocks of quarried flint, nodules, or water-worn pebbles which are collected for further chipping. Differences observed between chipping processes are sometimes related to the raw material utilized.

1. Primary flaking refers to the shaping of a block or nodule of flint into a core.

a) Primary flaking rejects are the flakes struck off the raw material to prepare a nucleus. The term *decortication flakes* applies to a particular form of primary-flaking reject. They are struck from a natural irregularity of a nodule or from a pebble and are detached transversely from one of the narrow ends. The surface of cleavage obtained in such a manner serves as a striking platform to take off a longitudinal flake. Cortex covers the entire outer face of these flakes. Since they are detached first, they are called *primary decortication flakes* (Fig. 1). When the cortex covers only a part of the outer face the flakes are called *secondary decortication flakes* (Fig. 2). The difference between primary and secondary decortication flakes is based on the fact that primary flakes were usually discarded. Secondary flakes were, in many instances, selected to be used as a naturally backed knife.

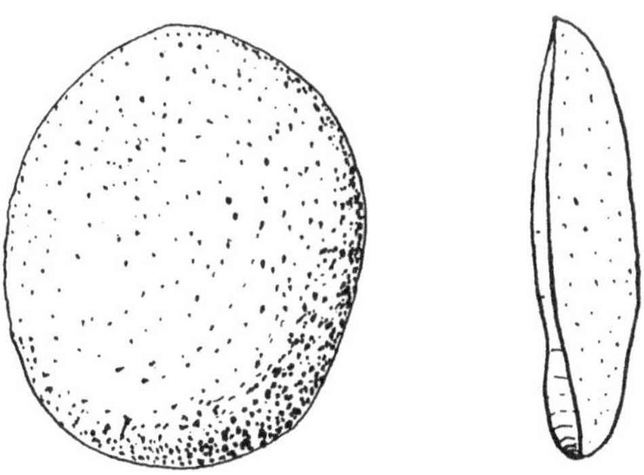

Fig. 1. Primary decortication flakes.

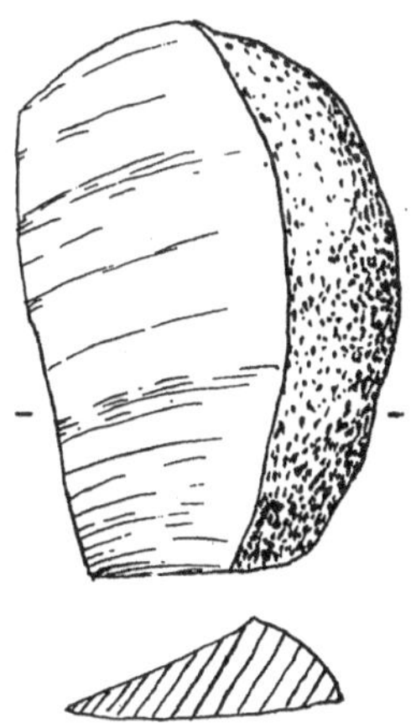

Fig. 2. Secondary decortication flakes.

b) The term *core* refers to a block, or nodule, from which flakes are detached.

Unprepared core is the term used when primary flaking is restricted to the preparation of a striking platform. There is no systematic shaping of the lateral edges. Flakes are struck by more-or-less flat flaking.

Prepared core differs from the preceding category by the presence of a systematic lateral preparation. Several processes of lateral preparation exist to shape the raw material into a pyramidal, discoidal, or conical form.

The *nucleus* is a waste or worn-out core from which no more flakes can be struck (Witthoft, 1957).

A single-ended core has only one striking platform; a double-ended core has two platforms prepared at two opposite ends.

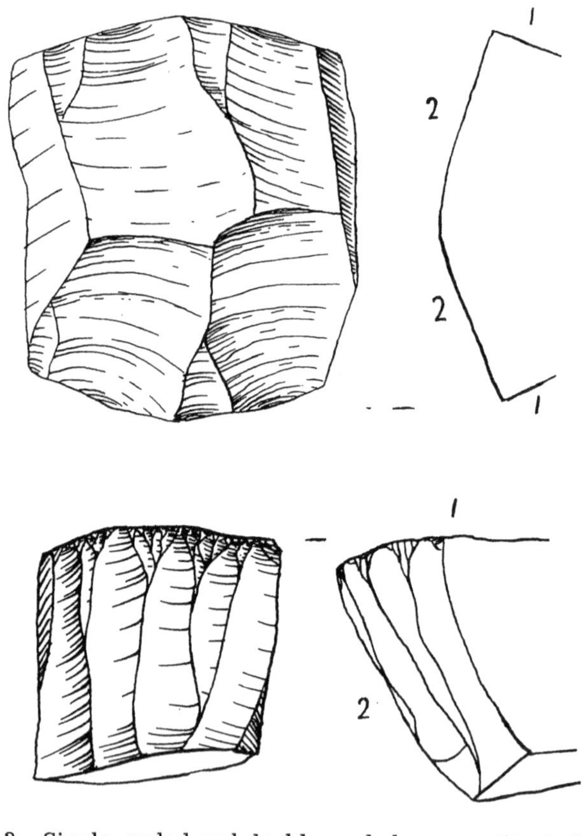

Fig. 3. Single-ended and double-ended cores: (1) striking platforms; (2) surfaces of cleavage.

Polymorphic core is the term applied to a form on which two or more adjacent platforms are prepared.

c) A block tool is one which is prepared from a block of flint by means of primary chipping. It is then ready for use as a tool without further alteration. Choppers and chopping tools are examples of block tools.

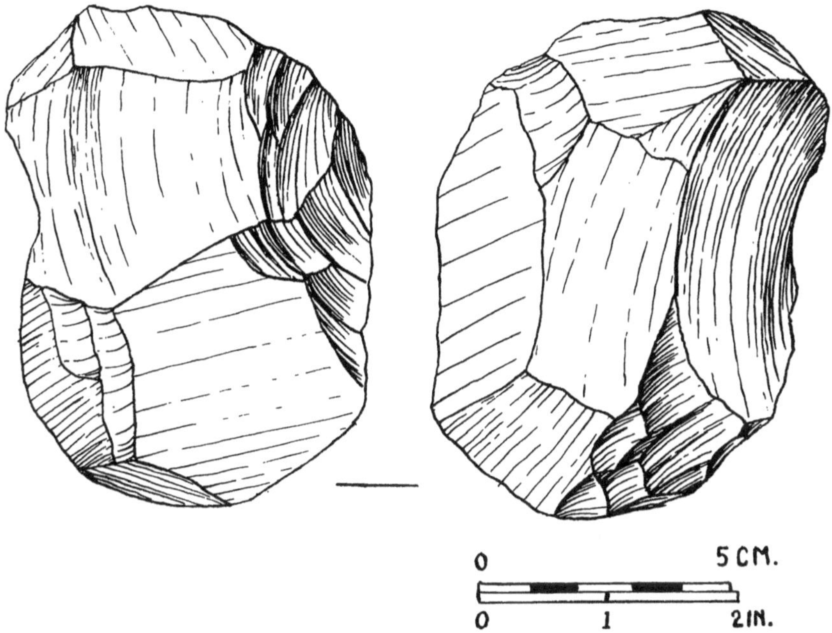

Fig. 4. Chopping tool. Specimen from Snyders site, surface collection.

2. Secondary Flaking refers to the processes of knapping flakes from a core. Definitions of flint-knapping processes are given by Witthoft (1957).

a) Blank flakes are those flakes selected to be modified into tools. Discarded flakes which were not suitable for use constitute the secondary-flaking rejects. The selection of flakes is characteristic of an assemblage, since one particular flake might be selected in one assemblage and discarded in another. Figure 5 shows the descriptive attributes of a flake.

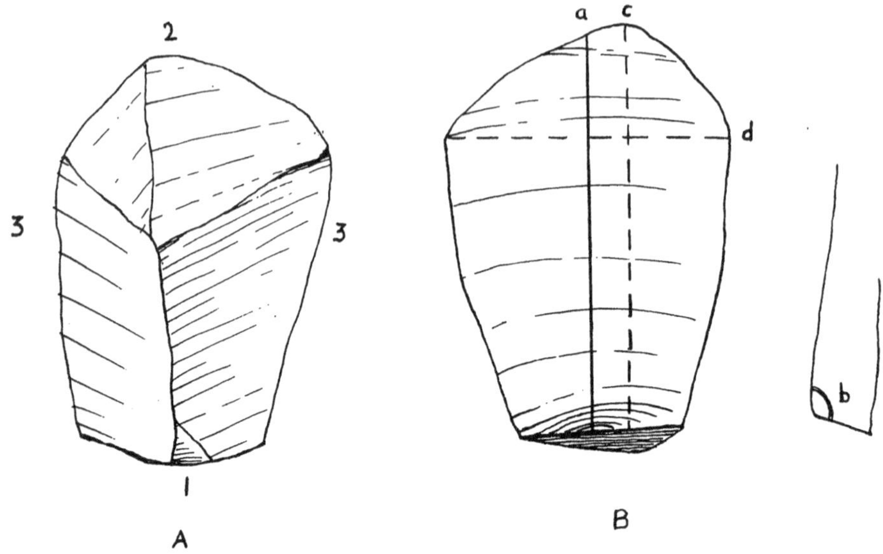

Fig. 5. Attributes of a flake: (A) outer face; (B) inner face; (a) axis of percussion; (b) striking angle; (c) axis of maximum length; (d) axis of maximum width; (1) proximal edge; (2) distal edge; (3) lateral edges.

b) The shape of a flake is described by considering the orientation of the lateral edges relative to the longitudinal axis with the proximal (bulbar) end as a reference point: (*a*) expanding, (*b*) converging, (*c*) parallel (Fig. 6).

Variations of the width-length ratio make possible differentiations between particular types of flakes such as, a *rectangular flake* with a w./1. ratio over .65, a *blade* with a w./1. ratio below .35 (Fig. 7).

It should be specified, however, that blade-like flakes occur in almost any assemblage. The use of the term *blade* should be restricted to the products of a systematic flaking technique. In that case, blades are the selected materials to be modified into tools. A large proportion of flakes exist in most of the so-called blade assemblages. For example, the relative proportion in Capsien and other blade industries of North Africa is one blade to 11 or 15 flakes.

The distinction between blades and bladelets is based on a bimodal distribution of measurements of length taken on an entire sample from a single industry.

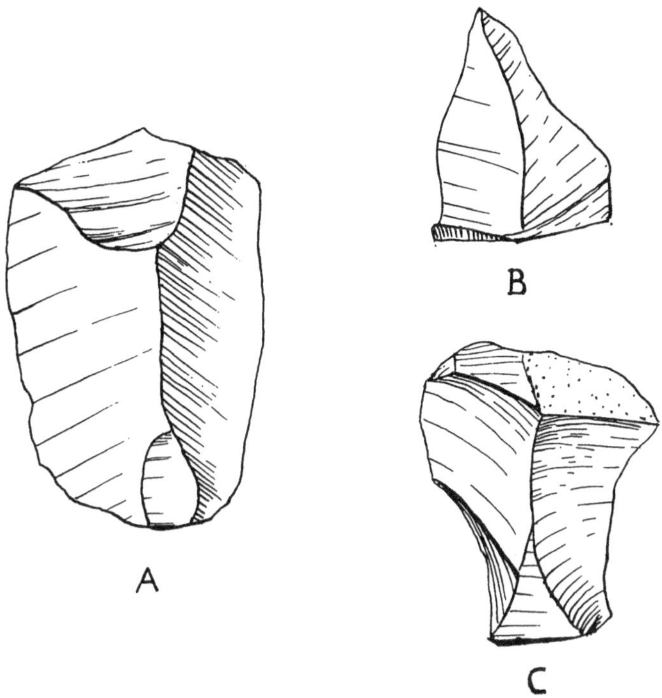

Fig. 6. Flake showing shape of lateral edges in relation to the longitudinal axis: (A) parallel edges; (B) contracting edges; (C) expanding edges.

B. Retouching

1. Marginal retouching is the term applied to any type of trimming, unifacial or bifacial, flat or steep, regular, or alternate that is restricted to the edges of an artifact.

2. Bifacial retouching covers all surfaces of an artifact.

3. Chips result from bifacial retouch. These chips are sometimes utilized.

4. Primary retouching refers to the shaping of a tool from a blank flake.

5. Secondary retouching can be:

a) Secondary modifications made on bifacial artifacts, such as the notching or fluting of a projectile point.

b) Pressure of wear or crushing over a retouched edge.

c) Reworking of a tool.

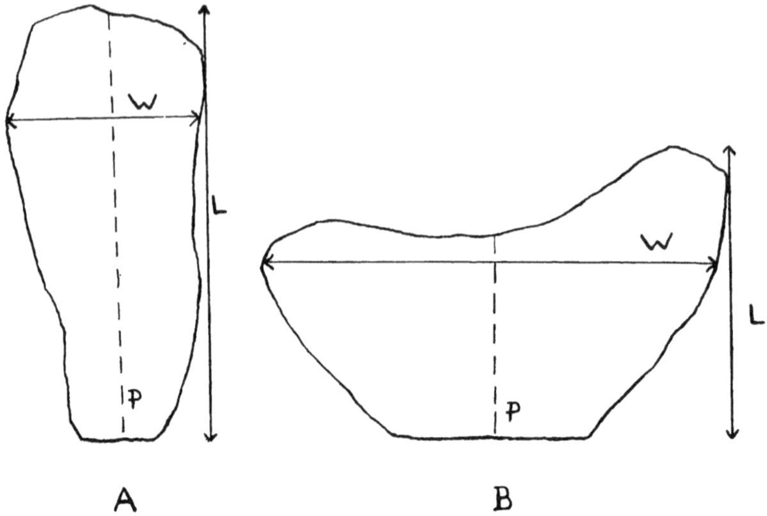

Fig. 7. Relation of width-length ratio: (A) lamellar flake; (B) rectangular flake; (W) width, (L) length, (P) axis of percussion.

C. Finished Artifacts

The following terms refer to the discrete attributes of finished artifacts:

a.) working area: (*a*) shape of the working edge (bevel, double-bevel point . . .); (*b*) placement of the working edge in relation to the longitudinal axis of the artifact (transverse, lateral); and (*c*) shape of adjacent edges.

b) hafting portion (if any) or base: (*a*) shape of lateral edges (converging, parallel); (*b*) shape of the base (round, tapered).

c) Junction of the working and hafting portions (if any).

D. Measuring Technique

Measurements are taken by inscribing the artifact into a quadrangular figure. The striking platform is placed at the base and the axis of percussion is perpendicular to the base.

The geometric description of an artifact is based on an analysis of the relation of the lateral and transverse edges to the longitudinal axis. The *longitudinal axis* is the median line drawn from the point of percussion of a flake tool, or medial point of the base of a bifacial tool as shown in Figure 9.

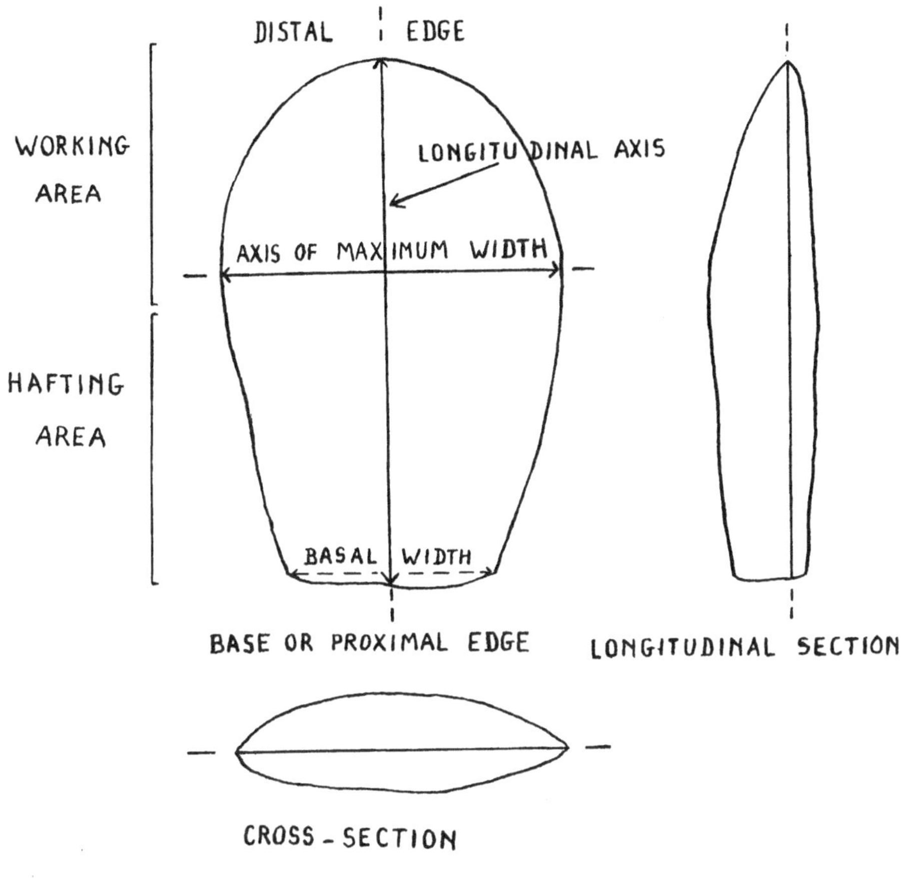

Fig. 8. Attributes of a tool.

The *working edge* is described in terms of its relation to the longitudinal axis.

These definitions are utilized to give a coherent and homogeneous description of all the artifacts present in an industry.

Functional terms, such as "scrapers" or "hoes," are avoided in the formal classification, since little is known of the actual function of many artifacts. The necessity of using technological definitions instead of common terms has been previously discussed (Gardin, 1958), and needs no repetition.

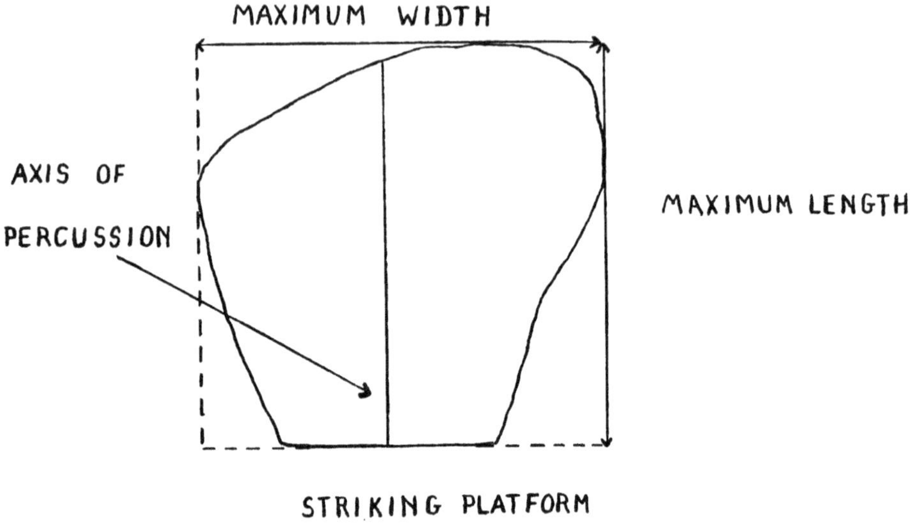

Fig. 9. Measurement of an artifact.

DESCRIPTION OF THE KNAPPING TECHNIQUES OBSERVED IN THE INDUSTRIES

From the standpoint of knapping techniques, Hopewell industries can be conveniently divided into two main classes, one composed of large, thick flakes, the other of thin blades. The blade assemblage is homogeneous and clearly constitutes a distinct technical unit as will be described later. There is heterogeneity in both form and technique represented within the flake assemblage.

A. Flake Assemblage

Artifacts are assembled on the basis of metrical similarities. They also share in common a certain number of discrete attributes: (*a*) a broad, flat striking platform; (*b*) a wide angle of percussion—the striking angle varies between 95 and 120 degrees at Snyders site, between 115 and 130 degrees at Worthy-Merigan site; and (*c*) a prominent bulb. These attributes suggest that anvil chipping was likely to have been the predominant technique utilized in their production.

Two attribute classes were utilized to separate the flakes into categories. These categories are classified according to the shape of the lateral edges in relation to the axis of percussion on the one hand, and the presence, or absence, of primary chipping on the other.

Category A: Flakes struck from unprepared cores

A1) Tabular flakes.-- Tabular flakes have a quadrilateral cross section; both inner and outer surfaces are flat and are parallel, as shown in Figure 10. These flakes are made from chert or poor quality white flint at Snyders and of yellow flint at Worthy-Merigan. The characteristic by-products associated with tabular flakes are long, narrow splinters with triangular cross sections (Fig. 11*A*) and flakes with flat outer surfaces (Fig. 11*B*). A few lumps of white chert (3 pieces) with a quadrilateral cross section were found in the Snyders collection. They can be interpreted as tabular chipping nuclei.

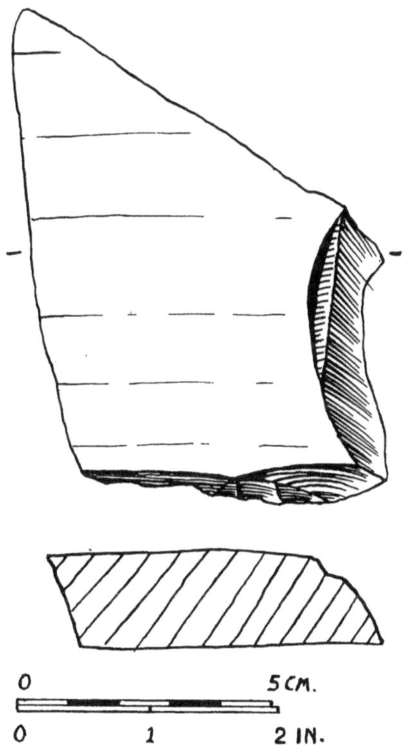

Fig. 10. Tabular flakes. Specimens from Snyders site surface collection.

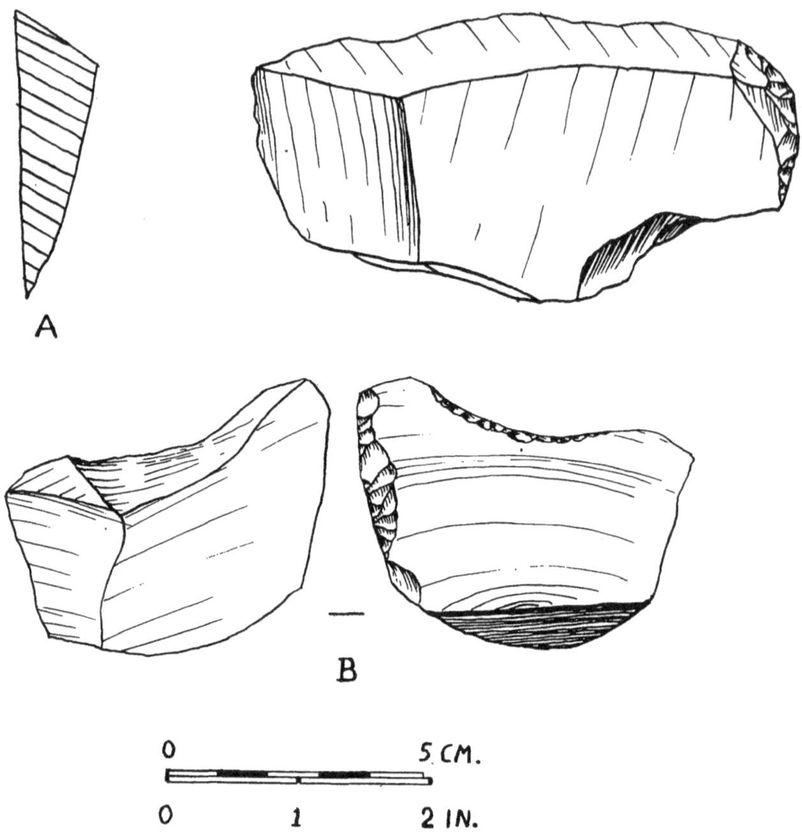

Fig. 11. By-products of tabular chipping.

A2) Tabular flakes from broken nodules.—Nodules are split into two or more sections. The broken surface is used as a striking platform. The method of chipping is similar to that which produces tabular flakes (Fig. 11, A1) but the raw material differs (Fig. 12).

Category B: Flakes from prepared cores.

B1) Parallel-sided flakes.—Parallel-sided flakes are large, thick pieces with a scalene triangular cross section.

B2) Rectangular flakes.—Rectangular flakes are smaller than B1 specimens. The lateral edges are parallel, or slightly expanding, in relation to the longitudinal axis. Specimens from categories B1 and B2 are found at Worthy-Merigan and Manker sites. They can be related to the same chipping technique. No cores have

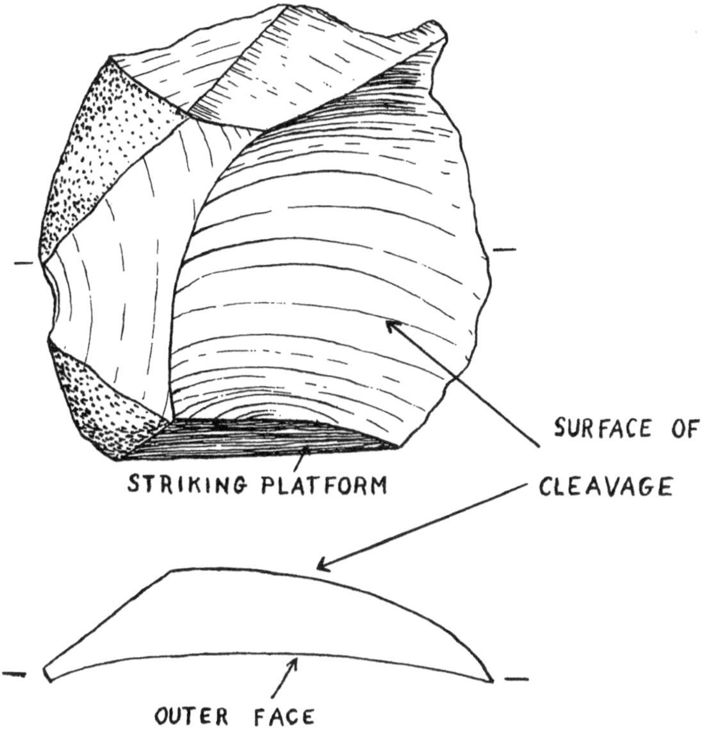

Fig. 12. Broken nodule. Specimen from Worthy-Merigan Mound.

been found in the collections studied here. One can assume, however, that these flakes were detached from the edges toward the center of a more-or-less pyramidal-shaped core (Fig. 13).

B3) Lamellar flakes.—Lamellar flakes are thinner and more regular in shape than the two preceding categories, B1 and B2. The width-length ratio (around .42) and the approximate symmetry of these flakes are traits intermediate between those of a flake and those of a blade (Fig. 14). The cores were prepared in a manner similar to that of the blade core, but they lack the careful preparation of the striking platform that characterizes the blade core. That difference is made clear by a comparison of the core illustrated in Figure 14 with the blade core shown in Figure 15 and described below. The striking angle is narrower than the one observed on B1 and B2 flakes (95-100 degrees). Hammerstone chipping may have been used instead of anvil chipping in making lamellar flakes.

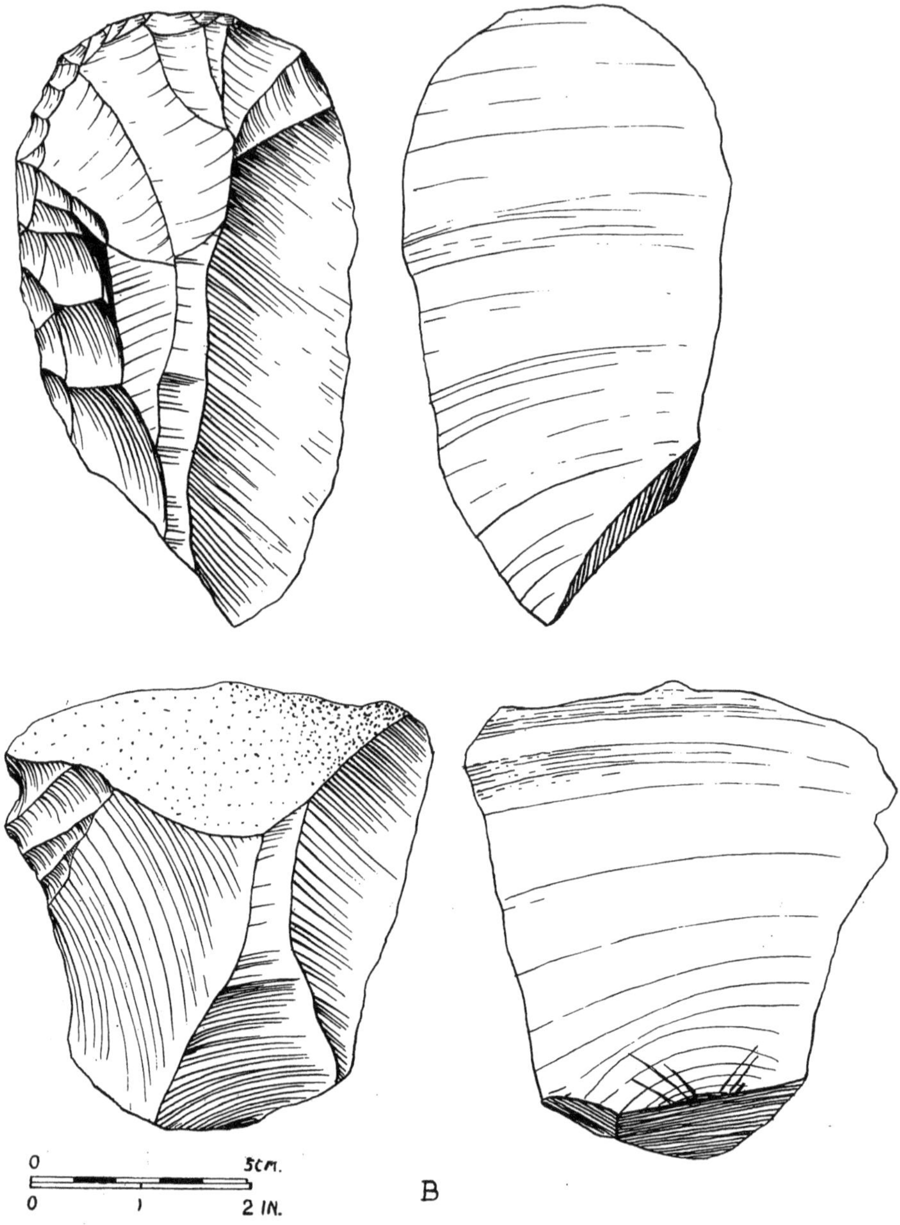

Fig. 13. Flakes from prepared cores. Types Bl and B2. Specimens from Worthy-Merigan Mound: (A) flake type Bl, the base is broken as well as the left lateral edge; (B) flake type B2.

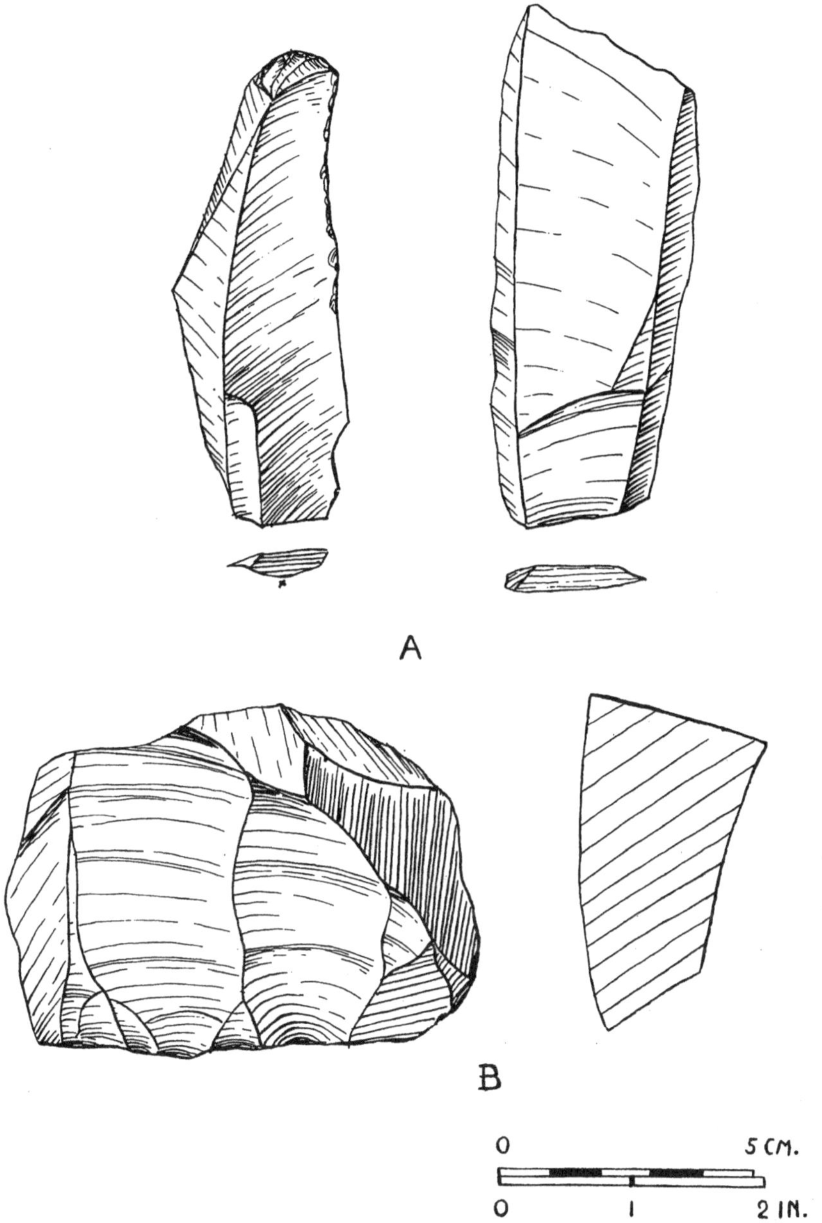

Fig. 14. Lamellar flakes. Specimen from Snyders site: (A) lamellar flake; (B) associated core.

Flakes in the B1 and B2 categories are predominant at Manker site and Worthy-Merigan, while A1 and B3 are the common types at Snyders. A2 (broken nodules) are present among Worthy-Merigan material and also are occasionally found in other sites. A few specimens are present at Snyders and Sconce-Schudel.

The raw material utilized at Snyders is white chert and white-pink flint. That used at Manker and Worthy-Merigan is yellow flint. More data would be necessary to establish a systematic relationship between raw material and chipping techniques, considering that the materials from Manker are a surface collection and that most of the material from Worthy-Merigan comes from a mound cache. Whether each of these different techniques—tabular chipping, prepared cores B1 and B2, and lamellar flaking, represents a particular tradition, or one aspect of a single technical complex, remains an open question. Further study of rejects and unmodified flakes from abundant excavation units will be necessary before we can give a definite answer. Therefore, categories of flakes are not considered in the present classification of chipped-flint industries although these divergencies are mentioned in descriptions.

B. Blade Assemblage

A table of width and length measurements taken from a particular group of blades shows little variation between specimens (Tables I and II). Such a homogeneous assemblage suggests the utilization of a single technique of flaking. Most Hopewell industries furnish more elements for the definition of that group than they did for the flake assemblage.

The few preserved cores show that large lumps of flint were utilized at first. They were shaped into a rough pyramidal form by anvil chipping. The base of the core, prepared by striking off one or two flakes, was used as the striking platform. One of the largest samples in The University of Michigan Museum of Anthropology collections comes from Knight mound Number 4. Its base measures 18.5 cm by 9.5 cm; the maximum height is 13.6 cm. Negative marks left by detached blades range from 8 to 11 cm in length. Bladelets of that size are rare but do occur occasionally. Another specimen from Snyders has the following measurements: base, 9.2 by 4.5 cm, height, 5.1 cm, negative marks between 4 and 5 cm.

The presence of these artifacts is evidence that the cores were originally quite large. Before they were reduced to the size of the

TABLE I

SNYDERS SITE BLADES

DISTRIBUTION OF WIDTH MEASUREMENTS
(In millimeters)

Classes	Observed Numbers
0. — 5	0
5.1 — 10	3
10.1 — 15	43
15.1 — 20	86
20.1 — 25	46
25.1 — 30	14
30.1 — 35	2
35.1 — 40	...
Total	194
Mean = 18.3	

TABLE II

SNYDERS SITE BLADES

DISTRIBUTION OF LENGTH MEASUREMENTS
(In millimeters)

Classes	Observed Numbers
25.1 — 30	0
30.1 — 35	14
35.1 — 40	20
40.1 — 45	43
45.1 — 50	41
50.1 — 55	27
55.1 — 60	27
60.1 — 65	8
65.1 — 70	6
70.1 — 75	4
75.1 — 80	4
81.1 — 85	...
Mean = 48.7	

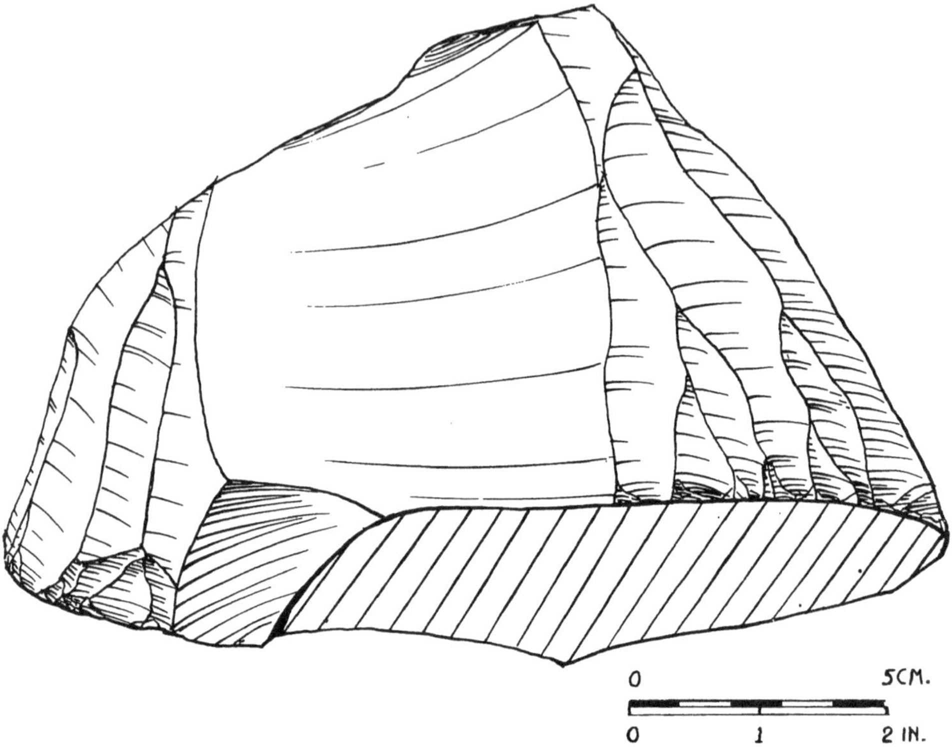

Fig. 15. Large blade core. Specimen from Knight Mound No. 4

nuclei, a great many blades could be produced. This observation explains, in part, the abundance of bladelets as compared with the relative scarcity of small cores or exhausted nuclei. The proportion of nuclei from Snyders excavated units is .05 per cent. The eventual utilization of small-sized nuclei as tools will be described later.

When the raw material used was small-sized pebbles, as in the Poverty Point complex, preliminary trimming was not extensive (Ford and Webb, 1956, and collections in The University of Michigan Museum of Anthropology). A primary flake was struck from one of the narrow ends. Then the surface of cleavage so obtained was used as a striking platform. In the special case of Poverty Point and Jaketown sites, pebbles provided so little material that no further preparation was possible. Consequently, most of the bladelets have a part of the cortex remaining on the upper face. The percentage of cores is 0.7 per cent at Poverty Point and 7 per cent at Jaketown site (Ford and Webb, 1956, p. 77). Both greatly exceeding the percentages observed at Snyders.

Once the cores were shaped, bladelets were detached by flat flaking. The percussion tool was likely to be an antler or wood flaker. The point of impact of the percussion tool on the platform was determined by a careful preparation which consisted in trimming the ridges left by previously detached bladelets. When the

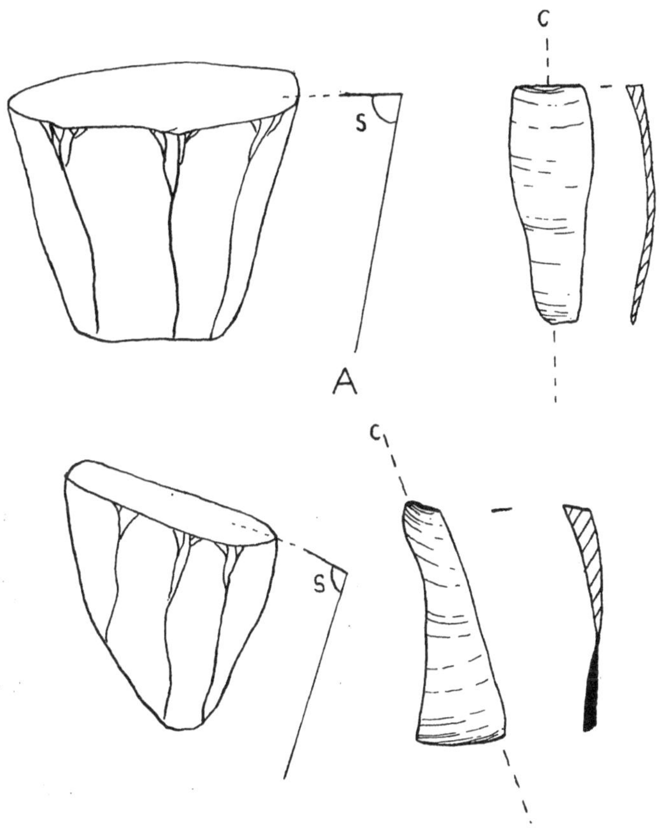

Fig. 16. Techniques of blade chipping. Variations of the axis of curvature (c) in relation to changes of the striking angle (s).

platforms were oblong, as frequently occurred, flakes were struck back and forth from the narrow ends. Because of the semispiral movement described by a series of blows, the striking angle, which at first measured around 75-85 degrees, had a tendency to get smaller while the curvature of the inner face of the bladelets increased. Then a new platform had to be cut. A variety of transverse flakes resulted from this operation. These chipping flakes were often used as end scrapers.

Blade technique would normally produce square-ended and converging-ended artifacts according to a certain rhythm of alternation. The proportion would be approximately three square-ended

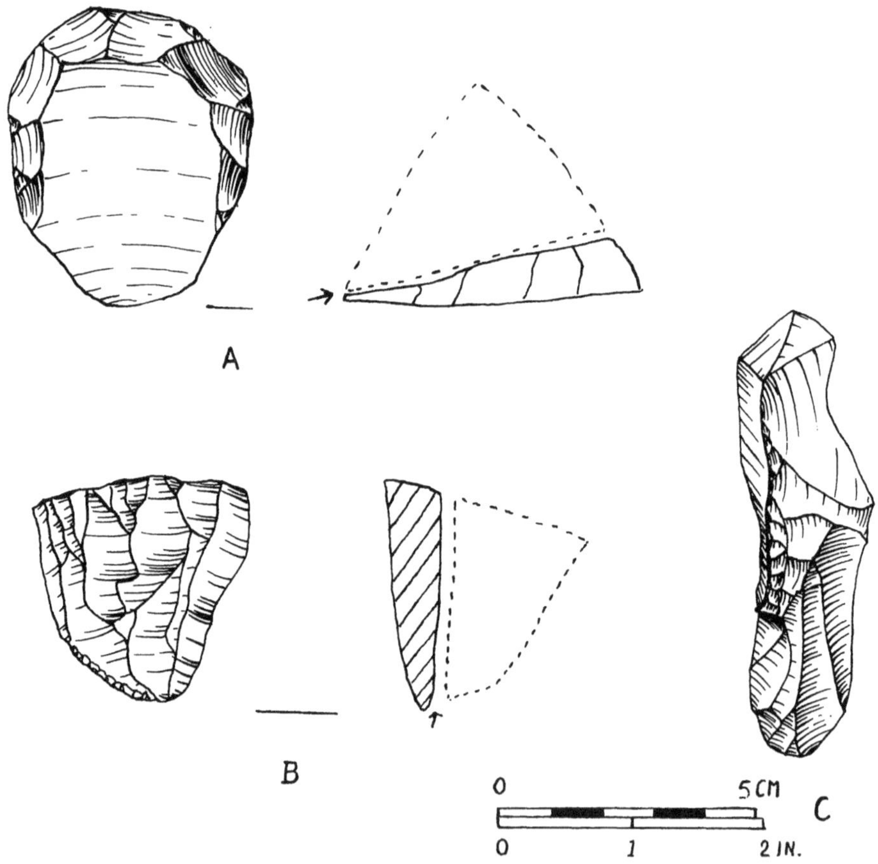

Fig. 17. By-products of blade chipping: (A) horizontal flake; (B) vertical flake; (C) crest blade.

to one triangular bladelet. Variations in handling the percussion tool, however, as well as defects of raw materials caused numerous misshapings of the bladelets. There is no significant relationship within Hopewell assemblages between the shape of a bladelet and a particular placement of the retouching on its edge. This fact renders useless a classification based on these factors. When used to make bladelets, flat flaking tended to cause a slight curvature of the inner face. This concavity is more pronounced when the bladelets are thinner. In Hopewell assemblages, the axis of curvature is, in most cases, normal to the striking platform; it follows the longitudinal axis. Mostly because of the material used, the Poverty Point blades differ in that respect from the Hopewell group. They are generally characterized by an oblique axis of curvature as shown on Figure 16.

DESCRIPTION OF THE MODES OF RETOUCHING

A. Over-all Bifacial Retouching

Several processes of percussion flaking were utilized to produce bifacially retouched artifacts. Celts from the Snyders and Manker village sites and "cache-blades" from Worthy-Merigan mound furnished abundant material for a description of bifacial retouching. The first step was to shape the flake blank into a geometric form. Working edges and base were subsequently modified according to the particular type of tool that was needed: knives, celts, and the like.

The common process of bifacial retouch is illustrated below (Fig. 18). Chips are removed from a lateral edge toward the center of the surface to be modified. When the lateral edge is flat and thick as occurs on tabular flakes there is no preparation for a striking platform (Fig. 18A); the natural edge is used as such. On the other hand, when the lateral edge is too irregular or too thin to provide a suitable platform, a series of short and abrupt chips are removed along the edges, resulting in an acute angle to the surface to be modified (Fig. 18B).

Scars left on the artifact often terminate in a hinge fracture and a few examples of resolved flakes can be observed (Fig. 19).

There are several ways to apply this basic technique of retouching in order to obtain rectangular, oblong, or discoidal artifacts:

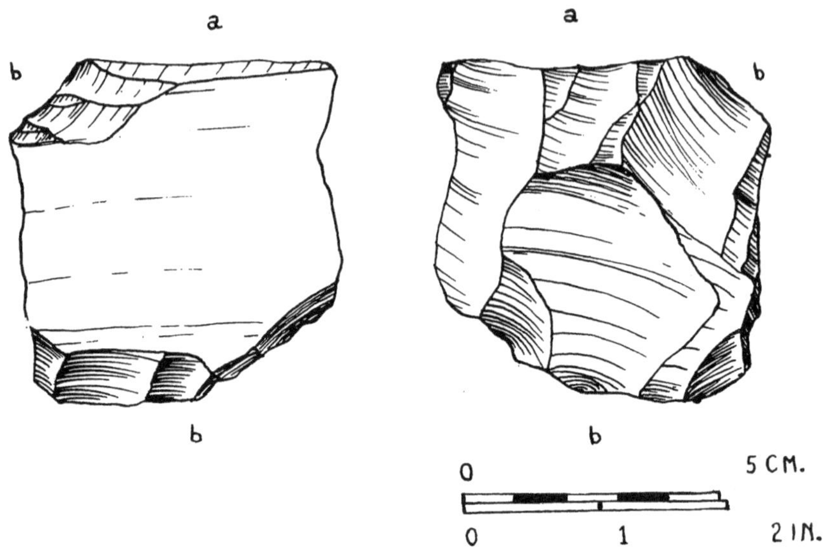

Fig. 18. Bifacial retouching: preparation of the striking platform. Specimens from Worthy-Merigan Mound: (a) flat striking platform, the natural edge requires no preparation; (b) prepared platforms.

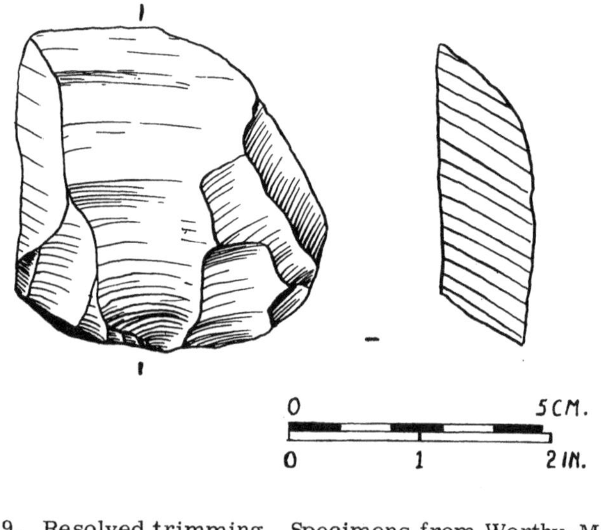

Fig. 19. Resolved trimming. Specimens from Worthy-Merigan Mound.

1. Rectangular artifacts (Fig. 20).—A single lateral edge is used as a striking platform to modify one surface. The artifact is then turned over. The lateral edge opposite the initial platform is utilized to retouch the other surface. As a result, the cross section of the retouched artifact is a parallelogram.

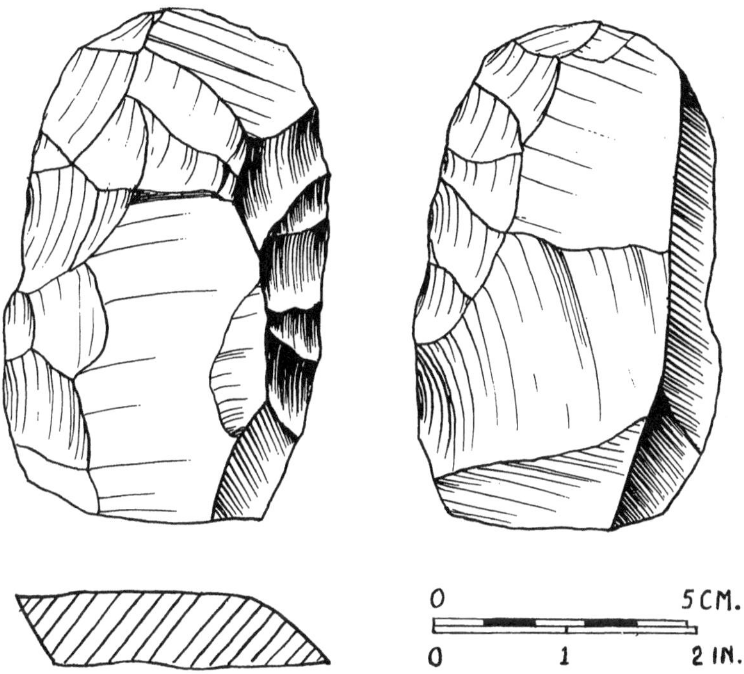

Fig. 20. Rectangular artifact. Specimens from Worthy-Merigan Mound.

2. Oblong artifacts.—Two platforms are prepared on two opposite lateral edges. Chips are removed from these platforms to modify one surface. In order to modify the other surface, the artifact is turned over. The same process is repeated on the remaining two edges (Fig. 21).

3. Discoidal artifacts.—The striking platform is prepared on one of the surfaces (outer or inner face) by taking off a series of adjoining short and steep chips all around the edges. Broad chips are subsequently removed from the edges toward the center of the

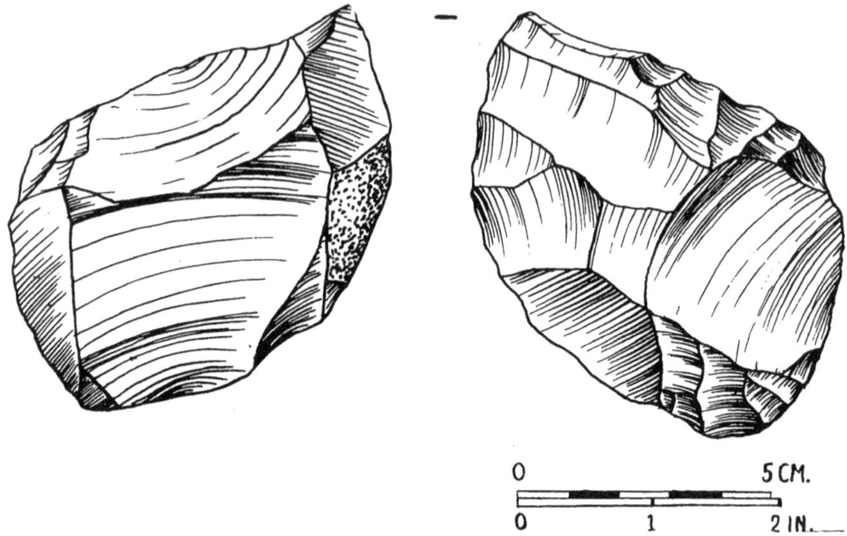

Fig. 21. Oblong artifact. Specimen from Manker site.

opposite face. The process leaves the central area of the initially worked face unretouched. Figure 22 illustrates the technique applied to blank flakes which have a naturally flat face not requiring modification. The flat face is considered to be the internal face, and the convex retouched surface the external face. The central ridge left on the external face was often removed by taking off a longitudinal flake from the distal end.

4. Chips from bifacial trimming.—Most chips obtained by bifacial chipping are characterized by a flat and oblique striking platform and a well-marked bulb of percussion (Fig. 24). They are irregularly shaped, with either converging or expanding edges. Some specimens are thinner with a diffuse bulb that suggests the utilization of a bone or antler flaker in the process of preparation. The exact proportion of bone and hammerstone flaking is impossible to evaluate. Both implements were used at Snyders and Manker, but hammerstone flaking was the only technique used to make the blades at the Worthy-Merigan cache.

The three processes of making bifacial artifacts that have been described above are not considered to be rigid categories. Many variations can be observed between specimens. These differences are caused mainly by defects or malformations which can be

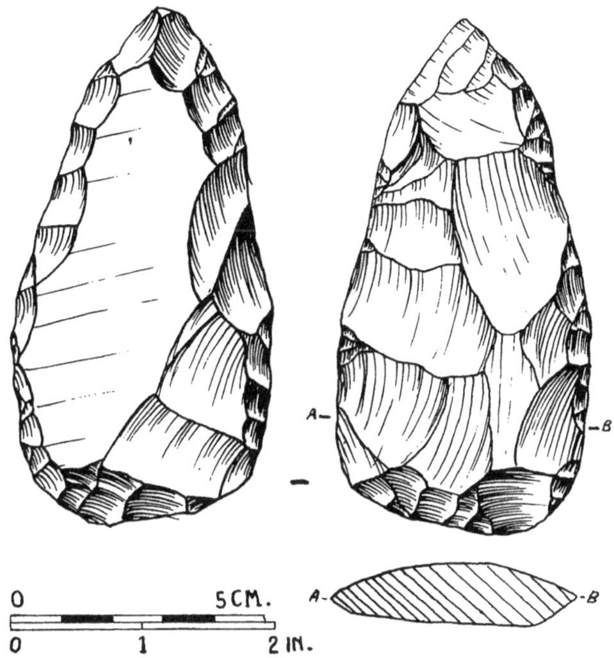

Fig. 22. Discoidal artifacts. Specimens from Snyders site.

observed on the blank flake itself. All three categories are present within each assemblage. Their relative proportion cannot be evaluated since only a small number of specimens were found during the excavations at Snyders. The other artifacts came from selected collections.

The utilization of chips as a substitute for blades will be discussed below (p. 48). Similar techniques to produce either bifacial blanks or core and flakes assemblages can be observed in other industries from either Archaic or Post-Hopewell periods. Further comparative studies will be necessary to give a complete picture of the origin and development of that technique.

The second step in bifacial retouching was to finish the working edge. It was modified with special care by taking off long, lamellar chips by the use of a bone or antler flaker. To obtain a transverse edge, the chips were removed from the distal edge with the axis of percussion parallel to the longitudinal axis (Fig. 26). A point was produced by removing chips transversely to the longitudinal axis (Fig. 25). Lateral edges were regularized by semiabrupt percussion flaking.

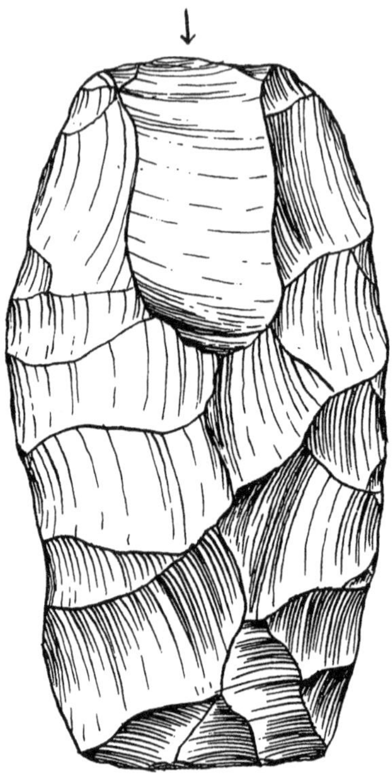

Fig. 23. Long flake taken from the central ridge.

B. Flat-Pressure Trimming

So far as we can observe from unfinished projectile points or rejected blanks, pressure trimming was applied directly on regularly shaped flakes with little or no previous bifacial trimming (see preceding description of bifacial retouching). Therefore, whenever pressure flaking was required, blank flakes had to be carefully selected.

Bone or antler flakers were the tools used for pressure flaking. Hopewell pressure retouching is characterized by round or ovate scars perpendicular to the edges. This indicates a direct pressure with a minimum preparation of the point of impact which consists in smoothing the ridge left by the previous scar before taking off the next one. A more careful process producing longer and more regular scars was used to transform the blank into a projectile point. Rejects from the pressure-flaking technique are

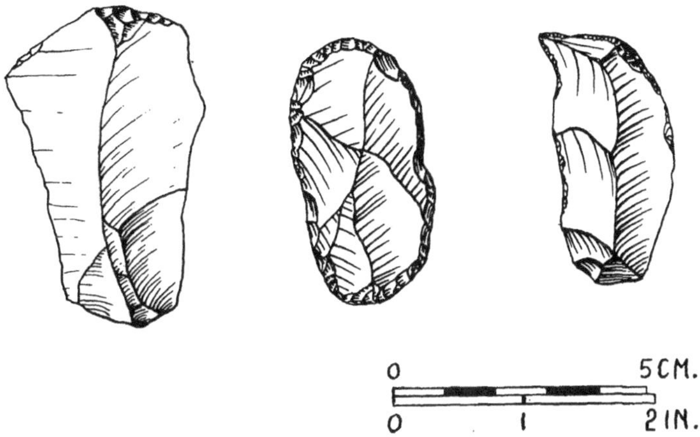

Fig. 24. Chips from bifacial trimming. Specimens from Manker site.

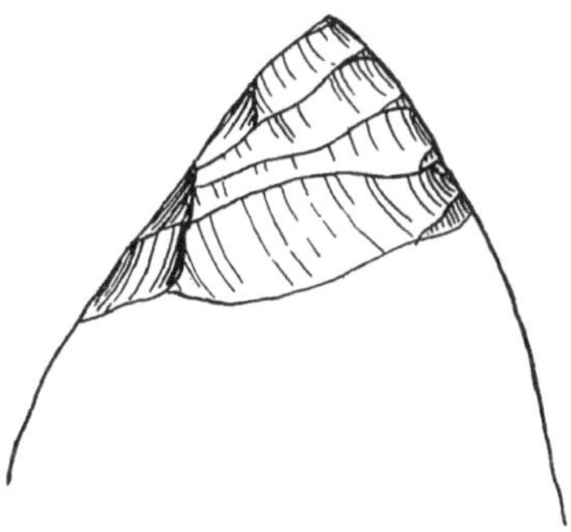

Fig. 25. Retouching of the working edge: point.

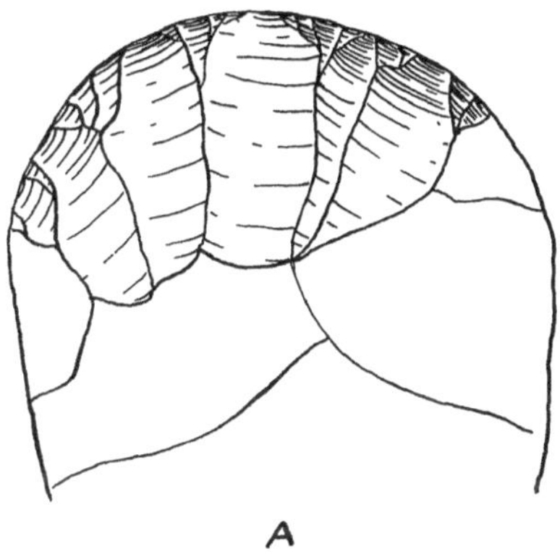

Fig. 26. Retouching of the working edge: transverse edge.

recognized by the smooth concentric ridges left on the inner face. They are small and irregularly shaped. Lateral notches were made by percussion.

C. Steep Marginal Retouch

Steep marginal retouch was used to produce a steep beveled edge (Fig. 27). It could be obtained either by percussion or by pressure. Percussion was more commonly utilized by Hopewell workmen. The most elaborate process in steep edging consisted in taking off long and narrow chips. The result was a perfectly shaped edge with convex profile and convex outline.

In most cases, because of a lack of preparation of the point of impact, the common type of steep edging is an irregular retouch in which lamellar and irregular scars alternate. As it appears on Hopewell specimens, crushing covers the original retouch and therefore is likely to be the result of wear, indicating a strong friction against a hard surface.

D. Edge Blunting

The modifications which can be observed on Hopewell bladelets are of three kinds, producing fine, steep, or crushed edges. Edge blunting may have been the result of pressure or percussion, in fact, most is due to wear pressure. Intentional retouching was

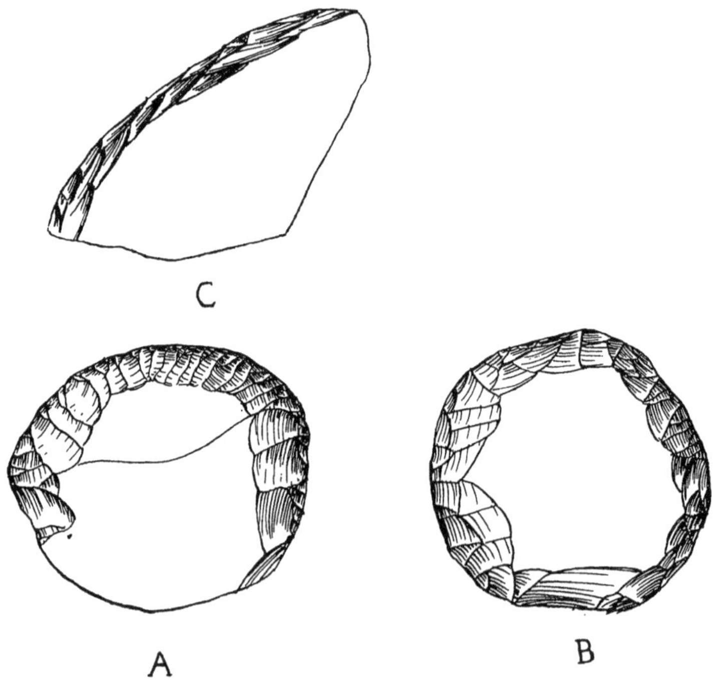

Fig. 27. Steep marginal retouch: (A) lamellar; (B) irregular; (C) crushing.

minimal. Hopewell blades and chips were tools in themselves. This trait differentiates them from Mesolithic and Upper Paleolithic blades. Old-world blades were blank flakes that were modified into various types of artifacts, such as the burin, graver and others. There is a tendency for the Hopewell fine pressure to be associated with a lateral position and steep retouch found on a blade end, but no specific conclusion can be drawn from the actual evidence.

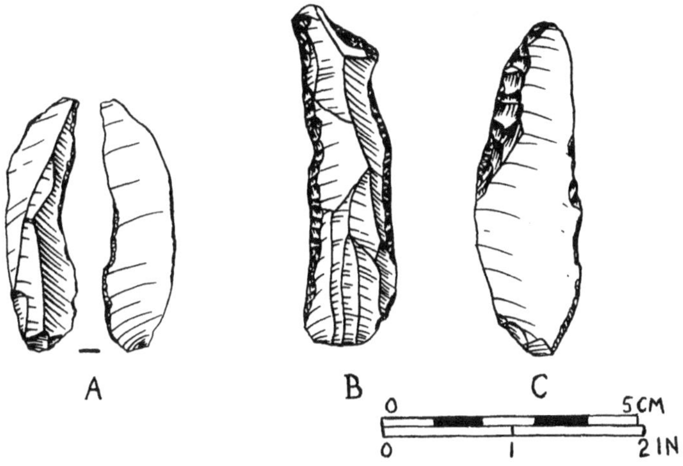

Fig. 28. Edge blunting of blades: (A) fine; (B) steep; (C) crushed.

The preceding description emphasizes the two features that are characteristic of Hopewellian flint industries, namely, a particular mode of bifacial retouching and the techniques of blade production. Both could have developed within a single tradition without any outside influence. On the basis of available evidence, an indigenous origin is postulated for the Hopewell techniques of blade production. This position is presently supported by a logical argument based on a well-established evolutionary sequence of flint-working techniques. Examples of such technical development can be found in northeastern Africa. There, blade industries of the late Stone Age have been found in direct contact with flake assemblages of middle Stone Age tradition. The Epi-levalloisian of Lower Egypt is characterized by the association of small blades and blade cores with the double-ended nuclei and lamellar flakes of Levallois tradition.

J. Desmond Clark demonstrates in his study of the Horn of Africa, that Magosian develops directly from local Stillbay in the same way that it developed in East Africa (Clark, 1954).

These examples are given to illustrate the fact already pointed out by Clark that similar ecology and the use of a certain type of raw material tend to result in a similar development of techniques. Further analysis of local Archaic assemblages will be necessary to test the hypothesis of the indigenous origin of Hopewell blades.

TYPOLOGICAL ANALYSIS OF THE ARTIFACTS

The analysis and classification of artifacts is based on two considerations: first, the modes of chipping and retouching, and second, the formal attributes suggestive of functional differences.

From the standpoint of the retouching and chipping techniques, which were described above, Hopewell artifacts from the sites studied can be grouped into the following classes:

- A1) Bifacial retouch associated with flakes B1, B2, A1, and A2.
- A2) Marginal retouch associated with flakes B3, occasionally A1 and B1.
- A3) Edge-blunted artifacts associated with blades and chips.
- A4) Wear pressure—all types of flakes, blades, and chips.
- A5) Unmodified artifacts.
- A6) Cores and by-products.
- A7) Rejects.

The description of functional characteristics is based on the attributes listed on page 10 (Fig. 9).

The functional classes, listed below, are based primarily on the placement of the working edge, or area, in relation to the longitudinal axis of the artifact (Fig. 29).

- B1) Points: lateral edges converging at one point along the longitudinal axis (Fig. 29A).
- B2) Straight-transverse working edge: the working edge is perpendicular to the longitudinal axis (Fig. 29B).
- B3) Obliquely-transverse working edge: the working edge is cut obliquely to the longitudinal axis (Fig. 29C).
- B4) Longitudinal working edge: the working edge is

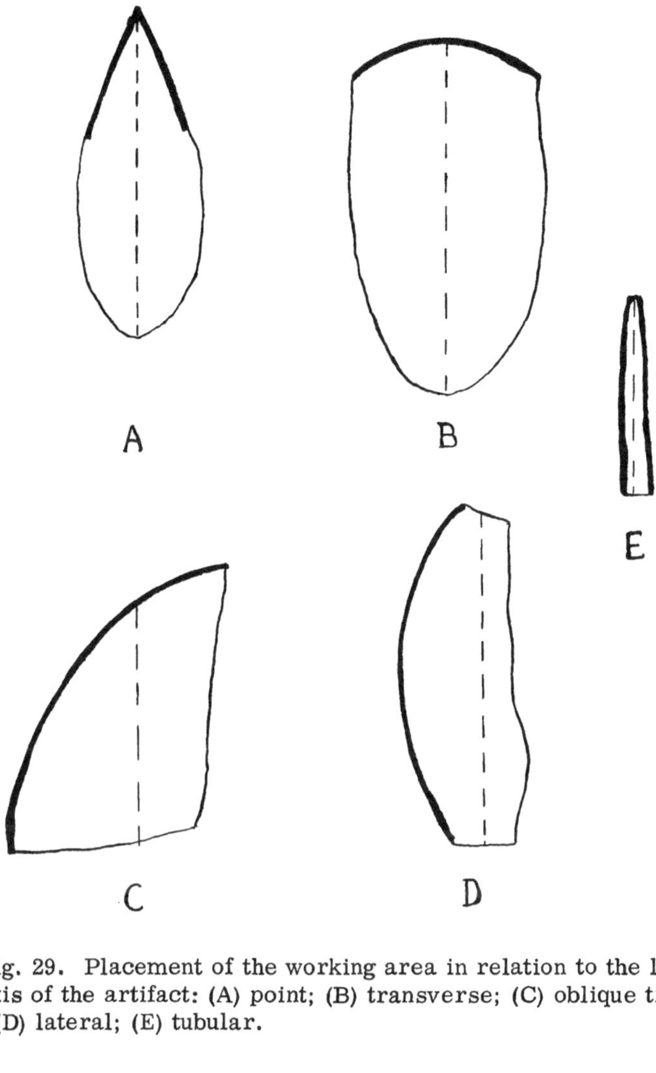

Fig. 29. Placement of the working area in relation to the longitudinal axis of the artifact: (A) point; (B) transverse; (C) oblique transverse; (D) lateral; (E) tubular.

parallel to the longitudinal axis (Fig. 29D).

B5) Tubular area revolving parallel to the longitudinal axis (Fig. 29E).

Groups of artifacts are defined on the basis of the interrelationship of these technical and functional attributes.

The next step in the analysis is to define types within each group. The typology is based on a description of lateral and proximal modifications, which were intended to prepare a way to haft or to handle the tool in relation to the shape of the working edge.

The group of projectile points (Classes A1 and B1) will be the subject of another study.

A. Bifacial Retouched Artifacts with Transverse Working Edge

The first group to be considered is characterized by bifacial retouching (Class A1) and a straight, transverse working edge (Class B2). This definition includes the artifacts commonly termed "celts" and "hoes."

Measurements.—Length, maximum and minimum widths, and thickness provide information on the general proportion of a tool. Two more measurements are taken to locate the area of maximum weight and its relation to both the distal and proximal edges of the artifact. They are: first, the distance between the axis of maximum width and the distal edge; and second, the distance between the axis of maximum thickness and the distal edge. Both distances are measured on the longitudinal axis.

Measurements were taken on materials from the Snyders and Manker sites (Table III). Specimens from Snyders are shorter and thinner than those from Manker. This fact can be related to the raw materials used: tabular flakes (A1) at Snyders, large-size flakes (B1, B2) at Manker. The relation between maximum and minimum widths shows a possible differentiation between parallel-sided and expanding-sided artifacts. The point of maximum thickness is always closer to the proximal end rather than to the point of maximum width. Measurements taken on artifacts from the Manker site indicate a positive correlation between the distance of maximum width to the distal end and the total length; also a low correlation is demonstrable between the distance of maximum thickness to the distal end and the total length. On the other hand, in a well-defined group of artifacts such as the Cahokia hoes, both distances appear to be independent of the total length. Measurements of Cahokia hoes are given in P. F. Titterington's notebooks, The University of Michigan Museum of Anthropology collection.

Numerical data do not provide enough information to define types, at least for the present. They do, however, suggest the presence of several types which can be described on the basis of discrete attributes.

Discrete Attributes.—The geometric description of the artifacts is based on the discrete attributes listed on page 10. Figures 30 and 31 illustrate the types of bifacial artifacts with a transversely placed working edge:

BT1) Working edge: double bevel, straight.
Lateral edges: convex-parallel.

TABLE III

MANKER SITE COLLECTION. MEASUREMENTS OF BIFACIALLY RETOUCHED ARTIFACTS WITH A TRANSVERSE WORKING EDGE
(In centimeters)

Specimen Number	Length	Maximum Width	Basal Width	Thickness	Distance of Maximum Width	Distance of Maximum Thickness
1 . . .	12.1	6.6	3.7	1.9	4.1	7.5
2 . . .	18.1	7.3	4.2	3.1	4.3	10.1
3 . . .	19.1	9.2	4.8	3.7	5.1	9.8
4 . . .	10.1	6.3	3.6	2.4	4.1	7.1
5 . . .	11.3	6.2	2.8	1.8	3.5	6.2
6 . . .	13.9	6.9	5.1	2.3	3.9	4.5
7 . . .	14.2	9.3	5.7	2.7	3.7	6.4
8 . . .	15.2	7.5	5.3	2.8	5.1	6.4
9 . . .	14.6	7.9	4.5	2.8	4.4	6.3
10 . . .	13.6	5.5	3.6	2.5	3.5	7.2
11 . . .	12.9	5.3	3.4	2.3	2.7	7.3
12 . . .	9.8	5.6	4.2	1.7	2.0	4.5
13 . . .	10.5	5.4	3.8	2.0	1.8	5.7
14 . . .	10.0	4.9	3.4	1.8	4.9	5.4
15 . . .	9.4	5.1	2.8	1.9	2.9	5.1
16 . . .	10.5	5.2	3.0	1.7	3.1	4.9

Numbers 12 to 16 are specimens with a single beveled end. Columns 5 and 6 correspond to measurements described in the text, page 21. The paired relation of the point of maximum width (5) and the total length (1) is expressed by the regression equation:

$$\hat{Y} = a + bX = 5.41 + 2.15X$$

which describes the straight line on a Cartesian graph best fitting the trend of the plotted points defined by the paired measurements as the X and Y coordinates.

The relation of the point of maximum thickness (6) and the total length (1) is expressed by the equation:

$$\hat{Y} = a + bX = 6.73 + 1.03X$$

Junction: no junction between functional and hafting part.
Base: modified round.
Cross section: biconvex asymmetric.

BT2) Working edge: double bevel, semicircular.
Lateral edges: convex-expanding.

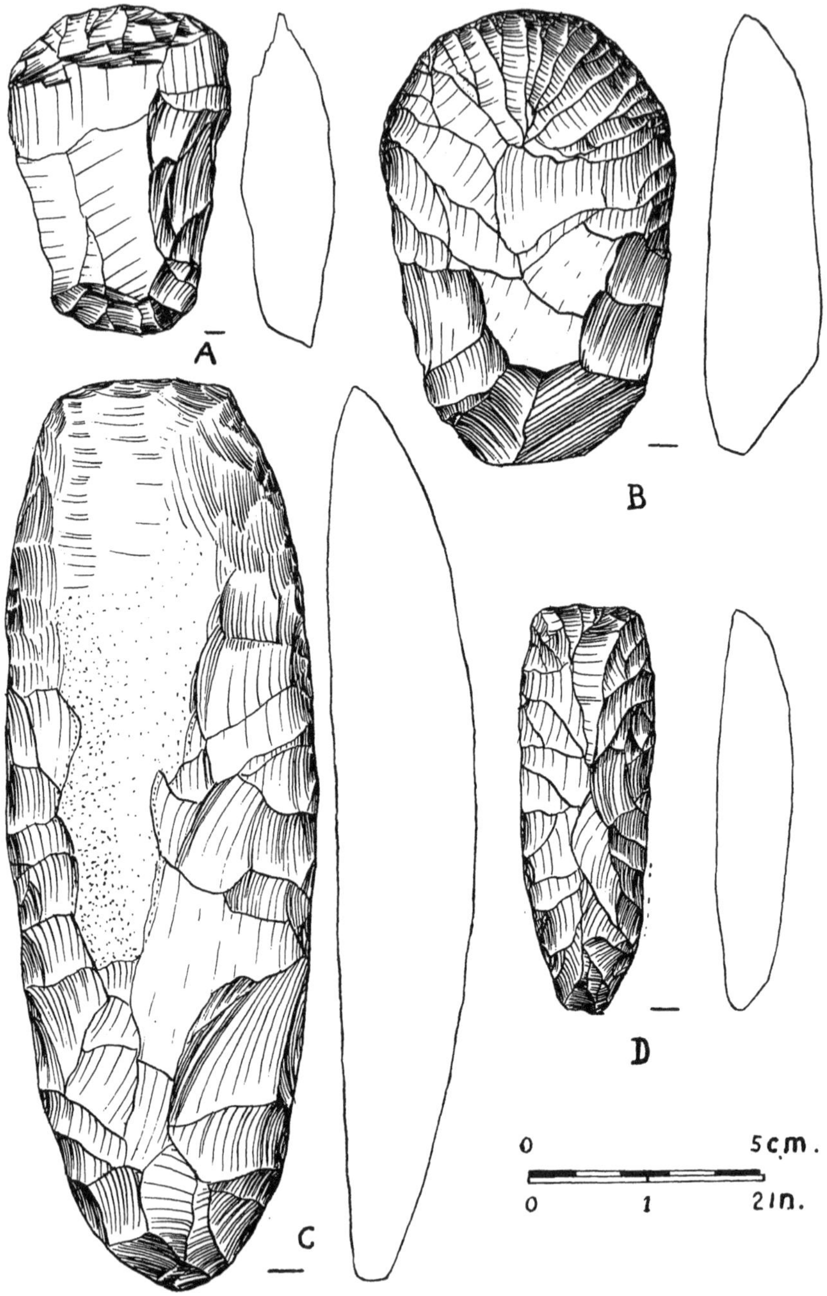

Fig. 30. Bifacial artifacts with a transverse working edge. Celts, types BT1, BT2, BT6, BT9. All specimens from Manker site: (A) BT6; (B) BT2; (C) BT1; (D) BT9.

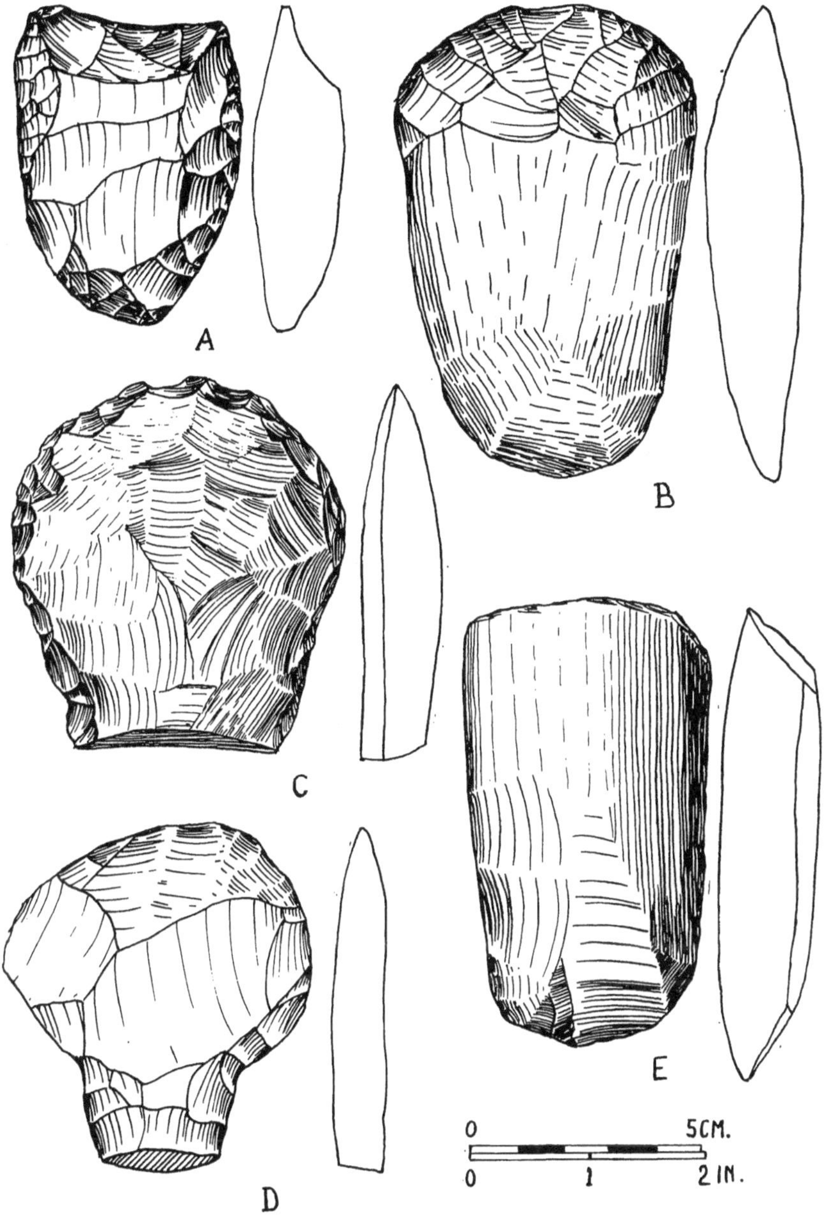

Fig. 31. Bifacial artifacts with a transverse working edge. Celts, types BT3, BT4, BT5, BT7, BT8. All specimens from Snyders site: (A) BT8, (B) BT3, (C) BT4, (D) BT5, (E) BT7.

Base: unmodified.
2a - no junction between functional and hafting areas.
2b - irregular lateral indentations.
Cross section: biconvex asymmetric.

BT3) Working edge: double bevel, convex.
Lateral edges: straight expanding.
Junction: no junction of hafting and working areas.
Base: modified, convex.
Cross section: biconvex symmetric.

BT4) Working edge: double bevel, convex.
Lateral edges: working area: convex parallel; hafting area: straight-expanding.
Junction: marked by a re-entrant angle.
Base: modified, round.
Cross section: biconvex symmetric.

BT5) Working edge: double bevel, convex.
Lateral edges: working area: convex-parallel; hafting area: straight-expanding.
Junction: junction between working and hafting areas, shoulders.
Cross section: biconvex symmetric.
(Bases are broken)

BT6) See below.

BT7) Working edge: single bevel cut off the internal face.
Lateral edges: convex-parallel.
Junction: no junction between working and hafting areas.
Base: modified round.
Polishing: external face, completely polished, in opposition to the light polishing of internal face.
Cross section: plano-convex.

BT8) Working edge: single bevel, concave (gouge end).
Lateral edges: convex-expanding (short blade).
Base: modified round.
Little or no polishing.
Cross section: plano-convex.

BT9) Working edge: single bevel, straight or convex.
Lateral edges: straight parallel (narrow blade).
Base: modified round.
Cross section: plano-convex.

BT6 has the same general characteristics as BT1, except that it has a short blade with a chipped and crushed working edge. Specimens included in this category might be interpreted as worn-out artifacts. They are kept separately for the present. Broken fragments, mostly proximal portions, complete the assemblage of bifacial blades with transverse working edges. The two first types are present at Manker site only. There are three specimens of type BT1, and six of type BT2. Types BT3, and BT7, BT8 and BT9 are well represented in almost every site. Types BT4 and BT5 exist only at Snyders site. The preceding analysis demonstrates the presence of several forms among the bifacial blades. The last three types differ from the first six by their working-edge profile, which is a single bevel.

One can observe on a large percentage of the double-beveled specimens a wear polish that extends on both external and internal faces of the working area. The edge itself is often resharpened or crushed. The presence of this kind of polishing suggests a strong and continuous friction in the ground.

A light polish of the internal face of the hafting portion indicates that these artifacts were hafted. A slight curvature can be observed as the proximal portion of the inner face of types BT1, BT2a, and BT3. It suggests that the internal face rested on a handle either beveled or hooked. This mode of hafting is more adapted to digging sticks than it is to hoes.

Types BT2b, BT4 and BT5 are modified in such a way as to adapt the plain blades of the preceding types to more specialized modes of hafting. Type BT2b has lateral indentations, BT4 and BT5 are stemmed. Type BT2b can be compared to some laterally notched hoes found at Cahokia (from Titterington's notebooks). The stemmed specimens are related to the spuds present in later industries, although the specimens present at Snyders are smaller. It is interesting to note that type BT5 is marked with a broken base. This observation might suggest an inadequate mode of hafting.

Because of the small number of specimens present in the collections, the significance of the distribution of these types can only be indicative. More data will be necessary to determine whether the differentiation between the types of bifacial blades has a cultural significance.

The single beveled types are present in every assemblage. High polish is restricted to the external face. The internal face is smoothed but does not show the same polish. The external face polishing is different from the one observed on the other bifacial tools. It would be possible to consider it as an intentional modification, although there is no other example of intentional polishing among Hopewell artifacts. It is more satisfactory to suppose that these artifacts were polished by wear.

A specimen of type BT7 was found at the Aaron Pulcher site, St. Clair County, Illinois (The University of Michigan, Museum of Anthropology collection). It was collected by J. B. Griffin and A. C. Spaulding in 1955. It can be attributed to the Late Woodland occupation of the Aaron Pulcher site (J. B. Griffin, personal communication).

Very similar artifacts are described by M. Maxwell (1951, p. 120): "There is a high glossy polish on the plane surface of these tools similar to the polish on agricultural artifacts and occasionally there are polished areas along the high spots of the convex surface. It has been suggested that these artifacts were used in one of the final steps in dressing soft skins." These artifacts belong to the lower and middle levels of the Sugar Camp Hill site, Williamson County, Illinois.

Because of their single, beveled edge and the particular type of polishing, it seems logical to assume that these tools were used for hide working. Whatever their function might be, these artifacts are widely distributed among the Woodland industries of southern Illinois.

The group of bifacial artifacts with a longitudinal working edge is not represented among industries of the village site. Specimens of the longitudinal working edge found in these collections are marginally retouched. This group is mentioned, however, since bifacial "knives" exist in the mound burial complex.

B. Perforators (Class A3 and Class B5)

A very steep edge retouch is utilized to modify the working area into a narrow blade with a square or rhomboidal cross section. The distal end is a flat surface, measuring 3 to 7 mm in diagonal. Most of the perforators are made from reworked projectile points with the exception of a few specimens which are modified blades. Perforators are classified into categories on the basis of two classes of attributes: shape of the lateral edges and presence or absence of hafting preparation. The following types were observed:

- A1) Plain blade with parallel lateral edges.
- A2) Plain blades with converging edges and straight base.
- B1) Parallel edge blades with hafting preparation (reworked projectile points).
- B2) Converging edges with hafting preparation.

Because of the small size of the sample available for study, very little can be said on the nature of the differences observed between the categories of perforators. These variations could be interpreted either as cultural or as functional traits.

C. Marginally Retouched Artifacts (Class A2) with Transverse Working Edges (Class B2)

This group of artifacts includes most of the end scrapers (Fig. 33). Blades with end retouch will be described later. The blank flakes commonly utilized to make scrapers are lamellar flakes and by-products of tabular chipping. The latter exists only at Snyders site. Three of the specimens found at Snyders are made on transverse flakes chipped from a blade core. In every industry, there are some examples of scrapers made out of bifacially chipped blanks; but in that case, the blanks are treated as flakes and modified by a secondary retouch similar to that used on raw flakes. Consequently, the function of the artifact is not affected whether the raw materials are flakes or blanks. The presence of scrapers made of bifacial blanks must be mentioned, however, since it shows the extent of reutilization of inadequate or broken bifacial artifacts.

For a functional analysis of the scrapers, the most significant attribute is the varying convexity of the beveled end. These variations can be estimated by measuring the working length, that is, the distance measured on the longitudinal axis between the distal end and the axis of maximum width of the functional area (Fig. 32).

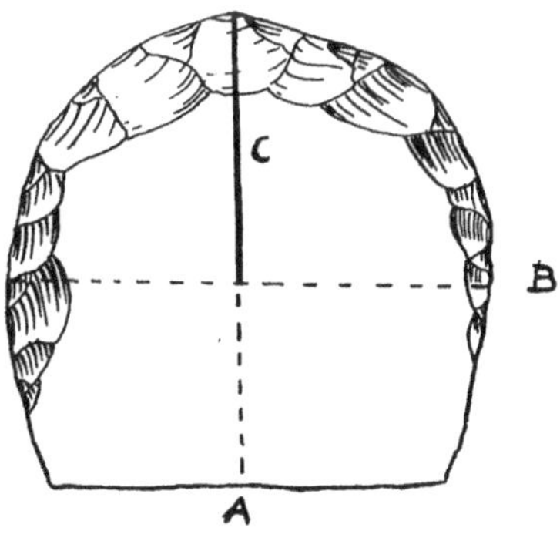

Fig. 32. Measurement of working length for end scrapers: (A) dotted line, maximum length; (B) dotted line, maximum width of the functional area; (C) full trait, working length.

Measurements taken on a series of artifacts from Snyders site show that two types of working edges can be recognized. Working lengths are distributed as follows:

TABLE IV

SNYDERS SITE END SCRAPERS

DISTRIBUTION OF WORKING LENGTHS

Classes in Millimeters	Observed Numbers	Expected Numbers
0.1 – 5	2	1.64
5.1 -- 10	3	4.50
10.1 – 15	14	10.12
15.1 – 20	11	15.91
20.1 – 25	12	17.50
25.1 – 30	12	10.79
30.1 – 35	16	7.62
35.1 – 40	2	2.91
		.88

Number of specimens - 72.
Mean = 22.
Standard deviation s = .08.
X^2 = 15.69.
Expected X^2 at .02 level of probability, 15.033.

This comparison shows that the actual frequency distribution of the working lengths of the end scrapers differs markedly from the distribution expected of a random sample drawn from a population of end scrapers having normal distributed lengths with the same mean and standard deviation as the actual sample. From the cultural point of view, this suggests that the makers of the artifacts had more than one pattern in mind. The total lengths are normally distributed as shown in Table V. There is no significant association between working lengths and total lengths.

On the basis of numerical evidence, two classes of working edges are separated. A third class of circular artifacts is added for the purpose of the description. Measurements of semicircular and circular artifacts vary within the same range, but the former are single-ended tools where the latter are double-ended.

The definition of types is based on the relationship of the

TABLE V

SNYDERS SITE END SCRAPERS

DISTRIBUTION OF LENGTH MEASUREMENTS

Classes (In millimeters)	Observed Numbers
30.1 – 40	2
40.1 – 50	10
50.1 – 60	26
60.1 – 70	19
70.1 – 80	6
80.1 – 90	5
90.1 – 100	1
100.1 – 110	1
110.1 – 120	1
120.1 – 130	1

Number of specimens - 72.
Mean = 63.

three classes of working end and the different modes of lateral and proximal modifications.

The edges and base are sometimes left unmodified. When retouching occurs, it can be either a steep marginal retouch similar to the one used to make the working edge or a flat internal retouching. The flat internal retouching is concentrated on the bulbar area. It is intended to flatten and to regularize the internal face when the bulb of percussion of the blank flake is too prominent. This mode of retouching has been called "composite" to separate this group of artifacts from specimens made of bifacial blanks. Therefore, the classes of lateral and proximal modifications are:

a) no modification
b) "composite" retouching of bulbar area
c) lateral retouching:
  (*c* 1) parallel
  (*c* 2) contracting
  (*c* 3) converging
  (*c* 4) shouldered and stem
  (*c* 5) corner notched (exclusively on worked bifacial blanks)

Table VI shows the relation between working edges and lateral modifications:

TABLE VI

SNYDERS SITE END SCRAPERS

CORRELATION BETWEEN CLASSES OF WORKING ENDS AND MODES OF LATERAL RETOUCHING

	No Modifications	Composite Proximal Retouch	Lateral Modifications				
			Parallel	Contracting	Converging	Shouldered	Corner-Notched
Convex-ended . .	6	. .	11	12	3	3	. .
Semi-circular-ended . .	7	9	. .	7	. .	. .	6
Circular	5	2	. .	. .	. .	. .	. .
Total	18	11	11	19	3	3	6

Total number of specimens - 72.

The ten types listed below are representative of the variety of Hopewell end-scrapers:

1) convex-ended, no lateral or proximal modifications
2) convex-ended, lateral edges modified, parallel
3) convex-ended, lateral edges modified, contracting
4) convex-ended, lateral edges modified, converging
5) convex-ended, lateral edges modified, stemmed
6*a*) semicircular, no lateral or proximal modifications
6*b*) semicircular, composite proximal retouch
7) semicircular, lateral edges modified, contracting
8) semicircular, corner notches
9) circular

The presence or absence of polishing has no direct relationship to any type: half of the specimens in each category show a more-or-less advanced stage of wear polishing. The random distribution of such wear polishing suggests that all the categories belong to a single unit adapted to the same function, probably hide working. The two different classes of working edges are related to the use of two different tools when the modifications observed on proximal and lateral edges are related to the modes of hafting.

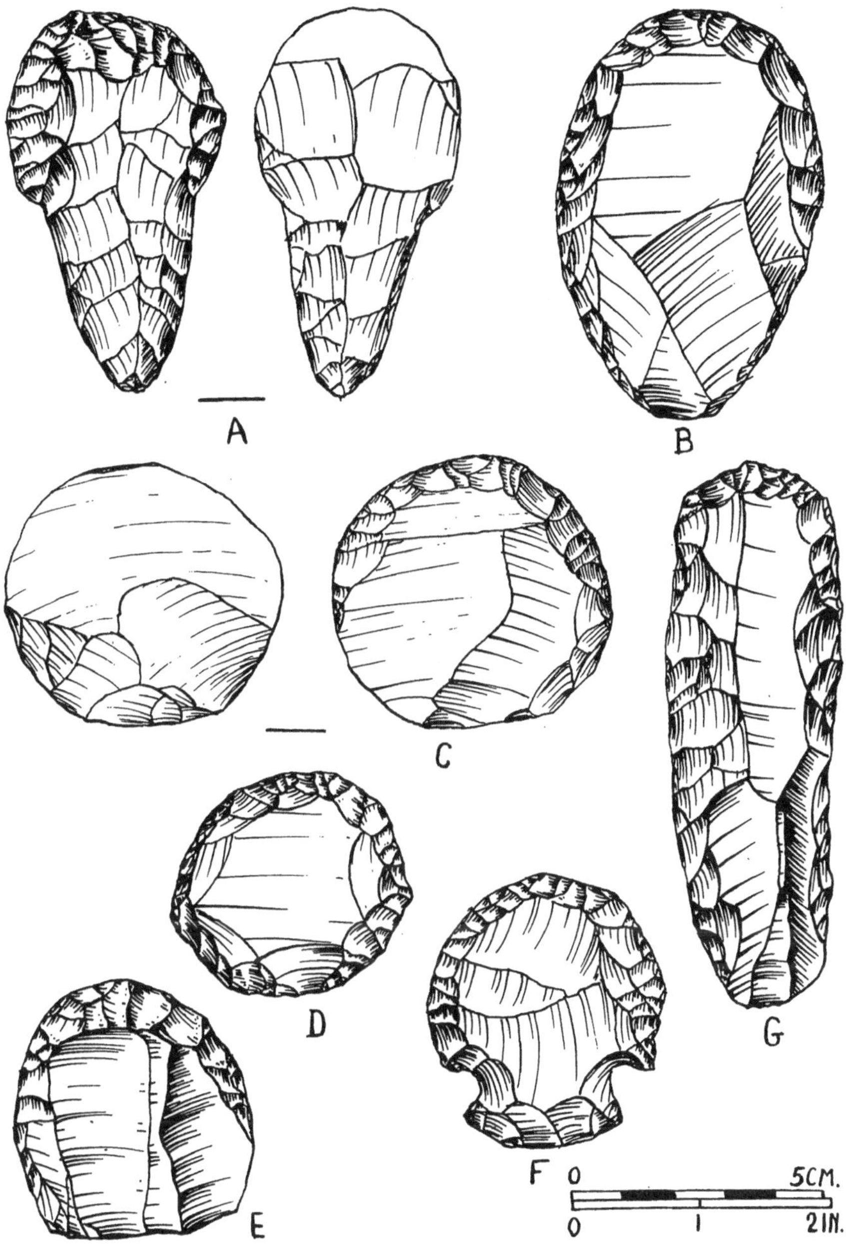

Fig. 33. End scrapers: (A) type 5, (B) type 7, (C) type 6*b*, (D) type 9, (E) type 6*a*, (F) type 8, (G) type 2.

D. Marginally Retouched Artifacts with Longitudinal Working Edge

These artifacts are often referred to as side scrapers. Their functional edge is convex and parallel to the longitudinal axis. With the exception of a few specimens (2 at Snyders) which are prepared by fine lamellar retouching, the functional edge is modified in a rough and irregular fashion.

The edge opposite to the working part forms a "back." Large, deep scars are made to produce a steep, serrated edge. This edge does not show the light polish by wearing which is present on the functional edge. This observation suggests that these large-sized tools were held in the hand.

Side scrapers were found at the Snyders site, but they are not present in the other collections. Seven specimens are unifacial. They are made of flint lamellar flakes. Flat scars on the inner face and polishing of the working edge are evident signs of wear that might suggest the utilization of these tools for cutting hard substances such as wood, or for fleshing game.

There are 10 zigzag-edged scrapers made on tabular flakes. Cutting edges are polished by wear. Backs, also modified by alternate chipping, are straight (3 specimens) or convex (7 specimens).

Six more pieces are made of lumps of flint which could be cores or fragments of cores. They differ from the specimens made of tabular chert by the lack of preparation of the back. Little can be said of the function of these artifacts.

E. Lamellar Flakes with Wear-Pressure Retouch

This group includes large lamellar flakes which were used, although they were not modified to produce a particular tool. The pressure from wearing is irregular and gives a serrated, crushed edge. The placement of this mode of retouching varies greatly from one specimen to another.

At Snyders site only a few specimens (10) are present in the surface collection while 61 were found among the excavated material. On most pieces, the retouching is scattered over all the edges. Some pieces are notched or denticulated.

F. Blades with Blunted Edges (Class A3)

Retouching on the edges appears on only a relatively small proportion of the blades. The excavated material from the Snyders Site (except Test Pit 8) is distributed as follows:

Unmodified bladelets:		
Complete specimens		113
Broken pieces:		
Distal portions	138	
Proximal portions	29	
Fragments	26	
Total		195
Bladelets with discontinuous scars		108
Bladelets with continuous retouching		145
Total		561

The main interest of the above list is to show the relatively large number of fragments of the distal portion as compared with the quantity of proximal pieces. This comparison might indicate that the proximal sections were used as tools though the distal fragments were rejected. This suggestion is supported by the fact that a large proportion of end-retouched blades are broken at the distal end.

A tool can be recognized only when the retouching presents a definite regularity and continuity along the edges. The discontinuous scars which appear on some of the blades might be the result of natural pressure under the ground as well as marks of wear or intentional retouching. There is no observable difference in size or form between the unmodified bladelets which apparently were rejected, and the ones which have been used. Placement of the retouching along the edges and ends is the most important characteristic for recognition of artifacts with blunted edges.

The end retouch is usually distal unless the proximal end is naturally thick enough to replace truncation or a break. The purpose of this preparation is to provide a sharp point supported by a blunted back. The point is the working part since it is associated with little, adjacent, lateral scars which under a microscope appear to be like small burin spalls. In case of converging-end retouch, the angle is the part which shows the wear. This leads one to suppose that those end-retouch bladelets were used as gravers. The different forms of end retouch seem to be the adaptation of each particular bladelet to its function. This would explain the multiplicity of the forms. There is no numerical evidence from the material described here that the various types of end retouching are real categories.

A certain number of the gravers are associated with lateral

preparation. A fine retouch around the base or any kind of bilateral, symmetrical retouching might be considered as hafting preparation. When the lateral retouching does not present any symmetry or regularity, it could be an indication of use as cutting tools.

Retouching located only on the edges is mostly notch or serration. It is irregular and composite. These artifacts were probably used to incise materials such as bird bones or light wood. The following categories have been used to compare various assemblages within the Hopewell complex. More categories should be established before considering other blade assemblages (Poverty Point, Cahokia). The four categories are:

A) Unmodified
B) Discontinuous scars
C1) Notched blades
C2) Laterally retouched blades
C3) End-retouched blades
C4) End and laterally retouched blades

Cores are conical, pyramidal, discoidal, or polyhedric. Their distribution does not seem to be significant.

Chips from bifacial retouching are occasionally used as blades. They have been classified in types on the same basis as the the blade assemblage:

A) No modification
B) Discontinuous scars
C1) Lateral retouch
C2) Notched
C3) End retouch
C4) End and lateral retouch

Unmodified flakes and waste of large and small assemblages complete the assemblage of chipped-flint industries.

DISTRIBUTION OF THE CHIPPED-STONE ARTIFACTS AND THEIR CULTURAL SIGNIFICANCE

A. The Snyders Site (Excavation Units Collection)

The first series of tables presented here shows the distribution of artifacts from Snyders site in respect to excavation units and levels. The location of each excavation unit is shown on the map in Figure 35. The five units dug along the creek, designated

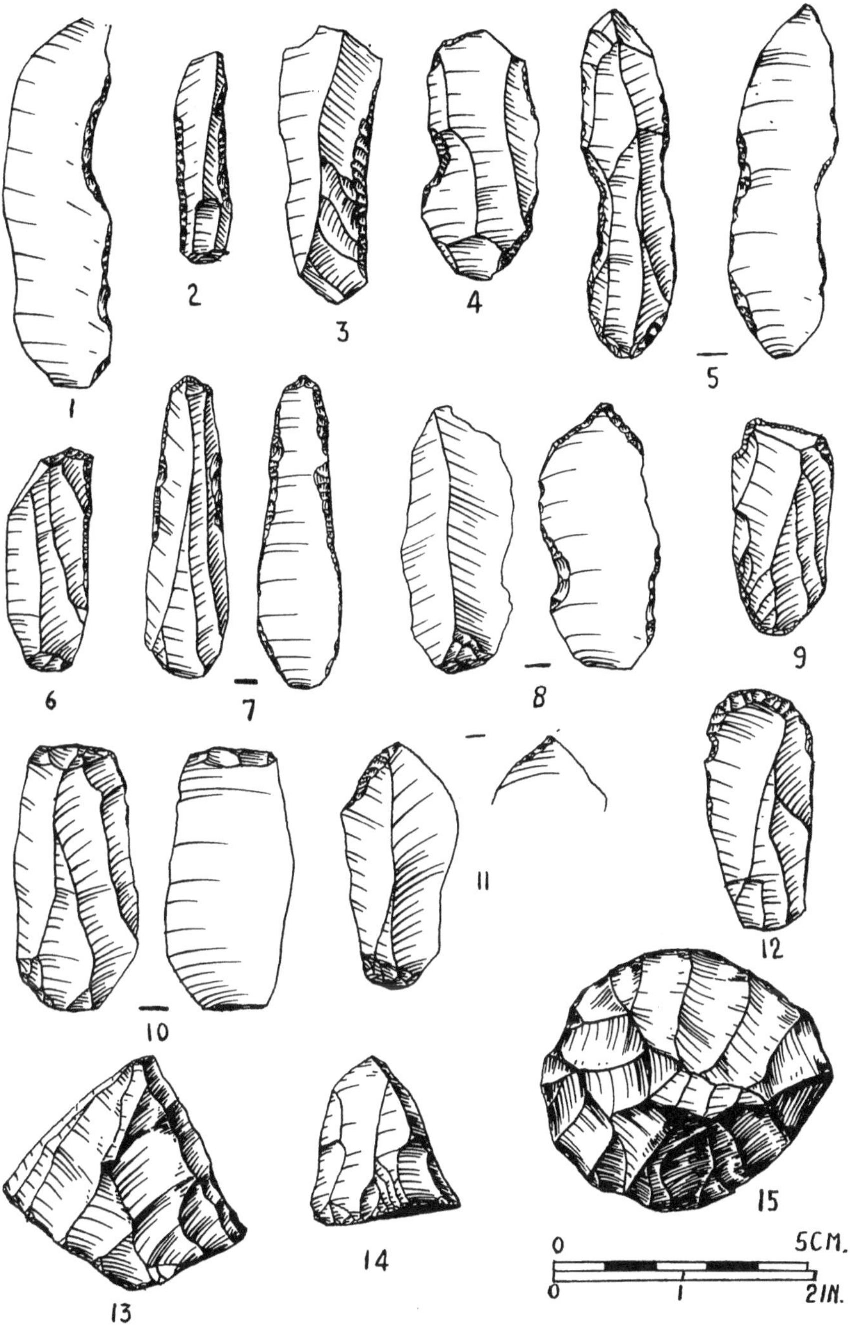

Fig. 34. Blades and blade cores (all specimens from Snyders site). Blade type Cl, Nos. 1, 4, 5; type C2, Nos. 2, 3; type C3, Nos. 10, 11, 12; and type C4, Nos. 6, 7, 8, 9; Nuclei, Nos. 13, 14, 15.

by the excavators as -5, -5R2, -5R3, 00, and 3, provide a good stratigraphic sequence. Nine levels are recorded. Because of the small number of specimens present in each square the data are pulled together into a single table. The amount of wasted information is negligible since these units constitute a single trench.

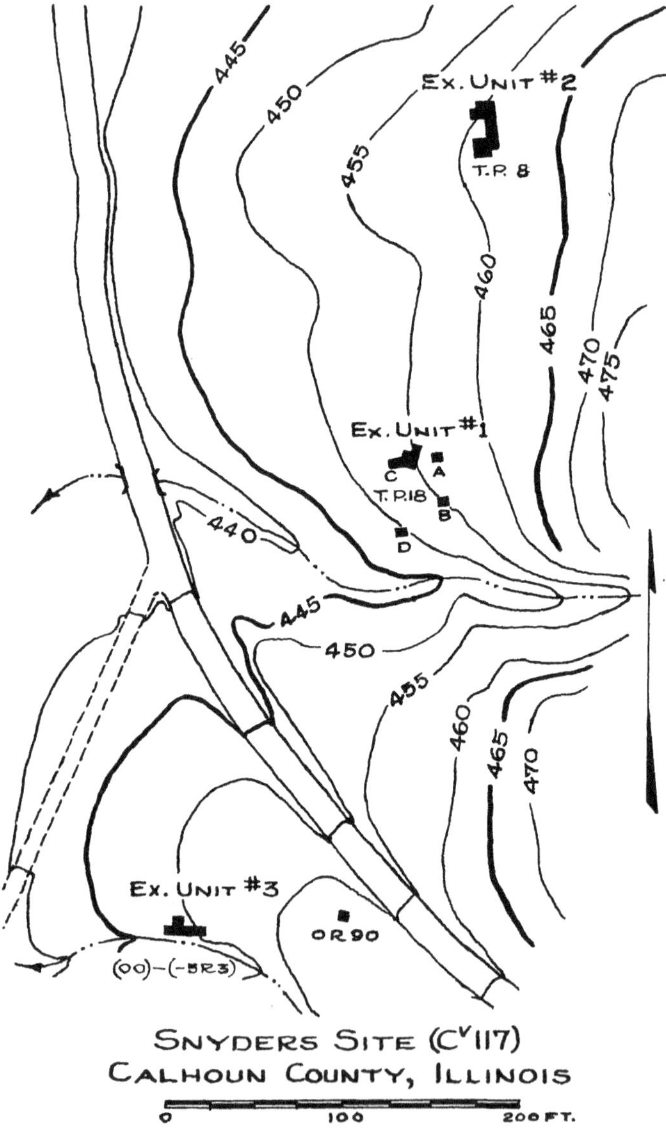

Fig. 35. Map of the Snyders site.

Ten classes of artifacts are selected to provide numerical data for a definition of the Snyders industry in terms of the chipping and retouching techniques:

1) Bifacially retouched artifacts
2) Marginally retouched artifacts (steep marginal retouch)
3) Flakes with wear retouch
4) Chips modified by edge-blunting retouch (Types B, C1, C2, C3, C4)
5) Unmodified flakes
6) Unmodified chips
7) Modified blades (types B, C1, C2, C3, C4)
8) Unmodified blades
9) Cores
10) Waste

TABLE VII

SNYDERS SITE

ARTIFACTS FROM UNITS -5, -5R2, -5R3, 3, 00

Classes	Levels									Total
	1	2	3	4	5	6	7	8	9	
1. Bifacially retouched . .	5	4	6	13	18	13	5	11	9	84
2. Marginally retouched . .	2	1	1	1	2	1	3	2	. .	13
3. Flakes with wear retouch	1	3	. .	3	3	2	3	. .	3	18
4. Modified chips	1	2	1	1	1	1	5	1	3	16
5. Unmodified flakes	1	2	1	. .	1	. .	3	. .	3	11
6. Unmodified chips	4	23	2	5	14	8	2	6	1	65
7. Modified blades.	4	5	11	15	5	5	9	5	. .	59
8. Unmodified blades	23	18	31	30	27	30	25	29	11	224
9. Cores	. .	. .	. .	. .	3	. .	2	. .	2	7
0. Waste	3	45	5	7	22	12	39	13	17	163
Total	44	103	58	75	96	72	96	67	49	660

One can observe from Table VIII that the proportion of unmodified artifacts and waste tends to be constant and that it is therefore independent of the stratigraphic sequence. Excavation unit 3 is taken here as an example.

TABLE VIII

SNYDERS SITE. EXCAVATION UNIT 3

DISTRIBUTION OF UNMODIFIED VERSUS MODIFIED ARTIFACTS

Unmodified Artifacts and Wastes	Others
Level 1 – 26	7
2 – 10	3
3 – 26	5
4 – 19	8
5 – 15	10
6 – 17	5
7 – 9	8
8 – 8	6

X^2 value at .20 level of probability 9.803 for 7 degrees of freedom.

Since a chi-square value as large as this can be expected in about 20 per cent of the samples drawn from a population having no association between population of unmodified artifacts and wastes and levels, there is no good reason to suspect a significant association here. Similar calculations need not be repeated for each square. As a consequence of this observation, the waste is not included in the following comparisons. On the other hand, there are substantial differences in the proportion of the various classes of artifacts. These differences concern, first, the interrelationship of the various artifacts and, second, the distribution by levels. The following calculations have been utilized to test whether the observable differences are significant (Table IX).

Since blades are the most important group numerically, the first comparison considers their distribution in relation to the other artifacts.

TABLE IX

SNYDERS SITE EXCAVATIONS

DISTRIBUTION OF BLADES IN RELATION TO OTHER ARTIFACTS

Levels	Blades	Other Artifacts
1	27	14
2	23	35
3	43	11
4	45	23
5	32	39
6	35	25
7	34	21
8	34	20
9	11	19

X^2 value at .001 level of probability = 26.128 for 8 degrees of freedom.

The large value of the calculated chi-square indicates that the distribution of blades by levels is highly significant. Next, the distribution of bifacial artifacts is compared to the flakes and chips (Table X).

TABLE X

SNYDERS SITE EXCAVATIONS

DISTRIBUTION OF BIFACIAL ARTIFACTS VERSUS FLAKES AND CHIPS

Levels	Bifacial Artifacts (Class 1)	Flakes and Chips (Classes 2, 3, 4, 5, and 6)
1	5	9
2	4	31
3	6	5
4	13	10
5	18	21
6	13	12
7	5	16
8	11	9
9	9	10
Total .	84	123

Total number of artifacts - 207.
X^2 = 16.92 at .05 level of probability degrees of freedom = 9.

The high value of the calculated chi-square shows that the distribution of bifacial artifacts in respect to levels is significant. These calculations answer the two questions mentioned above: (1) there are significant differences between the distribution of artifacts in respect to levels and (2) the calculations also emphasize the fact that each class of artifact varies independently as shown in Table XI.

TABLE XI

SNYDERS SITE EXCAVATIONS

DISTRIBUTION OF ARTIFACTS AND PERCENTAGES
(By Levels for Excavation-units 3, Squares 00, -5, -5R2, -5R3)

Levels	Bifacial Artifacts	Flakes Modified or Unmodified	Chips	Blades	Total by Levels (per cent)
1 . .	5 : 12.2	4 : 9.8	5 : 12.2	27 : 65.8	41 : 100
2 . .	4 : 6.9	6 : 10.3	25 : 43.1	23 : 39.7	58 : 100
3 . .	6 : 11.3	2 : 3.7	3 : 5.7	42 : 79.2	53 : 100
4 . .	13 : 19.2	4 : 5.7	6 : 7.9	45 : 67.2	68 : 100
5 . .	18 : 25.3	6 : 8.4	15 : 21.1	32 : 45.0	71 : 100
6 . .	13 : 21.6	3 : 5.	9 : 15.	35 : 58.4	60 : 100
7 . .	5 : 9.2	9 : 16.3	7 : 12.7	34 : 61.8	55 : 100
8 . .	11 : 20.4	2 : 3.7	7 : 12.9	34 : 63.0	54 : 100
9 . .	9 : 30	6 : 20	4 : 13.3	11 : 36.7	30 : 100
Total	84 : 17.2	42 : 8.6	81 : 16.5	283 : 57.7	490 : 100
Mean	9.3	4.6	9	31.3	

Blade maxima occur at levels 8 and 7 and at levels 4 and 3. On the other hand, chip maxima occur at levels 5 and then at level 2, and bifacial artifact maxima at level 8, level 6, and level 4. On the basis of these observations the following description of the stratigraphic sequence can be given:

Level 9 is characterized by a small number of blades, chips and flakes as compared to the relatively large number of bifacial blades.

The proportions of the four classes of artifacts between levels 8, 7 and 6 are constant with the exception of a significant decrease in bifacial artifacts at level 7. At level 5, the bifacial artifacts and the chips are abundant, but the number of blades decreases.

The highest proportion of blades is observed at levels 3 and 2 where the other three classes progressively decrease in number.

Level 2 is characterized by a distribution differing from the one observed in the lower levels: a low population of blades as compared to a relatively high proportion of chips and bifacial artifacts.

The most important difference is the negative correlation that exists between blades and chips. In spite of the fact that blades consistently outnumber the chips, the largest populations of chips occur when a substantial decrease in the number of blades can be observed at levels 5 and 2. This fact supports the observation suggested in the description, namely, that chips were utilized as a substitute for blades when the latter decreased in number. This statement becomes more evident when the Snyders industry is compared with collections from other sites (Table XVII, p. 66).

More data from a large number of Hopewell assemblages would make it possible to evaluate the mean and standard deviation for each population of artifacts. Then a comprehensive definition of Hopewell chipping techniques based on numerical variations will be possible. Presently, one can state that significant stratigraphic differences are observable at the Snyders site.

As stated previously, only a few specimens of tools were found in the excavations. Apart from the projectile points, bifacially retouched artifacts are represented by only two complete specimens of the spud-shaped category (Type BT5).

The distribution of end scrapers is shown in Table XII.

TABLE XII

SNYDERS SITE EXCAVATIONS. DISTRIBUTION OF END SCRAPERS

Types	1	2	3	4	5	6	7	8	9	Total
Level										
1 . . .	1	2	. .	. .	1	. .	. .	1	1	6
2 . . .	. .	. .	. .	. .	. .	. .	. .	. .	. .	. .
3 . . .	. .	. .	. .	. .	1	. .	. .	1	. .	2
4 . . .	. .	. .	. .	. .	. .	. .	. .	. .	. .	. .
5 . . .	1	1	. .	. .	. .	. .	. .	2	. .	4
6 . . .	. .	. .	. .	. .	1	. .	. .	. .	. .	1
7 . . .	2	1	. .	. .	1	. .	. .	. .	. .	4
8 . . .	. .	1	1	. .	. .	. .	. .	1	. .	3
9 . . .	. .	1	. .	. .	. .	. .	. .	1	. .	2
Total .	4	6	1	. .	4	. .	. .	6	1	22

The total number of end scrapers represents only 3.4 per cent of the industry, not counting waste. Types 6 and 7 are not represented. Type 8, reworked projectile points made into semicircular end scrapers, is the most common. This observation corroborates the assumption that bifacially chipped artifacts are more abundant than marginally retouched flakes. The proportion of modified blades is larger in the upper levels.

Tables XIII through XVII deal with the distribution of chipped flint artifacts within the other excavation units. They do not offer the stratigraphic sequence observed in the south trench. Test Pit 18 and Unit 1 occupied the central section, Test Pit 8 and Unit 2, the northern section.

Test Pit 18.—From a grand total of 727 artifacts, the largest percentages are found in levels 2 and 3 of section A, and pit B, section C. No bifacial artifacts were found in section A. With the exception of a few scrapers, the whole assemblage is composed of blades, chips, and rejects. On the other hand, eight projectile points were found in pit A, together with twenty-three blades and a few chips, but no rejects. Section B contains only one projectile point, four blades and a large number of chipping wastes. Section C has very little material, but a large number of artifacts were found in a deep pit (Pit B). Section D includes material containing a large proportion of rejects.

Unit 2.—The only important feature of Unit 2 is an oval pit of dark midden which had been dug in a layer of yellow clay. This pit contained a flexed burial. A total of thirty-eight artifacts were associated with the burial. Among them were seven projectile points, seventeen blades, one core, and a few chips and flakes.

The most noticeable difference that can be observed between the deep units and the other sections affects the proportion of unmodified artifacts. The unmodified artifacts represent 25 per cent of the whole assemblage in the deep units, but account for 70 per cent in the other sections. This difference affects not only the waste (artifact class 10) but the unmodified flakes, chips, and blades as well. On the other hand, there were very few tools.

Such a large differentiation suggests that the various units represent different modes of living.

B. Surface Collections

The surface collections are presented in a series of analytic tables which give the observed numbers of specimens for each type of artifact. These surface collections come from Illinois—

TABLE XIII

SNYDERS SITE. TEST PIT 18

Artifact Classes	Section A				Section B	Section C			Section D			Total
	Level 1	Level 2	Level 3	Pit A		Level 1	Level 2	Pit B	Level 1	Level 2	Pit C	
1 Bifacial	. .	. .	. .	8	1	3	2	8	. .	. .	4	26
2 Marginally retouched	. .	. .	. .	1	. .	. .	. .	2	. .	1	. .	4
3 Retouched flakes . . .	. .	5	. .	. .	. .	. .	1	1	. .	1	. .	8
4 Modified chips	. .	. .	. .	. .	. .	3	. .	3	. .	3	. .	9
5 Unmodified flakes . .	2	7	. .	1	. .	. .	. .	16	. .	. .	. .	26
6 Unmodified chips . . .	2	12	1	2	. .	4	. .	19	5	. .	6	51
7 Modified blades	1	2	3	3	. .	1	4	10	1	. .	1	26
8 Unmodified blades . .	9	33	32	20	4	1	9	47	7	8	7	177
9 Cores	. .	1	4	. .	. .	. .	. .	1	. .	. .	1	7
10 Wastes	26	61	91	2	59	. .	. .	99	11	38	11	393
Total	35	121	131	37	64	12	16	206	24	51	30	727

TABLE XIV

SNYDERS SITE – EXCAVATION UNIT I*

Artifact Classes	Levels			Feature 1			Total
	1	2	3	Level 1	Level 2	Level 3	
1 Bifacial	5	11	1	2	. .	1	20
2 Marginally retouched	3	. .	. .	. .	. .	. .	3
3 Retouched flakes . . .	. .	4	. .	. .	. .	. .	4
4 Modified chips	. .	. .	. .	. .	3	1	4
5 Unmodified flakes . .	. .	. .	. .	. .	. .	. .	. .
6 Unmodified chips . . .	. .	11	. .	. .	4	3	18
7 Modified blades	10	3	1	3	. .	. .	17
8 Unmodified blades . .	22	9	7	13	7	11	69
9 Cores	1	1	. .	. .	. .	. .	2
10 Wastes	95	97	62	15	. .	. .	269
Total	136	167	81	33	15	16	428

*Unit 1. The only remarkable feature of this ur is a roughly circular pit (Feature 1) which contains pottery sherds, bones, three projectile points, and thirty-five blades on a stone floor.

the Snyders, Knight, and Sconce Schudel sites in Calhoun County; the Manker sites in Pike County; and the Twenhafel site in Jackson County.

This mode of tabulation is chosen because rejects and unmodified artifacts were seldom collected. Consequently a typological analysis constitutes the most fruitful approach to the available data.

Following is an analysis based on the ten classes of artifacts utilized for presenting the excavated collection from the Snyders site.

TABLE XV

SNYDERS SITE. TEST PIT 8*

Artifact Classes	Section A			Section B			Section C			Section D			Total
	Lev. 1	Lev. 2	Lev. 3	Lev. 1	Lev. 2	Lev. 3	Lev. 1	Lev. 2	Lev. 3	Lev. 1	Lev. 2-3	Lev. 4	
1 Bifacial	4	1	. .	2	1	. .	1	3	1	2	. .	. .	15
2 Marginally retouched	. .	. .	. .	1	. .	. .	. .	1	. .	. .	1	. .	3
3 Retouched flakes . . .	. .	. .	. .	3	. .	. .	4	3	2	. .	. .	. .	12
4 Modified chips . . .	. .	. .	. .	. .	. .	2	. .	. .	2	. .	1	. .	5
5 Unmodified flakes . .	. .	6	. .	. .	4	. .	. .	3	. .	. .	. .	. .	13
6 Unmodified chips . .	. .	1	. .	. .	. .	. .	. .	4	3	. .	. .	. .	8
7 Modified blades . . .	. .	1	. .	2	2	. .	3	3	2	. .	. .	. .	13
8 Unmodified blades . .	2	5	. .	3	8	1	9	10	3	. .	1	. .	42
9 Cores	. .	1	. .	. .	. .	1	. .	1	. .	1	. .	3	7
10 Wastes	6	10	33	6	29	8	10	13	9	4	22	8	158
Total	12	25	33	17	44	12	27	41	22	7	25	11	276

*Test Pit 8. This pit is characterized by the general abundance of rejects, as compared to the number of modified artifacts. The modified artifacts constitute 9 per cent of the total.

TABLE XVI

SNYDERS SITE. EXCAVATION UNIT 2

Artifact Classes	Levels							Total
	1	Pit 1	2	Pit 2	3	4	5	
1 Bifacial	7	3	6	4	5	2	. .	27
2 Marginally retouched	1	. .	. .	. .	2	. .	. .	3
3 Retouched flakes . . .	5	1	3	1	1	1	. .	12
4 Modified chips	3	. .	. .	. .	. .	. .	. .	3
5 Unmodified flakes . .	. .	. .	3	2	6	. .	. .	11
6 Unmodified chips . .	6	6	2	1	9	. .	. .	24
7 Modified blades	8	. .	5	3	1	5	. .	22
8 Unmodified blades . .	21	7	24	7	21	1	. .	81
9 Cores	3	. .	1	1	1	. .	. .	6
10 Wastes	92	2	92	. .	128	. .	1	315
Total	146	19	136	19	174	9	1	504

DISTRIBUTION OF ARTIFACTS AMONG SURFACE COLLECTIONS

Snyders Site - Surface Collection

Group I

A. Projectile points—number of specimens: 189
B. Bifacial blades—number of specimens: 47
BT. 3—6 specimens

BT. 4—6 specimens
BT. 5—2 specimens
BT. 7—2 specimens
BT. 8—3 specimens
BT. 9—2 specimens
Fragments—18
Unfinished blanks—8

C. No specimens

D. Drills—number of specimens: 18

Group II

A. End scrapers—number of specimens: 75
A 1—11 specimens
A 2—11 specimens
A 3—12 specimens
A 4— 3 specimens
A 5— 3 specimens
A 6—12 specimens
A 7— 7 specimens
A 8— 6 specimens
A 9— 4 specimens
Fragments—6

B. Side scrapers—number of specimens: 23
1—7 specimens
2—16 specimens

Group III. Retouched flakes—number of specimens: 16

Group IV. Retouched chips—number of specimens: 13

B. Scattered scars: 13

Group V. Unmodified flakes—number of specimens: 16

Group VI. Unmodified chips—number of specimens: 21

Group VII. Modified blades—number of specimens: 252

B—bladelets with discontinuous scars—108
Cl—notched blades—none
C2—laterally retouched blades—none
C3—end-retouched blades—none
C4—end and laterally retouched blades—none

Group VIII. Unmodified blades—number of specimens: 308

Group IX. Cores and chipping wastes

A. Bladelets assemblage—21 conical:7
discoid:5
polyh.: 2
waste: 2

B. Large assemblage—5

Group X. Unclassified waste: none

Sconce Schudel Site, Calhoun County, Illinois—Surface Collection

Group I

A. Projectile point, number of specimens: 28
B. Bifacial blades—number of specimens: 4
B1 3—3 specimens
B1 7—1 specimens

Group II

A. End scrapers—number of specimens: 2
A 3—2 specimens

Group III. No specimens

Group IV. Mofidied chips—number of specimens: 16

C1—4 specimens
C2—6 specimens
C3—3 specimens
C4—3 specimens

Group V. Unmodified flakes—number of specimens: 6

Group VI. Unmodified chips—number of specimens: 29

Group VII. Modified blades—number of specimens: 34

B—10 specimens
C1—9 specimens
C2—9 specimens
C3—3 specimens
C4—3 specimens

Group VIII. Unmodified blades—number of specimens: 27

Group IX. Cores

A. 9 specimens

Group X. 7 specimens

Manker Site, Pike County, Illinois—Surface Collection

Group I

A. Projectile points—number of specimens: 61
B. Bifacial blades—number of specimens: 22
Bt1—3 specimens
Bt2—6 specimens
Bt3—2 specimens
Bt7—5 specimens
Fragments—6 specimens

Group II

A. End scrapers—number of specimens: 1
B. Side scrapers—number of specimens: 4
B2—4 specimens

Group III. Modified flakes—number of specimens: 7

Group IV. Modified chips—number of specimens: 11

C1—3 specimens
C2—3 specimens
C3—1 specimen
C4—4 specimens

Group V. Unmodified flakes: None

Group VI. Unmodified chips—number of specimens: 12

Group VII. Modified blades—number of specimens: 42

B. Discontinuous scars: 11 specimens
C1—11 specimens
C2— 7 specimens
C3— 4 specimens
C4— 9 specimens

Group VIII. Unmodified blades—number of specimens: 4

Group IX. Cores: None

Group X. Unclassified waste: None

Twenhafel Site, Jackson County, Illinois—Surface Collection

Group I

A. Projectile points—number of specimens: 13
B. Bifacial blades—number of specimens: 2
Fragments: 2

Group II

A. End scrapers—number of specimens: 4
   A.3—4

Group III. None

Group IV. Modified chips—number of specimens: 45 (thin, small flakes from pyramid cores or from bifacial trimming)

C1— 7
C2—13
C3—18
C4— 7

Group V. Unmodified flakes—number of specimens: 39

Group VI. Unmodified chips—number of specimens: 57

Group VII. Modified blades—number of specimens: 17
B —7 specimens
C1—4 specimens
C2—2 specimens
C3—1 specimens
C4—3 specimens

Group VIII. Unmodified blades—number of specimens: 1

Group IX. Cores—number of specimens: 4

A. Blades—conical cores: 4 specimens

Group X. None

Knight Site, Calhoun County, Illinois—Surface Collection

Group I

A. Projectile points—number of specimens: 30
B. Bifacial artifacts with transverse cutting edge—number of specimens: 7
   T1—2 specimens
   T3—3 specimens (one specimen was broken and reworked)
   T7—2 specimens
   Fragments: 9
D. Drills—number of specimens: 3

Group II

A. Marginally retouched artifacts with transverse cutting edge—number of specimens: 9
  A1—2 specimens (1 unifacial, 1 bifacial)
  A2—2 specimens (unifacial)
  A3—1 specimen (bifacial)
  A6—1 specimen
  A8—1 specimen
  A9—2 specimens

B. Marginal retouched artifacts with longitudinal working edge—number of specimens: 7
  B1 Unifacial—2 specimens
  B2 Bifacial edges—5 specimens

Group III. Modified flakes—number of specimens: 9

Group IV. Modified chips: None

Group V. Unmodified flakes: None

Group VI. Unmodified chips—number of specimens: None

Group VII. Modified blades—number of specimens: 74
  B —25 specimens
  C1—12 specimens
  C2—15 specimens
  C3— 9 specimens
  C4—13 specimens

Group VIII. Unmodified blades—number of specimens: 27

Group IX. Cores—number of specimens: 8
  Blade assemblage:
    conical—3 specimens
    conical, truncated—1 specimen
    discoids—2 specimens
    fragments—2 specimens

No statistical calculations are necessary to prove that the observable differences are exceedingly large and therefore are partly due to collecting errors.

A certain number of observations, however, are made available by means of Table XVII.

No complete specimens of bifacial celts were collected at Twenhafel (Class 1, Table XVII). The presence of two fragments suggests that bifacial celts were indeed rare. Types BT3 and BT7 are common to all the other sites. Stemmed types exist only at Snyders.

TABLE XVII

COMPARISONS OF SURFACE COLLECTIONS

Artifact Classes	Snyders Site			Sconce Schudel	Manker	Twen-hafel	Knight
	Excava-tions	Sur-face	Total				
1. Bifacial Artifacts . . .	185 12.39	254 25.3	439 17.58	32 20.65	83 50.61	17 11.72	39 22.54
2. Marginally Retouched Artifacts . . .	29 1.94	98 9.76	127 5.09	2 1.29	5 3.05	4 2.76	16 9.25
3. Flakes with Wear Retouch	61 4.09	16 1.59	77 3.08	. . . .	7 4.27	. . . .	9 5.21
4. Modified Chips	42 2.81	13 1.29	55 2.21	16 10.32	11 6.71	45 31.03	. . . .
5. Unmodified Flakes	70 4.69	16 1.59	86 3.44	6 3.87	. . . .	. . . .	. . . .
6. Unmodified Chips	225 15.07	21 2.09	246 9.85	29 18.71	12 7.32	57 59.32	. . . .
7. Modified Blades	164 10.99	252 25.11	416 16.66	34 21.93	42 25.61	17 11.72	74 42.77
8. Unmodified Blades	677 45.34	308 30.68	985 39.45	27 17.42	4 2.44	1 0.69	27 15.60
9. Cores	40 2.68	26 2.59	66 2.64	9 5.81	. . . .	4 2.72	8 4.63
Total	1493 100%	1004 100%	2497 100%	155 100%	164 100%	145 100%	173 100%

Relatively abundant at Snyders and Knight sites, the end scrapers are rare among the other collections. Type 8 (reworked projectile points) are present everywhere. The other semicircular-ended types are lacking at Manker, Twenhafel, and Sconce-Schudel sites. The end-scrapers, Types 6, 7 and 9, are well represented in the Snyders surface collection although they are not represented within the excavated material. Types 6 and 9 exist at Knight site, but do not exist in the other sites. Similar types of scrapers were found at the Raymond site (Maxwell, p. 241) and at the Dillenger site (Maxwell, Plate XXXI). A few scrapers were found at Sconce-Schudel and Manker. They belong to the convex-ended types.

The largest numerical differences affect the distribution of blades and chips. Modified and unmodified chips (Classes 4 and 6) amount to 12 per cent at Snyders, 13 per cent at Manker, 29 per cent at Sconce-Schudel and 70 per cent at Twenhafel. Twenhafel chips are made of a grey-blue flint but the blades are made of white flint. At the other sites, blades and chips are chipped from the same material, a pink-white flint. The fact that modified blades outnumber the unmodified at Sconce-Schudel and Manker is significant, since on the basis of the evidence observed at Snyders, one can suppose that sampling errors are responsible for this reverse distribution. If the specimens were collected at random, the differences would probably be smaller.

From the actual data, one can assume that the industry at the Knight site is closely related to that of the Snyders site. More variations can be observed between them and Manker and Sconce-Schudel, although the two latter sites can be assumed to belong to the same technical complex.

The differences observed at Twenhafel are numerous enough to suggest that this industry belongs to a different industrial complex.

More abundant collections from excavated sites will be necessary to evaluate the maximum individual variations that can possibly occur within a single technical complex. On this basis, it will be possible to define the range of variations that can take place within the type of industry represented at Snyders. Presently, these variations can only be suggested.

DISCUSSION

The chipped-stone industry of the Snyders site can be defined in terms of its flaking and retouching techniques; its main characteristics are clearly apparent in spite of a still incomplete numerical evaluation. Three sorts of raw materials are available at Snyders, slabs of white chert, blocks of pink-white flint, and nodules of blue-gray flint. The flaking techniques are adapted to each particular type of raw material. The chert is associated with tabular and lamellar flaking, which produces blank flakes easily modified by steep marginal retouching and bifacial trimming. The flints are knapped into more regular lamellar flakes well adapted to pressure trimming and blades that require little or no edge blunting.

It has already been mentioned that the whole industry

constitutes a homogeneous technological complex in spite of the metrical and formal differences that one can observe between specimens. The common technical processes taking place at the village site, namely, lamellar and blade flaking and bifacial retouching, are logically related. On the basis of this technical homogeneity, an indigenous origin is postulated for the blade assemblage.

The analytical description emphasizes formal differences between types of utilized artifacts. The types of scrapers appear to have a cultural significance. The semicircular scrapers found in the Snyders surface collections can be related to similar artifacts found at the Knight site and at the Sugar Camp Hill site, the Dillinger site, and the Raymond site in southern Illinois. This strongly suggests their association with late Hopewell or late Woodland occupations. The convex-ended scrapers are common to other Hopewell sites. The latter forms are found in the deep units J. B. Griffin identified as Hopewell on the basis of ceramic traits (Griffin, 1952). The former types occur in surface collections where Hopewell pottery is mixed with Jersey Bluff sherds. Single-beveled celts are associated with the semicircular scrapers in the sites just mentioned. It also exists at Manker and Sconce-Schudel where no semicircular scrapers are present. This observation suggests a wider distribution of the celt as compared to the semicircular scraper.

The stratigraphic distribution of blades and chips as compared to bifacial tools and marginally retouched tools shows significant differences by levels. More analytic descriptions will be necessary to give a clear definition of the stratigraphic distribution of chipped-stone industries, and more extensive analysis of artifacts to give an adequate picture of the functional distribution of an industry. The functional descriptions presented in this paper are proposed as temporary evaluation. They are mainly intended to show that the purpose of the typological analysis of the chipped-stone material will lead to a more comprehensive portrayal of the economy and technological environment of archaeological data.

REFERENCES CITED

Bordes, F.
1952. Stratigraphie du Loess et Evolution des Industries Paleolithiques dans l'Ouest du Bassin de Paris. L'Anthropologie Vol. 56, Paris.

Clark, J. D.
1954. The Prehistoric Culture of the Horn of Africa. Occasional Publications of the Cambridge University Museum of Archaeology and Ethnology, Vol. II. Cambridge: Cambridge University Press.

Ford, J. A. and Webb, C. H.
1956. Poverty Point, A Late Archaic Site in Louisiana. American Museum of Natural History, Anthropological Papers, Vol. 46, Pt. 1, New York.

Gardin, J. C.
1958. Four Codes for the Description of Artifacts: An Essay in Archeological Technique and Theory. American Anthropologist, Vol. 60, No. 2, Pt. 1.

Griffin, J. B.
1952. The Snyders Site, Calhoun Co., Illinois. The Greater St. Louis Archaeological Society.

Griffin, J. B. (Ed.)
1952. Archaeology of the Eastern United States. Chicago: University of Chicago Press.

McGregor, J. C.
1958. The Pool and Irving Villages. Urbana: University of Illinois Press.

McKern, W. C., Titterington, P. F. and Griffin, J. B.
1945. Painted Pottery Figurines from Illinois. American Antiquity, Vol. 10, No. 3, pp. 295-302.

Maxwell, M. S.
1951. Woodland Cultures of Southern Illinois: Archaeological Excavations in the Carbondale Area. Logan Museum Publications in Anthropology, No. 7, Beloit College, Beloit, Wis.

Struever, S.
1960. The Kamp Mound Group and a Hopewell Mortuary Complex in the Lower Illinois Valley. Unpublished thesis, Northwestern University, Evanston, Ill.

Titterington, P. F.
1938. The Cahokia Mound Group and Its Village Site Materials. P. F. Titterington, St. Louis, Mo.

Witthoft, J. W.
1952. A Paleo Indian Site in Eastern Pennsylvania, An Early Hunting Culture. Proceedings of the American Philosophical Society, Vol. 96, No. 4, pp. 464-95.

1957. The Art of Flint Chipping. Ohio Archaeologist, Vol. 7, No. 2, pp. 42-46. The Archaeological Society of Ohio, Columbus.

THE EASTPORT SITE
ANTRIM COUNTY, MICHIGAN

Lewis R. Binford and Mark L. Papworth

CONTENTS

Figures

Tables

DESCRIPTION OF SITE AND EXCAVATION

At Eastport, Michigan, there is a wide area of sand dunes and old lake beaches worked by wind and water into a rather complex formation of ridges and blow outs. This sandy area extends, at Eastport, from highway U. S. 31 westward to Traverse Bay. Much of the area is today being eroded by the wind. Many of the basin-shaped depressions formed by wind action contain evidence of aboriginal occupation in the form of fire-broken rock and flint fragments. Near the Eastporter Motel there is one such area which has yielded a large amount of flint debris and many flint artifacts. This site has been reported by G. W. Davis and E. V. Gillis in a recent article entitled "Grand Traverse Bay Archaic" (Davis and Gillis, 1959). Davis and Gillis' report concerns materials which they excavated from a dune area in the Eastport vicinity. As a demonstration of the richness of the worked flint in this area, there is reproduced from their article the following information:

"An area measuring 16 feet square produced the following quantities of artifacts: 440 pounds of flint chip fragments; 60 broken projectile points; 90 points finished to varying degrees; 50 spawls; 15 hammer stones; 5 anvil stones; 5 abrading stones; 20 thumb scrapers; and 1 fragment of slate gorget." J. B. Griffin and M. L. Papworth, from the Museum of Anthropology at The University of Michigan, further investigated the area with the aid of Davis and Gillis.

The site itself is situated on a fairly flat sand area sporadically in use as a barrow pit by the Antrim County Highway Department. The elevations above sea level of various old lake features in the area are of extreme importance to the interpretation of the archaeological data from this site. In the following interpretation, we have followed, with some modification, Jack L. Hough's *Glacial Geology of the Great Lakes* as the most recent and reliable source for this problem.

Ten thousand years ago, the last big stand of glacial ice in the Great Lakes blocked a deep cleft in the rocky wall of the Great Lakes basin at North Bay, Ontario. This stand of ice dammed the lake waters up to the level of the drainage sills at Port Huron and Chicago, which allowed the water to flow out of the great southern outlets at 605 feet above sea level. This stand of ice and the firm sill at Port Huron created a stable level of Lakes Michigan and Huron, which lasted long enough to create strong beaches at this

605-foot elevation in both lakes. These beaches mark the outline of Lake Algonquin, a single level, two-lobed lake, joined at the Straits of Mackinac by a narrows. The north shore of this narrows, as well as the northern shores of the two lobes (now Lakes Michigan and Huron) was formed by the retreating ice wall of the continental glacier. Because of the tremendous weight of this ice mass and the isostatic instability of the surface of the earth in its vicinity, the land was depressed hundreds of feet. At the time of Lake Algonquin, the area around Eastport was covered by the waters which stood at 605 feet. Since the retreat of the ice, the land has rebounded to the present elevations.

When the retreating ice uncovered the low sill at North Bay, the waters of Lake Algonquin flowed out of this new outlet to the Ottawa River and the St. Lawrence. The Algonquin beach was left high and dry. A number of weak beaches formed as the water lowered, each marking a temporary stand at their elevations. Simultaneously, the isostatic action of the land raised the Eastport area out of the water. The Algonquin beach line began to rise from its horizontal plane about 80 miles south of Eastport. At Eastport, the Algonquin beach is approximately 45 feet in elevation above the 605-foot hinge line to the south. At the beginning of this isostatic activity, the rate of recovery was more rapid than at present. In the northern part of the Lower Peninsula, the rate has decreased from about 4 feet per one hundred years in Algonquin times, to about 1 foot per one hundred years today.

Another gross morphological change in the Great Lakes took place close on the heels of this lowering from Lake Algonquin. The sill at North Bay stood at 180 feet above sea level. The land around North Bay was rising at only 4.7 feet per one hundred years. When the ice which covered this outlet disappeared, the water sought this new level. By 8250 years ago, the water in Lake Huron and Michigan had lowered to only 180 and 230 feet above sea level respectively. This is the Chippewa-Stanley low stage.

The land continued to rise in the area north of the Great Lakes, tilting the old shore lines still further, and gradually raising the low sill opening at North Bay. As this sill rose, the waters continued to flow through the North Bay outlet, but the lakes behind it steadily deepened. The rise in lake levels continued until the Port Huron sill at 605 feet was once again called into action; the North Bay notch rising until it forced the principle drainage back into its old channel to the south. Once the 605-foot outlet was again utilized, another pronounced beach was formed similar to that of Lake Algonquin. This "new" 605-foot beach is the Nippissing stage of the Great Lakes. It was formed approximately 4250 years ago. This date is extrapolated from radiocarbon dates of the rising Nippissing waters at Blackwell, Ontario, and also computed by W. R. Farrand on the basis of rates of upwarp at North Bay.

This second beach at 605 feet obscures, or merges, with the former Algonquin beach below the hinge line. North of the Algonquin hinge, the continuous rise of the land since Algonquin times allows the Nippissing beach to stand out sharply below the present elevation of Algonquin beaches. This is the situation at Eastport. The Algonquin beach in this area is at about 625 feet A. T. The Nippissing beach is carved at approximately 612 or 613 feet A.T. The surface of the site is 616 feet above sea level and the various features which we will discuss lie slightly below this elevation.

The site could have been occupied at any time since the retreat of the water from the Algonquin beach. We would suspect, however, that there was little or no serious habitation of the site until around Nippissing times. At the low-water stage of Chippewa, the site was likely a high sandy promontory far inland from the much reduced lake and similarly removed from major inland waterways. Suitable flint deposits were more accessible to the low-water hunters than this out-of-the-way hilltop. Also, there is no cultural material on the site which relates to periods much earlier than Nippissing times.

The surface of most of the site is covered by wind-blown sand of varying thickness. In places, this light sand has shifted to expose an old soil level varying in thickness from 4 to 10 inches, where it was observable. This old soil layer is a classic example of podzol. A relatively thin zone of intense leaching shows up as a light ashy-grey sand consisting of almost pure quartz. Beneath this layer, A_1 and A_2, podzol zones extend down into B_1 soil and gradually fade out to a disconformed grey sand which lies on top of waterlaid sands about 5 feet beneath the surface. The depth at which these waterlaid sands are clearly visible varies in different places around the site. This suggests a shifting and irregular topography contemporaneous, or nearly so, with a lake beach. It can be best visualized as a sand storm beach of Lake Nippissing, which stood at about 612 feet in this area piling up dune sands which were further reworked and shifted around by the wind.

Figure 1, A shows excavation Unit 1, which was dug 4.5 feet deep on the edge of a gently sloping blow out basin. Figure 1, B is a view of excavation Unit 2 dug 3.5 feet into the low center of the blow out. The sloping line of ragged calving which shows so clearly

A

B

Figure 1

in the wall of the pit in Figure 1, A is the layer of concentrated flint debris which brought Griffin and Papworth to the site. These two views illustrate the stratigraphic interpretation made here. The trowel in Figure 1, B marks the upper limits of clearly defined waterlaid sands. Above this point the gray disconformed sand extends up to the surface. The dark streaks are the bottom tips of vertical stains caused by the leaching of organic materials down from the podzol above. The A_1 and A_2 podzol zones are eroded away from above this level. Figure 1, A continues the sequence upward through the area of characteristic podzol staining to the dense soil zone which was the floor for the forest (probably pine) that formed the podzol beneath.

The ancient living surface, or at least the artifact-bearing layer, is above the waterlaid sands and the artifacts are not water-rolled. From this we judge that the living surfaces were never inundated completely by the Nippissing waters. Since the land has risen about 5 feet since Nippissing times, and the artifact zone, while variable on the site, is generally present at 614 feet, we must assume that the artifact level stood at 609 feet at Nippissing maximum. The present-day Great Lakes may annually vary 2.5 feet above or below their normal depths. Assuming this variation was also present during Nippissing times, our occupation zone would have been subject to storm and ice action, yet our artifacts show no indication of such hard usage. Therefore, we conclude that the artifacts were deposited at this elevation after the retreat of the Nippissing waters from the 612 foot A.T. maximum had begun—after 2200 B.C.

In dune sands such as are typical of the Eastport area, erosion sometimes results in the concentration of debris from different time periods at single levels. While some redeposition has undoubtedly taken place, evidence points to a rather rapid covering of the concentrated artifact zone by the sand above it. In the artifact-bearing level in Excavation Unit 2 there was a shallow basin-shaped depression 2 feet in diameter and approximately 2 inches deep, which was compactly filled with tiny trim flakes. Their consolidated position suggests that they were dropped where we found them and almost immediately covered with sand. This indicates a minimum of reworking of the original surface by wind as does the only occasional occurrence of artifacts above or below this level.

The materials recovered from our excavations consist entirely of flint and other stones. The unusual quantity of these materials would lead one to expect other sorts of things such as bone, charcoal, organic stains, and the like; but the extremely acid quality of podzol would make preservation of any organic material improbable.

FORMAL ANALYSIS OF THE RECOVERED MATERIAL

Introduction

Few archaeologists in the United States since W. H. Holmes have taken an active interest in writing and publishing analyses of quarry materials and flint-working debris in a comprehensive and detailed manner. Descriptions of the materials found at quarry and workshop sites are vital and useful, as are lithic analyses of the quarried stone, but more important for dealing with problems of culture history are the techniques by which artifact forms are manufactured. We mean, of course, the stone-working technologies of the Stone Age cultures which exploited these quarries. American archaeologists have long been aware of the temporal durability of those attributes of artifacts which reflect manufacturing processes. The basic techniques of manufacture in pottery-making weaving, or in the production of skin clothing are much more firmly fixed than elements of decoration or the final shapes of the pieces produced. Many people have suggested that the same must be true of flint artifacts. Such attributes as relate to these basic motor habits should be recognizable on finished flint tools and even more apparent in the debris which is the by-product of their manufacture.

This analysis has been carried out to answer questions about the way in which the raw material was modified into finished artifacts. The procedure followed was to select certain attributes for investigation among the different classes of flint materials and to carry out a conventional typological study; that is, attempt to demonstrate a clustering of attributes. Once the types of flakes, modified forms, cores, and similar articles had been established, certain inferences were made concerning the functional relationships between the types and classes with respect to the original question, "how was the raw material modified into finished artifacts?" For instance, in the case of flakes the formal variation observed for certain attribute classes was believed to be indicative of different flint-working processes. These were the form of the longitudinal section, the form of the surface of the striking platform (faceted, nonfaceted), the angle between the striking platform and the internal face of the flake, the pattern of scarring on the external face of the flake and the shape of the lateral edges of the flake.

Examination of a sample of flakes was carried out initially for one of these attributes. This was the form of the surface of the striking platform and the sample was split into faceted and non-faceted forms. Subsequently, these two samples were examined for each of the attribute classes listed above. As will be shown in the results of this analysis there were definite clusterings of particular manifestations of the attribute classes. One form was recognizable that has a faceted striking platform and reticulate scars on the external face, concavo-convex longitudinal section, a striking angle of around 109 degrees, and excurvate lateral edges. This was segregated from flakes with the nonfaceted striking platform, a striking angle of around 101 degrees, expanding lateral edges, a straight longitudinal section, and scars on the external face that were roughly parallel to the direction of force which removed the flake. Other types of flakes were recognized but these two are mentioned to demonstrate what is meant here by a cluster of attributes. The inferences concerning the functional relations between these two types and other recognized types is best discussed in the body of the report. We have attempted to avoid inferences concerning the particular motor habits employed in producing the observed formal differences. For instance, Witthoft (1957) discusses free flaking, flat flaking, and resolved flaking. Others have argued about the distinctions between percussion flaking and pressure flaking. We have attempted to avoid these inferences by merely demonstrating the differences between forms of flakes and attempting to relate these forms to the cores from which they were derived, and secondarily to study the sequence of modifications ultimately resulting in a finished artifact. This procedure has been followed because the attributes which some archaeologists believe to be indicative of such techniques as pressure flaking are questioned by other archaeologists, but demonstrable formal differences can not be argued about as such. At the present unsophisticated stage of the analysis of flint-working, arguments about the attributes indicative of particular motor habits can obscure the value of this type of analysis and relegate the study of flint materials to the level of "expert opinion." We have attempted to answer the question "what formal modifications were made in the raw material during the process of manufacturing artifacts?" Others have attempted to answer this question plus the additional question of, "how was this accomplished in terms of particular motor habits?"

The results of the analysis are presented as inferences. We have arranged the demonstrable types of cores and flakes in terms of inferences about their functional relationship to one another and with regard to the process of the modification of the raw material into finished Pomranky points. (See Binford, *The Pomranky Site*, pp. 149-92). Some archaeologists may care to argue with these inferences but any argument on this level is not an argument against the formal types that have been recognized. These are demonstrable as clusters of attributes and as such are meaningful for comparisons between assemblages regardless of the validity of the inferences about their functional relationships.

Chipped-stone Artifacts

Raw Material

Seven different types of raw material were represented in the sample of materials from the site. By far the greatest preponderance of material, both flakes and artifacts were Eastport chert. Of the seven types observed at least five can be considered exotic to the site in that they are not represented in the chippage nor in the nodular material occurring on the site.

Eastport chert is a light-gray to buff-colored chert with dark gray wavy laminae combined into a larger even-banded pattern. The chert is opaque with a dull surface. Cavities are rare, but when present, are small and orientated with the laminae lined with a waxy, subtranslucent chert and occasionally having internal clusters of quartz crystals. This material occurs in the form of relatively small angular nodules that is locally available in drift washed by the Nippissing and higher Algonquin waters and along the present shores. This material has its source in (Silurian) outcrops along the south shore of the Upper Peninsula, north of Lake Michigan, and was apparently transported to the south by the Valders or earlier ice advances. Eastport chert is widely available in glacial deposits in the northern part of the Southern Peninsula of Michigan. The pieces which are readily available at the site are quite small and much rolled. These were the major source of raw materials which the occupants of this site sought and worked on the site.

Bayport chert is a medium- to light-gray opaque chert with a shiny to dull surface. There are numerous fine cavities lined with white opaque chert and internally, oftentimes, clusters of quartz crystals occur. Fossils occur and include crinoids and bryozoans. The chert is banded, but not consistently so. Bands are medium width (5 mm) to very narrow and are generally concentric with the surface of the given nodule. The nodules occur in the Upper Grand Rapids formation of Bayport limestone, ranging in size from the size of a marble to nodules 8 inches in diameter. The larger nodules are rare. Known sources of this material available to the aborigines are in Huron, Arenac, and Tuscola Counties. (Dustin, 1935, pp. 465-75, 1927; and Ellis, 1960.)

Type E—See *The Pomranky site* for description, p. 156).

Type O is a whitish, massive, uniformly colored opaque chert with a dull surface. Cavities and fossils are absent. The sources and distribution of this material is unknown.

Type R is a medium, bluish-gray opaque chert with a slightly shiny surface. There are parallel narrow streaks and isolated cavities lined with white opaque chert. Fossils are absent. The sources and distribution of this material is unknown.

Type S is a black massive chert with occasional small splotches of a light-gray to cream-colored opaque chert. Cavities are rare, fossils are absent, and the surface is dull.

Pomranky Points (manufacturing stages, Fig. 2)

Initial modification of the raw material.—The small nodules of Eastport chert were initially modified by the removal of decortication flakes from one of the tabular ends of the nodule. The other known technique for the initial modification of nodular material is to split the nodule either lengthwise or across the middle with the resulting relatively flat scar being used subsequently as a striking platform (Leakey, 1960, p. 33). The complete absence of split nodules and the preponderance of decortication flakes from the ends of the angular nodules suggests that, at this site, the first step was to remove the weathered cortex from an end of the nodule and subsequently to use the smooth, relatively flat surface of the nodule itself as a striking platform. The initial steps in knapping were accomplished with a hammerstone. The complete absence of anvils (Davis and Gillis, 1959 [the five anvil stones reported originally are questioned by the present authors]) from the sample as well as the fact that all of the measured flakes, including the decortication flakes, have a striking angle of less than 120 degrees, suggests that the anvil was not used during any stage of manufacture of artifacts. (Witthoft, 1957; Oakley, 1958.)

Utilization of the nodular raw material.--Holmes has indicated that at some sites nodular materials were directly modified into tools (Holmes, 1919). This procedure was not common at the

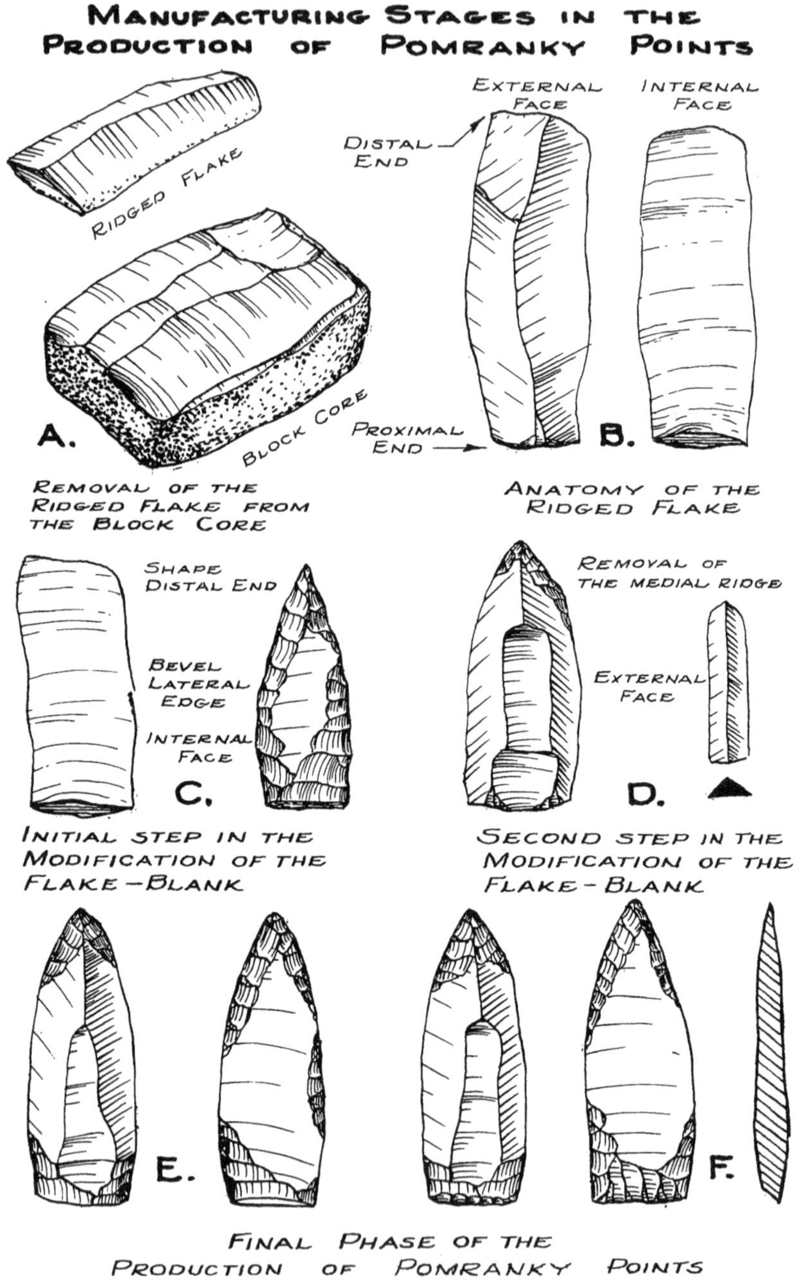
MANUFACTURING STAGES IN THE PRODUCTION OF POMRANKY POINTS
RIDGED FLAKE
BLOCK CORE
A.
REMOVAL OF THE RIDGED FLAKE FROM THE BLOCK CORE
EXTERNAL FACE
INTERNAL FACE
DISTAL END
PROXIMAL END
B.
ANATOMY OF THE RIDGED FLAKE
SHAPE DISTAL END
BEVEL LATERAL EDGE
INTERNAL FACE
C.
INITIAL STEP IN THE MODIFICATION OF THE FLAKE-BLANK
REMOVAL OF THE MEDIAL RIDGE
EXTERNAL FACE
D.
SECOND STEP IN THE MODIFICATION OF THE FLAKE-BLANK
E.
F.
FINAL PHASE OF THE PRODUCTION OF POMRANKY POINTS

Figure 2

Eastport site. Nodules were modified into cores from which flakes were derived, some of which were subsequently modified into tools. The dominant type of core is designated the "block core" (Fig. 3). The term "core" is used here to specifically refer to any block of raw material prepared so that flakes could be removed in a systematic manner for later use as blanks for artifacts. The block core is characterized by a relatively flat straight face from which flakes were removed. The particular form of the block cores from the Eastport site is, to some extent, a function of the peculiarities of the materials utilized. For instance, block cores are known which were manufactured from chunks of quarried rock, or from large split nodules. In these cases, the block cores are much larger and have more than a single striking platform. The block cores from the Eastport site are small and generally worked from only one striking platform.

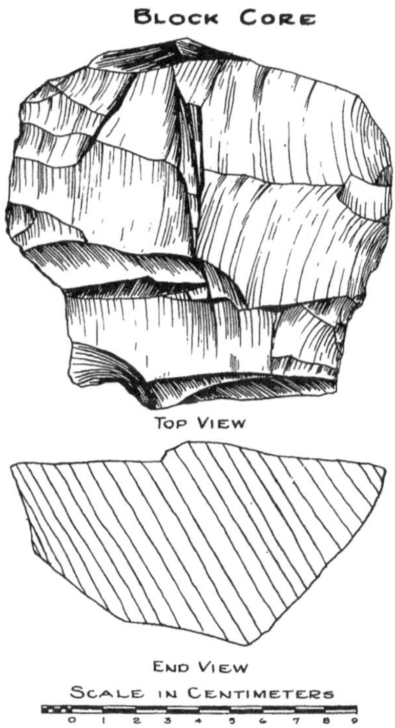

Figure 3.

Classification and analysis of the flakes derived from cores.--In the process of working a block core there are two classes of flakes that can be removed: (1) flakes removed incidental to the production of flake blanks, and (2) flake blanks. Blanks are those forms of modified raw material which are worked into artifacts. Of the incidentally produced flakes, there are three major types present at the Eastport site.

The first type (expanding flake, Fig. 4), is characterized by the presence of small flake scars on the external face opposite the bulb of percussion. These scars are the result of the striking platform having been trimmed prior to the removal of the flake. The lateral edges of these flakes invariably expand toward the distal end which is generally in the form of a hinge fracture. The angle between the striking platform and the bulbar face (the striking angle) is 101 degrees with a standard deviation of 4.32 degrees for the sample from this site. The striking platform is never faceted or bruised and in roughly 60 per cent of the sample the striking platform is the cortical surface of the nodule. The mean width of the striking platform on expanding flakes for the Eastport sample is 1.83 cm with a standard deviation of .84 cm. The longitudinal section of this type is straight and the point of maximum thickness is generally near the distal end. The scars on the external face of the flake are generally parallel to the axis of percussion. Occasionally, flakes are observed which have all the attributes of this type and exhibit odd lateral projections or roughly parallel flake scars that run laterally across the flake. These are interpreted as the result of the utilization of a new striking area on the edge of the core.

The second type of flake at the Eastport site that is incidentally derived from the block core will be called a "fluted" flake or blade (Fig. 4). These are characterized by the presence of opposing positive and negative bulbs of percussion and two longitudinal scars on the external face of the flake. The fluted flakes are generally parallel-sided or only slightly expanding below the medial region of the flake. The width of the striking platform is generally greater than on triangular flakes. The platforms of these flakes have a mean width of 2.45 cm with a standard deviation of .93 cm. Occasionally, on very delicate specimens the striking platform will be rather diminutive and the lateral edges will expand quickly for a short distance, then become parallel, or in some cases, gradually contract. They have a uniform thickness and a straight longitudinal section.

Of the second class of flake blanks derived from the block

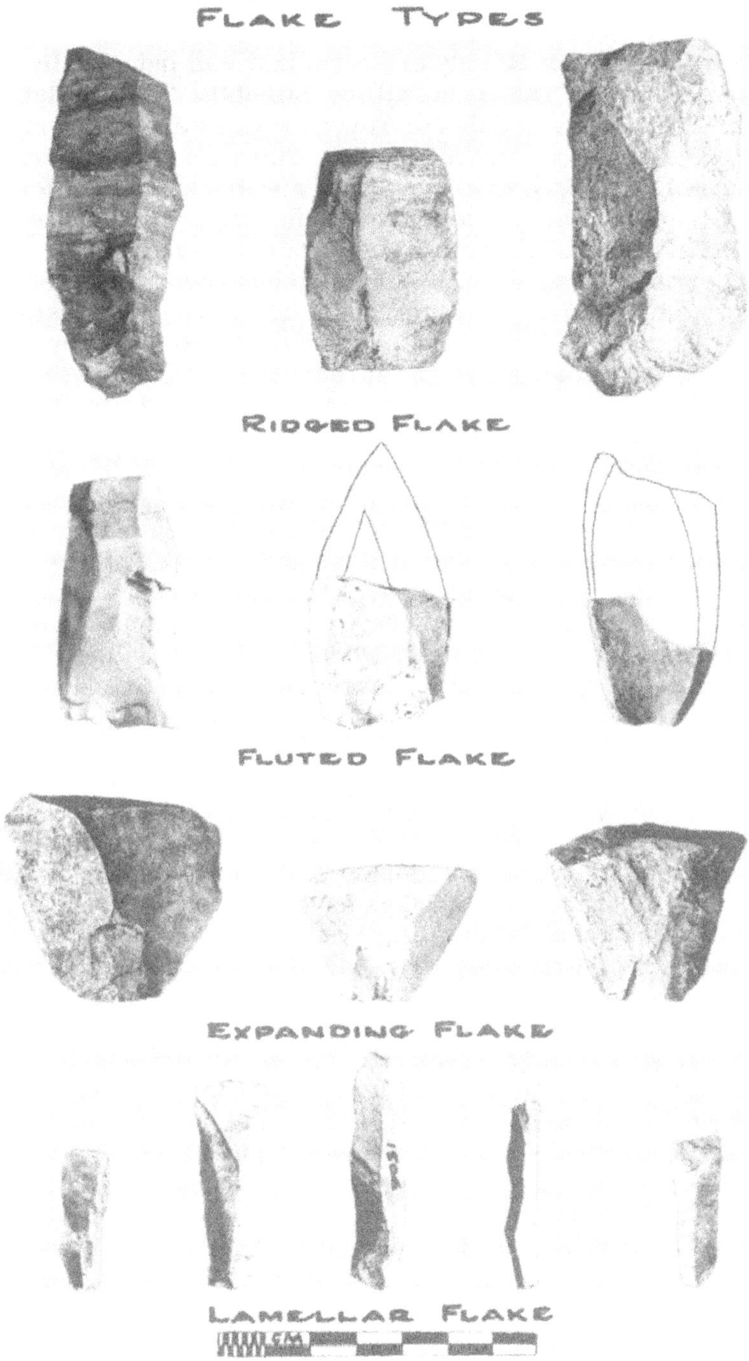
FLAKE TYPES
RIDGED FLAKE
FLUTED FLAKE
EXPANDING FLAKE
LAMELLAR FLAKE
CM

Figure 4

core, there appears to be only one form that was industrially important at this site. This form will be called the "ridged flake" (Fig. 4). Because the nodules or raw material were quite small and the block core was utilized with its characteristic flat face, it was frequently possible to remove with a well-placed blow a complete cross section of the core. When this was accomplished the detached flake was characterized by ends that have some of the original cortical surface. The flake also has several ridges running longitudinally down the outer face. These ridges were the scars left from the flakes previously detached from the core. When the cores were big enough, several flakes would be removed sequentially across the face of the core. This would result in the production of flakes with central ridges running longitudinally down the external face. The "peak" remaining on the face of the core as a result of flake removal was often the selected point of impact for the detaching blows. Bigger "bites" of the striking platform were taken when removing this form of flake and so they are much more massive than any of the other types. The lateral edges are generally parallel-sided and slightly convex in outline. In about 80 per cent of the sample the striking platform is as wide as the widest part of the flake. Occasionally, flakes with contracting lateral edges were produced. It is believed that this was the result of a slight change in the orientation of the striking platform or from the detaching blow having been delivered at a relatively acute angle to the striking platform. These constitute less than 1 per cent of the sample. The striking angle on this form of flake is not significantly different from the other forms mentioned--a mean of 102 degrees. Many of the ridged flakes have a relatively crude appearance, which is a result of the rather heavy-handed way that the core was worked. Obviously, what was desired was a rather large blank.

Probably incidental to the removal of blanks, small lamellar flakes were occasionally struck off (Fig. 4). It is postulated that these were removed when the point of impact for the detaching blow was quite close to the external edge of the striking platform. There are a fair proportion of the latter type present at the site, but in no case was there evidence that they had been used as blanks for the production of artifacts.

All of the varieties of flakes mentioned here were formed as blanks from which artifacts were manufactured. For instance, the scrapers found at the site are generally manufactured on expanding flakes. The most important blank at the Eastport site, however, is the ridged flake.

Initial step in processing the flake blank (Fig. 2, C).—The initial step in the modification of the blank seems to have been directed toward shaping it roughly into the correct size as well as accomplishing the necessary beveling of the edges to produce a bilaterally symmetrical longitudinal section. There were two alternative initial procedures depending upon the original size of the blank. In the event the blank was relatively massive, both beveling and reduction in size was necessary. This was accomplished by the removal of chips completely around the lateral edges of the blank. This procedure resulted in the removal of the original striking platform and frequently obscured to a great extent the medial ridge of the blank. Eighteen examples of this form of reject were present in the assemblage, constituting 17 per cent of the total sample of rejects from the site (Fig. 5).

If reduction in size was not necessary, because the original blank was roughly the correct size to start with, the production of the bevel and initial shaping were the only necessary requirements at this stage of manufacturing. In this event, transverse chipping across the internal or bulbar face was sufficient to produce the bevel and to remove the bulb of percussion (Fig. 2, C). The rough shaping was accomplished along with the beveling, although transverse chipping on the external face was sometimes necessary to produce the rough triangular shape with the tip opposite the old striking platform. Thirty-four per cent of the rejects from the site were of this form, that is, the original striking platform was still present and the medial ridge was not obscured (Fig. 5).

The interpretation that both of these forms represent alternatives in the first stage of modifying the blank is based on a comparison of the sizes of the two forms. Since the form that has the original striking platform obscured has been altered more than the form with the platform still present, it may be argued that the latter represents a more advanced stage of manufacture and consequently should be the smaller form. Table I presents the metrical data for the two forms together with an analysis of within and among sample variance.

Table I shows that for both length and width the means of the two samples are so different that the chances of the observed differences being the result of sampling vagaries is less than one in one hundred. Thus we can accept the means of the two samples as representing real differences in the populations from which they were drawn. By inspection of Table I, A., row 7, we see that for both length and width, the forms with the platforms obscured are larger than are the specimens with the platforms present. This is

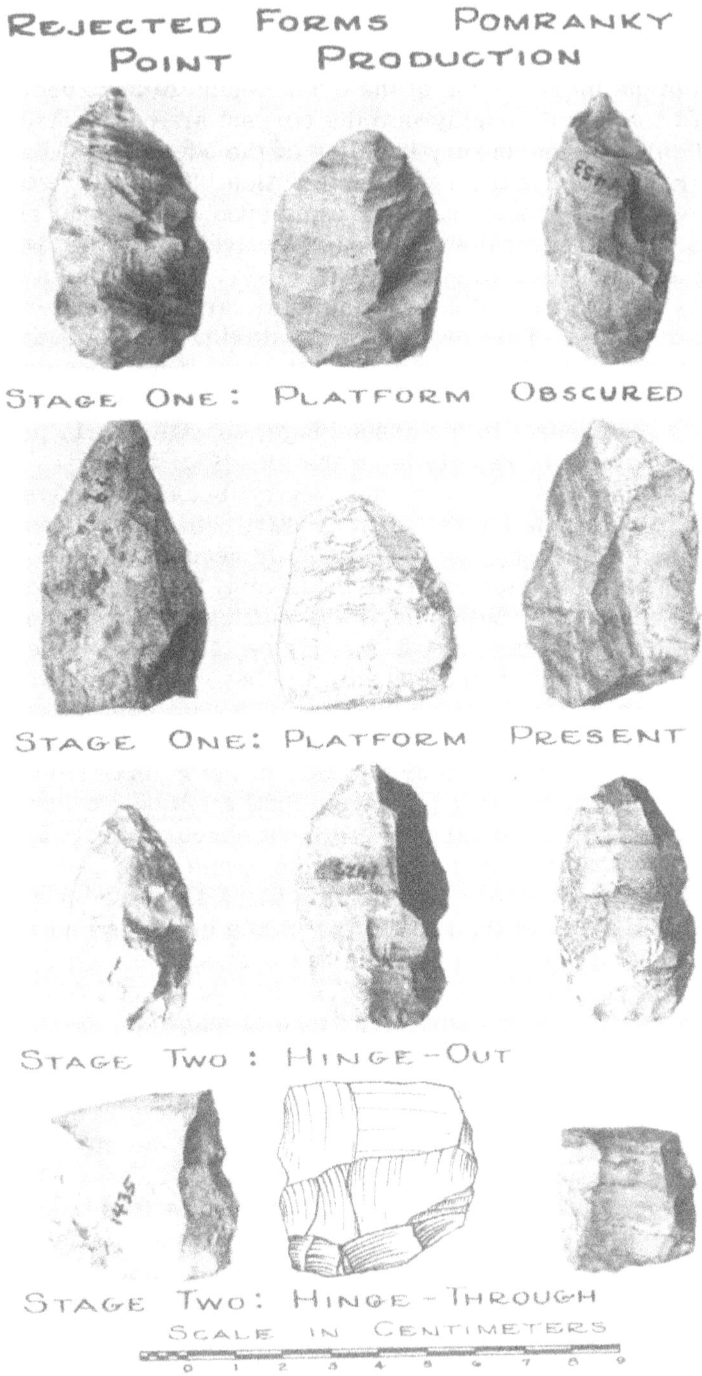
REJECTED FORMS POMRANKY
POINT PRODUCTION
1453
STAGE ONE: PLATFORM OBSCURED
STAGE ONE: PLATFORM PRESENT
STAGE TWO: HINGE-OUT
1435
STAGE TWO: HINGE-THROUGH
SCALE IN CENTIMETERS
0 1 2 3 4 5 6 7 8 9

Figure 5

TABLE I

VARIANCE ANALYSIS OF COMPARATIVE METRICAL ATTRIBUTES BETWEEN TWO CLASSES OF STAGE 1 REJECTS

A. Data for Each Sample
(In Centimeters)

Data	Obscured Platform		Platform Present	
	Maximum Length	Maximum Width	Maximum Length	Maximum Width
1. SX . . .	115.2	70.3	150.4	96.7
2. n	18.0	18.0	29.0	29.0
3. SX^2 . .	752.88	281.51	802.78	327.99
4. $\frac{(SX)^2}{n}$.	737.28	274.56	780.07	322.44
5. S^2 . . .	.92	.41	.81	.20
6. S	.96	.64	.90	.45
7. X	6.40	3.91	5.18	3.33

B. Within and Among Sample Variance of the Two Sample Lengths

	Degree of Freedom	Variance	(F)	Probability
Among sample	1	16.43	32.21	exceeds 1 per cent
Within sample	45	.51		

C. Within and Among Sample Variance of the Two Sample Widths

	Degree of Freedom	Variance	(F)	Probability
Among sample	1	3.62	12.92	Far exceeds the 1 per cent level
Within sample	45	.28		

the reverse of the situation expected if the specimens with the obscured platforms represented a more advanced stage of the processing of the blanks.

There is an alternative hypothesis: the forms with the obscured platforms do not represent a stage in the sequence of blank processing being presented here. On the basis of the data at hand this seems unlikely. There are no other artifacts present at the site that were processed through a series of stages and these do not appear to be finished artifacts. At present, the best interpretation seems to be that these two forms, one with obscured, the other with unobscured striking platforms, represent alternative methods of altering the blank during the first stage of processing. The alternative techniques are believed to be a function of the relative sizes of the original blanks. Very massive blanks were flaked completely around the lateral edges to reduce their size, as well as to roughly shape and bevel them. Less massive blanks were merely beveled and roughly shaped.

Second step in processing the flake blank (Fig. 2, D).—The second processing stage involves a reduction in thickness and further shaping of the blank. Shaping was accomplished by delicate transverse chipping along the lateral edges. Thickness was reduced by the removal of long longitudinal chips or flutes struck from the basal edge.

Normally, the removal of the longitudinal chips was accomplished by utilizing the remnants of the old striking platform as the platform for the removal of the "fluting" or longitudinal chips. In the event that the old striking platform had been removed in the course of reducing the size of the original blank, a new platform was prepared by beveling the end of the blank. Of the 51 specimens rejected at this stage, 14 (or 27 per cent) had secondarily prepared striking platforms while the remaining 37 (or 73 per cent) had vestiges of the original striking platforms which were utilized during the fluting stage. Two types of failure could occur at this stage. Either the longitudinal flakes would hinge out and fail to remove the central ridge or hump on the face of the blank, or the flake would hinge through the blank breaking it in half (Fig. 5). Only 12 per cent of the rejects had this latter type of failure.

In the event of successful removal of the medial ridge, the nearly roughed-out artifact would be further thinned in places where prominent scars remained. This was particularly true around the basal striking platform. In some cases, the longitudinal flute may have left prominent longitudinal scars; and if this was the case, transverse chipping would be utilized to remove them. Rejects discarded after successfully fluting the blank amounted to only 3 per cent of the total rejects from the site. In all cases they seem to have been rejected because of a relatively concavo-convex longitudinal section, which could not have been eliminated in the final retouching stage. Table II presents the summary and comparative data for the rejects in the fluting stage and those previously discussed as rejected during the initial stage of manufacturing.

It is interesting to note that the lengths of the two samples are

TABLE II

VARIANCE ANALYSIS OF COMPARATIVE METRICAL ATTRIBUTES BETWEEN STAGE 1 AND STAGE 2 REJECTS

A. Data for Each Sample (In Centimeters)

Data	First Stage Platform Present			Second Stage Fluting Rejects		
	Length	Width	Thickness	Length	Width	Thickness
1. SX . .	150.4	96.7	47.9	221.1	135.0	60.7
2. n . . .	29.0	29.0	29.0	43.0	43.0	43.0
3. SX^2 .	802.78	327.99	82.31	1165.47	443.88	90.41
4. $\frac{(SX)^2}{n}$.	780.07	322.44	79.12	1136.86	428.87	85.69
5. S^2 . .	.81	.20	.11	.68	.36	.11
6. S . . .	.90	.45	.33	.82	.60	.33
7. X . . .	5.18	3.33	1.65	5.14	3:16	1.41

B. Within and Among Sample Variance of the Two Sample Lengths

	Degree of Freedom	Variance	(F)	Probability
Among sample	1	.09	.12	Does not exceed 1 per cent
Within sample	70	1.73		

C. Within and Among Sample Variance of the Two Sample Widths

	Degree of Freedom	Variance	(F)	Probability
Among sample	1	5.69	19.62	Far exceeds the 1 per cent level
Within sample	70	.29		

D. Within and Among Sample Variance of the Two Sample Thicknesses

	Degree of Freedom	Variance	(F)	Probability
Among sample	1	1.00	9.09	Exceeds the 1 per cent level
Within sample	70	.11		

not significantly different from one another, whereas the widths differ far more than would be expected if sampling vagaries were the only factors contributing to the differences between the samples. We must conclude that there is a real difference in the populations sampled with respect to widths. This is what would be expected from an inspection of the rejects, for those of the second stage show a greater modification along lateral edges as evidenced among other criteria by a greater overlapping of flake scars, etc. The data on the thickness of the two samples shows that even though the removal of the medial ridge had not been successful in the specimens rejected at the fluting stage, there had nevertheless been a reduction in thickness.

Throughout the steps in the manufacturing process mentioned thus far, a single mode of working flint is indicated. In all cases the chip scars are relatively deep with prominent negative bulbs of percussion and tend to be expanding. This is interpreted as being the result of the utilization of a hammerstone for the removal of the chips.

Chips incidentally produced during the process of modifying the flake blank.—Before going on to the discussion of the final stage in the processing of blanks into artifacts, the form of the chips incidentally produced during the processing of the blanks will be considered. Only a single type of chip has been interpreted as being the result of the modification of primary blanks although several varieties are identifiable.

The most striking characteristic of a chip is the presence of reticulate scars on the external face. Reticulate scars are those that run across the face of the chip in haphazard directions. Seventy-eight per cent of the total sample of reticulately scarred chips share another characteristic: they have a concavo-convex longitudinal section. Roughly 50 per cent of the total sample have faceted striking platforms. This is the result of the removal of chips from the lateral edge of a partly completed artifact. The edge which serves as the striking platform has had chips removed from both faces, therefore, chips subsequently removed will many times be faceted or show the scars from chips removed from the opposite face of the artifact. The striking angle on these chips is 109 degrees with a standard deviation of 3.63 degrees.

In general, chips with reticulate scars are much smaller than are the types mentioned as being in all likelihood derived from the working of cores. Table III shows a comparison of the relative size as measured by the weight of the total sample of chips with reticulate external surface and faceted butts as opposed to ridged and triangular flakes.

TABLE III

COUNT AND RATE RATIOS FOR TWO CLASSES OF FLAKES

	Count	Total Weight (In Ounces)	Mean Weight Per Spall (In Ounces)
Chips with reticulate scars . .	1549	133	.08
Flakes with parallel scars	239	118	.49

In establishing a typology of flakes such as is presented here it must be kept in mind that there will be found flakes that were produced from cores that will resemble those produced from the working of bifacial tools and vise versa. Nevertheless, in a sample this large, the two distinct clusters of attributes described here seem to be valid.

Final step in processing the flake blank (Fig. 2, E, F; Fig. 6).-- The final stage in the production of the artifacts under discussion was not accomplished in the same manner as the previous stages. The chip scars on the surface of the finished pieces are very flat and those having their origin on the lateral edges tend to expand rapidly from the point of percussion and frequently run more than half way across the finished artifact. The distal ends of the scars occasionally exhibit diminutive hinge fractures, but this is relatively rare. The most common form is a clean cleavage at the distal end of the scar which overlaps smoothly with scars originating on the opposite edge, so that the face of the artifact is almost smooth and definite scars cannot be identified readily. Along the lateral edges there will frequently be small overlying scars that are lamellar or only slightly expanding in shape. These are not continuous along the lateral edge, but tend to be clustered and apparently represent the removal of diminutive irregularities along the lateral edge. The base is retouched somewhat differently. Longitudinal chips are taken off that are better defined and deeper than any other scars on the finished artifact. These scars tend to be lamellar and the negative bulbs of percussion are well defined (Fig. 6, C, D). They are arranged sequentially along the basal edge. About 50 per cent of the finished specimens are retouched in this manner on both faces, while the other half are retouched on only one face. Those that are retouched on only one face frequently

POMRANKY POINTS
A
B
C
D
E
F
G
H1
H2
SCALE IN CENTIMETERS
0 1 2 3 4 5 6 7 8

Figure 6

have a vestige of the bevel remaining from the old striking platform that was present on the basal edge during the fluting stage (Fig. 6, H).

With regard to the geometric outline of the finished artifacts the base is typically straight, although slightly convex bases are occasionally seen. Four different blade shapes occur in the sample. The normal form is ovate. That is, the lateral edges of the artifact describe slightly convex lines between the points of junction of the lateral edges with the basal edge and their point of intersection at the tip. In this form the maximum width must be at the base. The next most frequent form is excurvate. That is, the lateral edges describe gently convex lines as in the above form, but the point of maximum width is not at the base. Two examples of parallel ovate blade shapes were observed. These had lateral edges that described straight, parallel lines between the point of juncture with the basal edge and a point located forward of the medial section of the blade. At this point the lateral edges begin to converge to their intersection at the tip and describe slightly convex lines. One triangular specimen was noted. Triangular blade shapes are those whose lateral edges describe straight lines between their points of intersection with the basal edge and the tip of the artifact. Table IV shows the summary of information for the discrete traits of the finished artifacts broken up into two samples, complete specimens and basal specimens only.

TABLE IV

FREQUENCY OF OCCURRENCE OF OBSERVED ATTRIBUTES—POMRANKY POINTS

	Complete Specimens	Bases Only
Base shape		
straight	41	45
subconvex	3	5
Basal thinning		
one face	24	24
both faces	20	26
Blade shape		
ovate	28	38
excurvate	13	11
parallel ovate . .	2	0
triangular	1	1

TABLE V

VARIANCE ANALYSIS FOR COMPARATIVE METRICAL ATTRIBUTES BETWEEN STAGE 2 REJECTS AND FINISHED POMRANKY POINTS

A. Data for Each Sample
(In Centimeters)

Data	Second Stage Fluting Rejects			Third Stage Finished Pieces		
	Length	Width	Thickness	Length	Width	Thickness
1. SX .	221.1	135.0	60.7	224.7	106.0	31.7
2. n . .	43.0	43.0	43.0	44.0	44.0	45.0
3. SX^2 .	1165.47	443.88	90.41	1214.43	264.42	23.43
4. $\frac{(SX)^2}{n}$	1136.86	428.87	85.69	1147.50	255.36	22.33
5. S^2 . .	.68	.36	.11	1.56	.21	.02
6. S . .	.82	.60	.33	1.25	.46	.14
7. X . .	5.14	3.16	1.41	5.11	2.41	.71

B. Within and Among Sample Variance of the Two Sample Lengths

	Degree of Freedom	Variance	(F)	Probability
Among sample	1	.02	102	Does not exceed 50 per cent
Within sample	85	1.12		

C. Within and Among Sample Variance of the Two Sample Widths

	Degree of Freedom	Variance	(F)	Probability
Among sample	1	16.63	59.39	Far exceeds the 1 per cent level
Within sample	85	.28		

D. Within and Among Sample Variance of the Two Sample Thicknesses

	Degree of Freedom	Variance	(F)	Probability
Among sample	1	11.00	183.	Far exceeds the 1 per cent level
Within sample	86	.06		

No specimens showed evidence of grinding, nor were any specimens notched or showed any alteration to facilitate hafting.

Table V presents the metrical data on the Pomranky points together with a comparison with the rejects at the fluting stage of processing.

As was noted in the comparison of the rejects in the first and second stages, there is essentially no difference in the lengths of the two samples, whereas there is a great difference in the widths. The observed difference between the widths of the two samples compared in Table V could result from sampling vagaries alone in far less than one in one hundred samples drawn from the same population. The above information indicates that during the last stage of manufacture, the shaping of the lateral edges was accomplished simultaneously with the reduction of thickness. The basal retouch seems to have been carried out merely to make the base straight and the desired length was attained at a much earlier stage of manufacture.

What is referred to here as a "finished artifact" merely indicates that these were the end-product of the major manufacturing process at the Eastport site. It is the investigators' opinion, however, that these forms may have been later modified into notched projectile points.

Summary of manufacturing stages (Fig. 2).—The initial modification of the small nodules of Eastport chert was the striking off of decortication flakes in the preparation of a lateral face or a striking platform ultimately resulting in the production of a block core. The block cores at the Eastport site are characterized by the presence of only a single striking platform frequently being the original cortical surface of a roughly tabular nodule. Once the core was prepared flakes of two major classes could be removed: flakes incidentally removed in preparing the face of the core or accidentally struck off in the process of producing the desired flake form. These incidentally produced flakes are of three types, the fluted flake, the expanding flake and the lamellar flake. The dominant form of flake blank produced from the block core is the ridged flake. It was this form that was selected for subsequent modification into Pomranky points. The initial step in the modification of the flake blank was to modify the distal end into a rough point and to produce the necessary bevels along the lateral edge to produce a symmetrical specimen. This was accomplished by removing chips primarily from the internal face of the flake blank along the lateral edges. An alternative means was correlated with the original size of the flake blank. If the flake blank was massive, removal of the original striking platform may be required to obtain, roughly, the correct size at this point of processing. The next step was the removal of the medial ridge on the external face of the flake blank. This step has been termed the "fluting stage." This was accomplished by the removal of a longitudinally orientated chip utilizing either the remnants of the original striking platform at the proximal end of the flake blank or by the preparation of a striking platform at the basal edge of the specimen. The actual removal of the longitudinal chip may result in two types of failure: (*a*) breakage of the specimen resulting from the hinging out through the specimen of the longitudinal chip, and (*b*) failure of the fluting attempt to remove the medial ridge on the flake blank. If the removal of the longitudinal flake is successful the specimen is further modified by thinning of the proximal end by the removal of longitudinal chips and smoothing off the fluting scars by transverse chipping.

"Blanks"--Type A (Miscellaneous Items, Fig. 7, F, G)

A total of 29 specimens from the Eastport site were not assignable to any of the reject types previously described. All of these have the relatively massive chip scars with well-defined negative bulbs of percussion characteristically observed on the other reject types. An attribute which sets this form apart from other reject types (shared by all of the specimens of this type) is a relatively flat surface on one lateral edge that appears to be the remnants of an old striking platform. Twenty-four of the specimens in the sample have bases that are convex while the remaining five have straight bases. Of all the specimens of the latter shape the base is not at right angles to the longitudinal axis of the specimen. It generally runs from the lateral edge that has the flat "striking platform" at an angle of approximately 120 degrees to the longitudinal axis of the specimen. Eighteen of the twenty-nine specimens have an asymmetrical blade shape, one lateral edge being relatively straight while the other is convex. Flake scars originating on the straight lateral edge tend to be more pronounced and more or less dominate the face of the artifact. None of the specimens exhibit any cortical surface on the face. Table VI presents the metrical attributes together with a comparison with the smallest of the types of artifacts previously discussed--the finished Pomranky points.

With respect to all three measurements, it is observed that the differences between the two samples are greater than would be expected to arise as a result of sampling vagaries in more than one

TABLE VI

VARIANCE ANALYSIS FOR COMPARATIVE METRICAL ATTRIBUTES BETWEEN POMRANKY POINTS AND BLANK TYPE A

A. Data for Each Sample
(In Centimeters)

Data	Third Stage Pomranky Points			"Blanks" Type A		
	Length	Width	Thickness	Length	Width	Thickness
1. SX .	224.7	106.0	31.7	134.3	55.6	18.27
2. n . .	44.0	44.0	45.0	29.0	29.0	29.0
3. SX^2 .	1214.43	264.42	23.43	639.77	106.62	11.54
4. $\frac{(SX)^2}{n}$	1147.50	255.36	22.33	621.95	106.60	11.51
5. S^2 . .	1.56	.21	.02	.64	.07	.03
6. S . .	1.25	.46	.14	.80	.26	.17
7. X . .	5.11	2.41	.71	4.63	1.92	.63

B. Within and Among Sample Variance of the Two Sample Lengths

	Degree of Freedom	Variance	(F)	Probability
Among sample	1	3.96	3.33	Exceeds the expected value at the 5 per cent level
Within sample	71	1.19		

C. Within and Among Sample Variance of the Sample Widths

	Degree of Freedom	Variance	(F)	Probability
Among sample	1	4.23	32.54	Exceeds the expected value at the 10 per cent level
Within sample	71	.13		

D. Within and Among Sample Variance of the Two Sample Thicknesses

	Degree of Freedom	Variance	(F)	Probability
Among sample	1	.10	6.25	Exceeds the expected value at the 1 per cent level
Within sample	71	.016		

in a hundred samples drawn from the same population. Since in all cases the Blank Type A is smaller than the smallest of the reject series previously discussed it seems logical that they are in no way related to the production of Pomranky points of the type discussed above. Inspection of all the specimens of this type reveal that in no case is there evidence of use, so their status as rejects seems justifiable. The artifacts that were later manufactured on this blank is unknown. Some hint as to how they were produced may rest in a sample of small worked nodules present in the assemblage (Fig. 7). These are demonstrably small nodules that have been altered by the removal of decortication flakes on the broad faces of the nodule. In all cases the lateral edges of the nodule served as the striking platform for the removal of the decortication flakes. Although still easily recognizable as nodules these specimens share with Blank Type A the striking platforms on the lateral edges and the domination of the face of the nuclei by the flakes removed from the striking platforms on the lateral edges. If these two forms are related in a manufacturing sequence this would be an example of the modification of natural nuclei directly into an artifact, by-passing entirely the production of cores. Whether this is an alternative technique utilized by the makers of the Pomranky points characteristically found at the site or a different technique utilized by different people it is impossible to determine on the basis of available evidence. The fact that the Blank Type A specimens are significantly smaller than the finished Pomranky points is indicative that the Blank Type A specimens are unrelated to the manufacturing steps in the latter's production.

Notched Projectile Points (Fig. 8)

A total of 12 notched or stemmed projectile points were included in the sample of material from the Eastport site. Five of the 11 specimens were manufactured from stone not found on the site. Certainly these specimens were brought to the site by the people who left behind the workshop debris. Of the 11 specimens 6 can be identified as having been manufactured on flake blanks, 1 can be positively identified as having been manufactured on a Pomranky point blank and the remaining 4 can be said to have probably been manufactured on Pomranky point blanks. The latter 5 projectile points appear to constitute a type in the sense of a true cluster of attributes and for this reason they will be provisionally defined and termed the Davis Point.

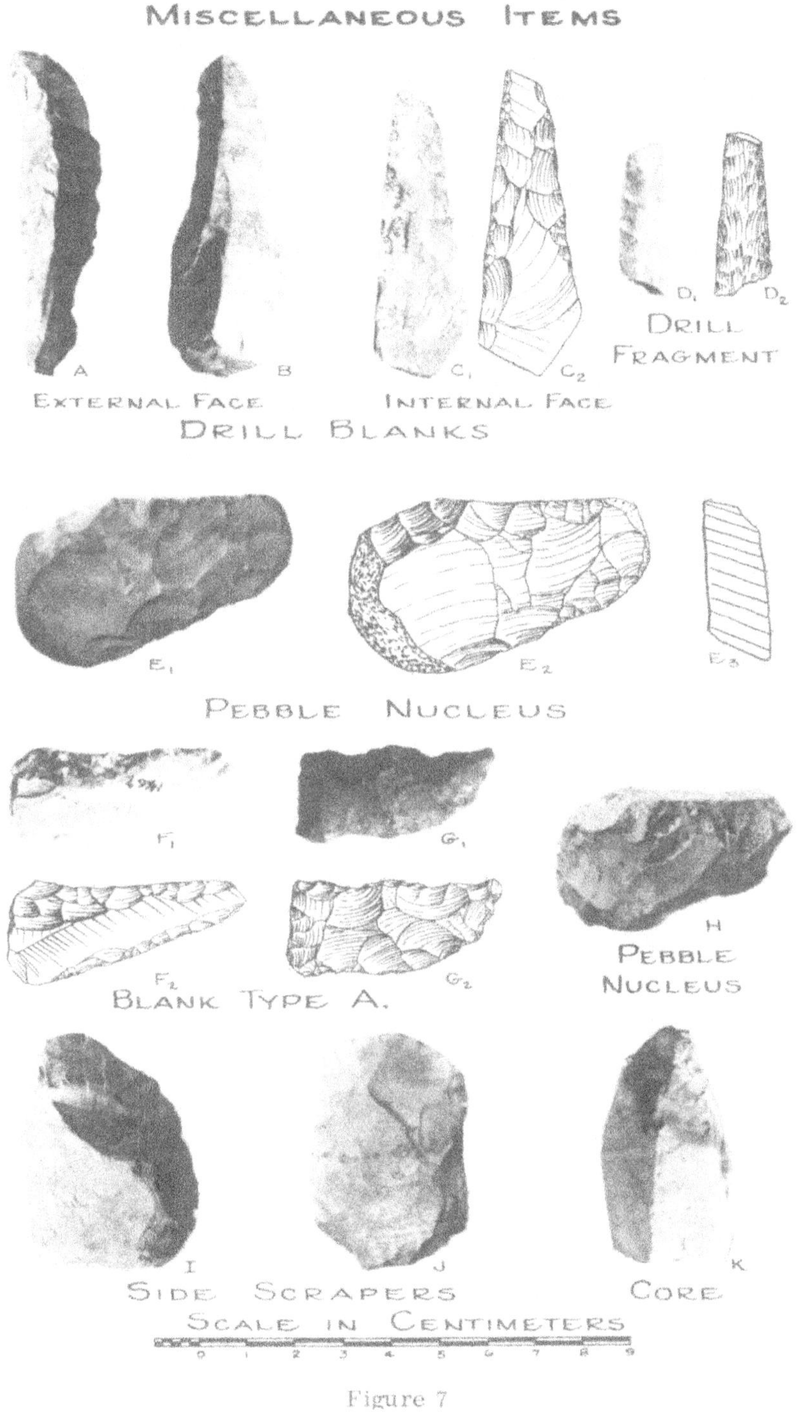
MISCELLANEOUS ITEMS
A
B
C1
C2
D1
D2
DRILL FRAGMENT
EXTERNAL FACE
INTERNAL FACE
DRILL BLANKS
E1
E2
E3
PEBBLE NUCLEUS
F1
G1
F2
G2
BLANK TYPE A.
H
PEBBLE NUCLEUS
I
J
K
SIDE SCRAPERS
CORE
SCALE IN CENTIMETERS
0 1 2 3 4 5 6 7 8 9

Figure 7

Davis Points (Fig. 8, A, B, C).—All share in common an ovate blade shape as well as a slightly convex base. Four specimens have grinding on the base while one is unground. Three of the 5 specimens have "side notches." That is, both the proximal and distal points of juncture of the notch articulate with the lateral edge of the point. Two specimens have "corner notches" and in this case the proximal point of juncture of the notch is coincidental with the point where the projected symmetry of the lateral edge of the projectile would meet the basal edge. Because the unmodified portion of the lateral edge below the notch on those "side notched" specimens is relatively undefined, it is likely that distinction in the placement of the notches has no stylistic significance. The chipping on the Davis points reveals that they were probably manufactured on secondary blanks. One of the specimens exhibits the unobscured remnants of the prepared striking platform utilized during the fluting stage of the manufacture of the Pomranky points produced at the site. This makes the identification of the blank form relatively certain. The other 4 specimens lack this very diagnostic feature but exhibit the relatively prominent longitudinal basal thinning scars as well as the characteristic "flat" flake scars typical of the chipping on the Pomranky points. In all cases the notches were produced by the removal of single opposing flake from each face of the projectile point. The notching scars always obscure lateral and basal thinning scars indicating that they were the last step in the production of the point. The lateral edges of all specimens have diminutive short lamellar scars that are continuous along the edges. These have been produced subsequent to the processing state represented by the Pomranky points found at the site. Metrical attributes are presented in Table VII.

TABLE VII

METRICAL ATTRIBUTES: DAVIS POINTS

	Haft Width	Basal Width	Shoulder Width	Total Length	Haft Length	Thickness	Stone Type
1.	1.8	2.0	2.6	. . .	1.0	.6	exotic
2.	1.5	2.2	2.0	4.5	1.0	.5	local
3.	1.6	2.3	2.6	. . .	1.0	.6	exotic
4.	1.5	1.7	2.1	4.2	.8	.4	exotic
5.	1.7	2.1	2.1	4.4	1.3	.8	local
Means	1.62	2.06	2.28	4.36	1.02	.58	

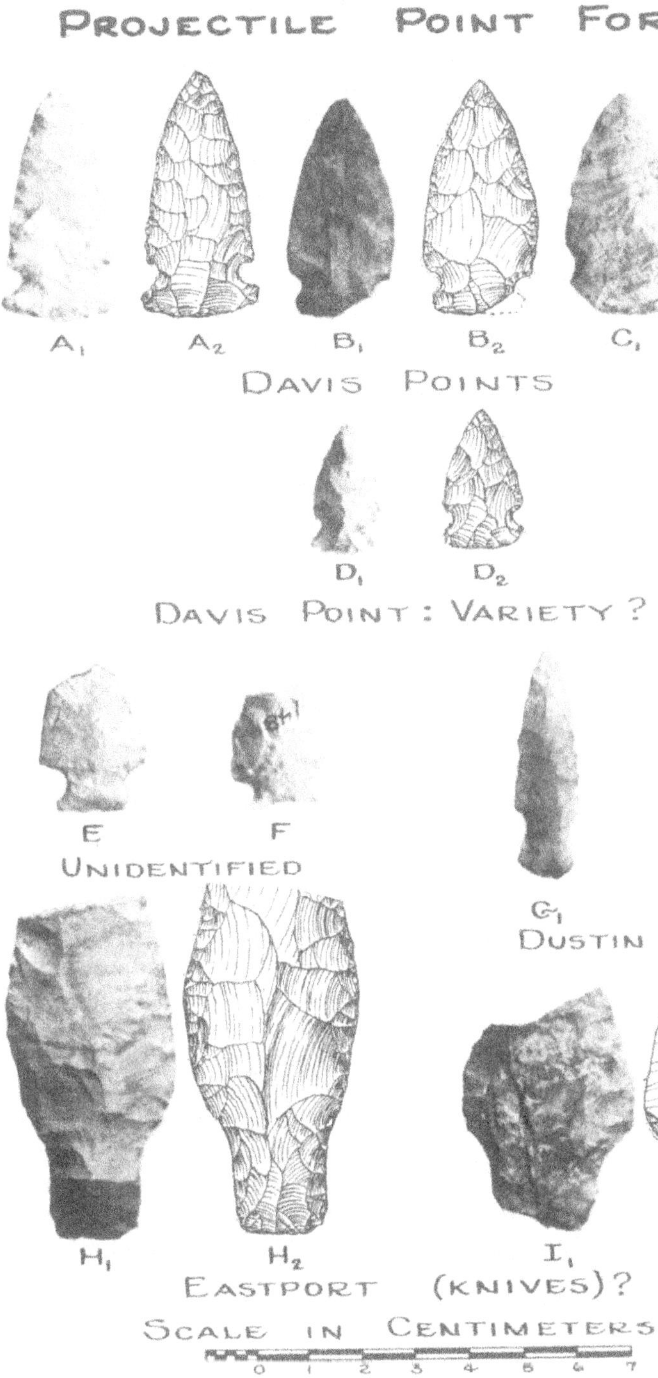
PROJECTILE POINT FORMS
A1 A2 B1 B2 C1 C2
DAVIS POINTS
D1 D2
DAVIS POINT: VARIETY?
E F
UNIDENTIFIED
G1 G2
DUSTIN POINT
H1 H2 I1 I2
EASTPORT (KNIVES)?
SCALE IN CENTIMETERS
0 1 2 3 4 5 6 7

Figure 8

Inspection of Table VII shows that 3 of the 5 specimens in the sample were manufactured of exotic stone indicating that they were probably brought onto the site as finished projectile points. All 3 of these points are broken, 2 lack tips while the other is broken in the haft element. These facts support the interpretation that they were brought into the site as finished pieces and discarded there after having been broken.

Although the sample is very small it is the opinion of the investigators that the information presented is sufficient to serve as a provisional type definition for the Davis point.

Davis Point Variety? (Fig. 8, D).—A single specimen which is almost identical in technical and geometric attributes to the sample of Davis points described above has not been included in the above sample because of its very small size. Given a large sample it may have been possible to show that this specimen was in fact within the size range of Davis points. It is my opinion, however, that it represents a variety of Davis points distinct from that previously described. This opinion is based on observations made on several large surface collections where similar forms were recognized and were demonstrably representative of a bimodal size distribution. This opinion is further supported by the presence of one of the very small specimens very similar to the one being discussed in association with a larger form of a different style as part of the grave furniture in an Old Copper burial at Riverside Cemetery, Menominee County, Michigan. It is believed that the size differences of the order being discussed may reflect functional differences.

Eastport "points" (knives).—Two large stemmed "points" (Fig. 8, H, I) were present in the sample. Both were manufactured of Eastport chert and hence were believed to have been manufactured locally. Both have expanding ovate blade shapes, with biconvex transverse sections and biplano longitudinal sections. Primary chipping is reflected in massive expanding scars. Secondary chipping is of the diminutive, expanding, triangular and lamellar forms. The blade is generally asymmetrical with a gentle convex edge with the opposite edge being less regular. Secondary chipping is much more in evidence along the gentle convex edge and evidence of some crushing and lateral abrasion is present on this edge. The base is straight or slightly convex and lacks grinding. Juncture is lateral-basal with all points being articulated with short arcs. The modified subelement of the tang is either parallel or slightly contracting. The "stem" was produced by multiple removal of chips from the lateral edge which tends to be continuous with the primary scars on the blade suggesting that the shaping of the blade and the production of the "stem" were a single operation. Secondary scars occurring along the edges of the haft element tend to be conchoidal in form and continuous. Metrical attributes are given below.

TABLE VIII

METRICAL ATTRIBUTES: EASTPORT KNIVES
Figure 8, H, I

(In Centimeters)

	Haft Width	Basal Width	Shoulder Width	Total Length	Haft Length	Thickness
H. . .	1.7	1.7	3.0	. . .	2.2	1.0
I. . . .	2.2	1.7	3.3	. . .	2.0	.8
Mean .	1.95	1.7	3.15	. . .	2.1	.9

Dustin Point (Fig. 8, g).—A single specimen of a type recently defined from materials recovered from the Saginaw area was present at the site. This point type has been defined on the basis of a large sample of points from the Dustin collection housed at the Museum of Anthropology, The University of Michigan and from collections owned by Ralph Stroebel of Saginaw. It is typologically within the range of the projectile points typical of the Lamoka focus of New York. The Lamoka complex is well dated at approximately 2500 B.C. by "carbon fourteen" determination. Although no sites have been excavated in Michigan that can be identified as belonging to the Lamoka focus, artifacts such as the beveled adz and Dustin points occur in Michigan's Lower Peninsula and it is believed that a cultural complex is present in Michigan which is quite similar stylistically to the Lamoka focus. The presence of this single specimen is interesting for it is the only reported specimen of this type from the west coast of Michigan and it is the best evidence that the Eastport site or area is a multicomponent location.

Unidentified Specimens (Fig. 8, e, f).—Three specimens of undefined types complete the sample. All have in common a small size, yet all differ in the form of juncture, shape of the base, and in technical attributes of flaking. The meaning of these forms in terms of site interpretation is not known, nor are similar forms described from other sites in Michigan. Until other forms are known and a larger sample is available their typological status must be left undetermined.

Artifacts with Transverse Working Edges

As has been the case with the artifacts discussed thus far, scrapers can be analyzed with respect to the type of blank upon which they are manufactured. Scrapers lend themselves to this kind of analysis quite readily because, generally, the blank is not completely obscured in the process of tool manufacture.

Type A (Fig. 9, A, B, C, D).--Scrapers of this type are manufactured on flake blanks of 2 types, triangular flakes and fluted flakes. They have a working edge that is convex in plan view and beveled unifacially into a gently sloping edge. In the sample from the Eastport site there are 10 specimens of this class. Six of the 10 have flake scars which completely cover the external face of the blank. Seven have a few flake scars on the internal face of the blank generally clustered along the lateral edge near the base of the scraper. These appear to have been placed so as to remove the bulb of percussion on the blank and to slightly bevel the lateral edge. On 8 of the 10 scrapers, the striking platform on the flake blank is unobscured, 1 is broken and the remaining specimen has had the original striking platform obscured. All specimens have lateral edges that expand from the base toward the working edge. Two of the 10 specimens are manufactured of flint exotic to the site and this is taken as evidence indicative of their having been manufactured elsewhere and introduced into the site as finished artifacts.

Type B (Fig. 9, E, F).—Scrapers of this type are manufactured on triangular flakes and fluted flakes. All examples have the internal face of the primary blank unaltered. The base of the scraper is the original striking platform on the blank. The working edge is much less convex than on scrapers of Type A and the working edge is "snub nosed," that is the working edge is very steep. In all cases the lateral edges expand from the base and the point of maximum width is the point of juncture between the lateral edges and the working edge. There were no specimens of this type manufactured of exotic flint.

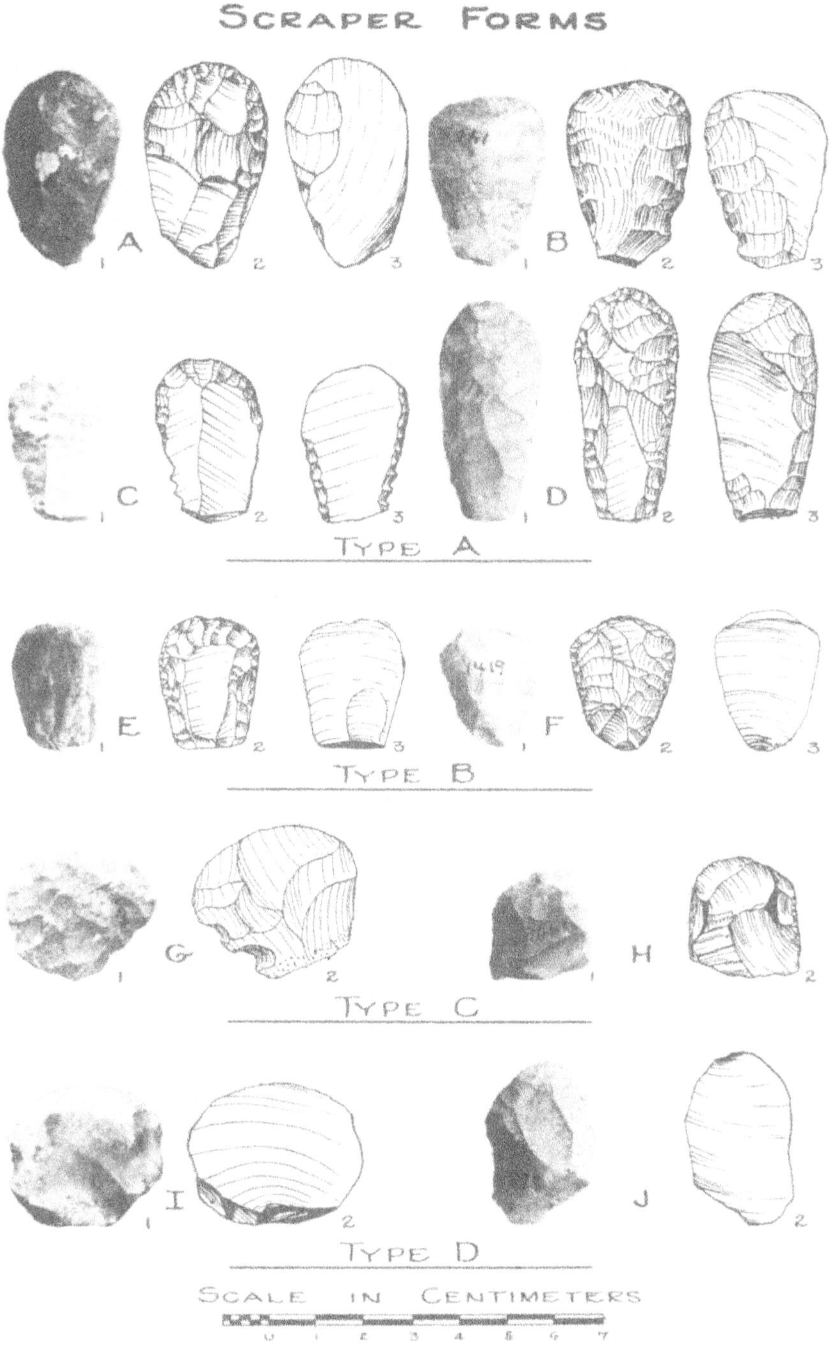
SCRAPER FORMS
A
B
C
D
TYPE A
E
F
TYPE B
G
H
TYPE C
I
J
TYPE D
SCALE IN CENTIMETERS
0 1 2 3 4 5 6 7

Figure 9

Type C (Fig. 9, G, H).—Two specimens manufactured of exotic flint occurred in the sample that had "snub nosed" working edges but were bifacially chipped. No identifiable remains of the original blank were found. In both cases the plan view of the specimen is much less symmetrical than in the other types described.

Type D (Fig. 9, I, J).—A total of 5 specimens occurred that exhibited reticulate scars on the external surface of the blank. In three of the cases a marked concavo-convex longitudinal section indicated that they had probably been manufactured on blanks that were produced incidentally during the modification of bifacial tools. These had a much less symmetrical plan than was characteristic of Types A and B. The working edge is not as steeply beveled as Types B and C. None of the specimens exhibited any modification on the internal face of the blank. Only 1 of these was manufactured of exotic material. Table IX summarizes the data on flint and scraper types.

TABLE IX

STONE TYPES: SCRAPERS

Scraper	Local Flint	Exotic Flint	Total
Type A	8	2	10
Type B	3	. .	3
Type C	. .	2	2
Type D	4	1	5
Total . . .	15	5	20

Artifacts with Lateral Working Edges

Type A (Fig. 7, I).—Two specimens were manufactured on massive decortication flakes and exhibited rather wide working edges chipped onto the external surface of the blank. Battering, and to some extent, evidence of "use grinding" was on the working edge.

Type B (Fig. 7, J).—Four specimens with working edges along the lateral edge of a blank were present in the assemblage. All four were produced on flakes derived from working cores. One specimen exhibited a high polish on the internal face along the lateral working edge. The other three lacked this polish and the working edges were on the external face of the blank.

Drill (?) and Drill Blanks (?) (Fig. 7, A, B, C, D)

One broken section of what may be the blade of a drill was recovered from the excavations. It is beveled so that a pronounced ridge runs medially along the longitudinal axis of both faces.

What may be the blanks upon which drills were manufactured were recognized as a distinctly modified form of ridged flake. On the external face of the specimens the characteristic ridge remains unaltered. On the internal face of the specimen, however, practically the entire face has been modified by the removal of transverse flakes. No attempt to bevel the blank was noted and the cross section is distinctly triangular. The very narrow dimensions of this form of modified ridged flake together with their characteristically long slender form made it plausible to interpret these as the blanks upon which drills were manufactured.

Notched Reject (?)

A single specimen that appears to be a notched blank rejected at the fluting stage is present. At first glance this looks like a notched scraper but what would be comparable to the working edge is broken. At present the significance or function of this specimen is uninterpretable.

Polished Stone

Worked Slate

A single fragment of slate with numerous incisions was recovered. Whether this is a fragment of a "finished" artifact is difficult to determine.

Pecked Stone

Hammerstones

A total of nineteen hammerstones were recovered. All specimens were simple rounded cobbles of a fine-grained stone that had been battered on the edges. The distribution of the total sample with respect to weight classes is given in Table X.

Although the sample is too small to demonstrate a multimodal distribution, inspection will suffice to indicate that there are

TABLE X

WEIGHT CLASS FREQUENCY: Hammer Stones

Weight Class (In Ounces)	Tabulation of Occurrence	Modal Grouping
2.5 - 3.5	4	1
3.5 - 4.5	. .	. .
4.5 - 5.5	4	2
5.5 - 6.5	3	. .
6.5 - 7.5	. .	. .
7.5 - 8.5	3	. .
8.5 - 9.5	3	3
9.5 - 10.5	1	. .
10.5 - 17.5	. .	. .
17.5 - 37.5	2	4

probably four modal clusters with respect to weight. The smallest with a mean weight of 3.0 ounces, the next with a mean weight of 5.4 ounces, the next with a mean weight of 8.6 ounces and another of over a pound. It is well known that for accomplishing different flint-knapping tasks the weight of the hammerstone is as important a factor as is the way in which the striking platform is prepared, and so on. The presence of four weight classes of hammerstones and the nature of the flake scars on all of the specimens indicate that percussion with the hammerstone, and possibly with an antler flaking tool, was the only technique employed in the production of the artifacts at this site.

Cores

Three examples of truncated blade cores were found at the site (Fig. 7, K). This type of core has been reported to be characteristic of the Paleo-Indian assemblage at the Shoop site and at other fluted point sites in the East (Witthoft, 1957, p. 476). The specimens from the Eastport site have well-defined striking platforms at the apex of the rough core with the ridged flake scars running down the circular expanding face of the core. As explained by Witthoft, flakes or "blades" removed from this type of core tend to expand and have parallel or single longitudinal ridges. No other core types were recovered. From the presence of certain blade forms, however, we suspect that the pyramidal core was worked occasionally by the occupants of the site.

ANALYSIS AND INTERPRETATION OF THE RELATIVE DISTRIBUTION OF THE VARIOUS ARTIFACT FORMS

Thus far the total artifact sample from the Eastport site has been discussed as a unit. Actually, the total assemblage from the site was obtained from four different provenience units. The Museum excavations at the site were concentrated on the blowout region described above (pp. 73-76). Three provenience units at the site are designated Excavation Units 1, 2, and 3. Although the materials recovered in these excavations amounted to a large sample, very few finished artifacts were recovered. The majority of the artifacts available to this study were obtained in excavations by Davis and Gillis from a wooded section between the blowout area and the beach. This material is designated "Loan Collection" in the following table. The latter sample, although quite extensive, was a selected one in that the entire sample of flakes, chips, and broken rock excavated was not available for study. Table XI presents a break-down of the total assemblage available to this study by provenience unit.

Inspection of Table XI will reveal that the majority of the materials included in this study were obtained from the areas of uncontrolled excavations. It is from those areas that we do not have a complete sample. Therefore, the relative proportions of artifacts to flake types is probably meaningless. Comparison of the flake types from the excavation units, however, reveals that there are obvious differences between the units. Because of the small sample from Unit 3, only the two units designated Excavation Units 1 and 2 were treated statistically. A chi square value of 31.49 was calculated for the comparative frequencies of core derived flakes for Units 1 and 2. This value far exceeds the expected value of chi square at the .01 per cent level of probability. Therefore, we can be very confident that the observed difference in relative type frequencies is not a result of sampling vagaries. The observed difference probably reflects concentrations in the site of materials derived from certain specific flint-knapping stages. Whether differential occupation of the site by peoples employing different flint-working techniques contributed to this particular difference in flake frequency cannot be determined on the basis of available data. Certainly what this observation does provide is the basis for the recognition that any further work carried out at this site should be done under conditions of maximum control so that the problem of multiple occupation, areas of industrial specialization on the site, etc., can be solved.

TABLE XI

MATERIALS BY PROVENIENCE UNITS

Artifacts	Excavation Units 1	2	3	Loan Collection	Total
Cores (block)	14	14	4	26	58
Core derived flakes					
Triangular flakes	58	25	6	20	119
Fluted flakes	66	35	2	26	129
Lamellar flakes	42	14	3	14	73
Blanks					
Decortication flakes	37	40	18	67	162
Ridged flakes	17	35	3	22	87
Modified primary blanks					
Stage one					
Obscured platform	...	1	1	18	20
Platform present	...	1	1	36	38
Stage two fluted	...	1	...	51	52
Postfluting rejects	...	...	1	4	5
Pomranky points					
Complete	...	...	...	44	44
Bases only	...	...	...	50	50
Tips only	...	...	1	54	55
Chips incidentally produced in blank modification					
Faceted	149	349	15	271	784
Nonfaceted	259	146	11	359	775
Transversely flaked nuclei	...	...	...	7	7
Blank Type A	...	...	...	29	29
Projectile points					
Davis points	...	...	...	5	5
Davis points variety	...	...	...	1	1
Dustin points	...	...	...	1	1
Eastport "points"	...	...	...	2	2
Unidentified	...	...	...	3	3
End Scrapers					
Type A	...	...	...	10	10
Type B	...	...	1	2	3
Type C	...	...	...	2	2
Type D	...	...	...	5	5
Side Scrapers					
Type A	...	...	...	2	2
Type B	...	...	1	1	2

TABLE XI

MATERIALS BY PROVENIENCE UNITS

	Excavation Units				
Drills and blanks					
Drill	. . .	. . .	1	. . .	1
Drill blanks	1	. . .	. . .	5	6
Notched reject	. . .	. . .	. . .	1	1
Worked slate	. . .	. . .	. . .	1	1
Hammerstones	. . .	. . .	. . .	17	17
Truncated core	. . .	. . .	. . .	1	1

INTERPRETATION OF THE RECOVERED MATERIAL

Interpretation of the Cultural Significance of Diversity of Forms Observed Among the Artifacts

The functional relationships between the various forms representative of the steps in the manufacture of Pomranky points has already been presented and needs no further elaboration. The presence of pebble nuclei and exotic blank Type A at the site raises the question of the relationship between the two forms and the relationship of these forms to the sequence of manufacturing stages leading to the production of Pomranky points. There is a fairly clear formal similarity between the pebble nuclei and the exotic blank forms suggesting that the exotic blank forms were fabricated directly from pebble nuclei and not manufactured on flake blanks. Whether the exotic blank forms were subsequently manufactured into Pomranky points cannot be ascertained for certain. That they were is suggested by the recognition of several varieties of Pomranky points each suggestive of slightly different processes of manufacture (Binford, pp. 149-92). The presence of a high frequency of obliquely orientated bases and the absence of distinct longitudinal scars originating along the basal edge of occasional specimens suggest that some of the Pomranky points were manufactured by the direct modification of a small pebble nuclei directly into the finished specimen. This is further supported by the demonstrably smaller size of the specimens lacking distinct longitudinal chip scars (Saginaw variety). Thus, on the basis of this argument, it is proposed that an alternative means of fabricating Pomranky points was the direct modification of pebble nuclei into finished pieces as represented at the Eastport site by Blank Type A and the pebble nuclei.

At the Pomranky site (Binford, p. 173) a third method of production of Pomranky points was recognized. That was the modification of an expanding flake into a Pomranky point with the finished piece orientated with respect to the flake blank so that the bulb of percussion was located along the lateral edge roughly at the point of juncture between the lateral edge and the basal edge. The presence of several specimens at the Eastport site exhibiting the typical transverse scar along one face of the basal edge which represents the unaltered edge of the original flake blank suggests that this mode of manufacture was also practiced. It has been suggested that the recognized differences in the manufacturing procedure may be related to the size and nature of the raw material utilized. This is supported by the strong correlation between formal differences at the variety level of differentiation and stone type (Binford, p. 164). Thus, it is reasonable to suggest that all of the recognized manufacturing sequences thus far recognized for the production of Pomranky points was practiced at the Eastport site but that, by far, the dominant technique was that involving the modification of a ridged flake into the finished piece.

Turning now to the problem of the function of Pomranky points, we can say that there is nothing in their formal composition suggestive of anything other than a utilitarian or technonomic usage. In the current literature Pomranky points are normally referred to as "mortuary blades" (Ritchie 1955, p. 42). Ritchie comments: "Prevailing evidence sustains the view that the sole purpose for which they [Pomranky points] were designed and used was as mortuary offerings, hence they may more appropriately be referred to as 'mortuary blades'." Indeed, all well-documented or professionally excavated finds of large numbers of Pomranky points have been associated with burials. The reported occurrences, however, of Pomranky points in Ontario, New York, and Michigan leave some question as to their exclusive occurrence with burials and also their exclusive function as mortuary offerings as opposed to their inclusion as part of the necessary equipment for carrying on life in the next world. For instance at the Andrews site in Saginaw County, Michigan, Pomranky points occurred in small numbers associated with several burials. In the same burials were notched projectile points obviously manufactured on Pomranky points. In this case the only difference between the Pomranky points and the notched points was the production of a notch to facilitate hafting. The dominant factor involved in hafting points of all kinds is the material selected for the haft. The width of the shaft or handle dictates the necessary width between the notches, otherwise the lashing attachment will simply not be secure or durable. Notching would seem, in most cases, to be the final step in the preparation of the tool and was accomplished as the tool was mounted for use. It is suggested here that Pomranky points while in some contexts certainly were utilized as mortuary blades were not exclusively produced for such use. The recognition of Davis points as having been manufactured on Pomranky points is supported by a similar recognition in the case of the specimens from the Andrews site. It is suggested here that Pomranky points are "secondary blanks," that is, nearly completed projectile points which could be notched at the time of hafting. That they were utilized as mortuary goods both in the form of necessary parts of the tool kit for use in the afterlife and mortuary offerings when they occur in burials in excessive quantities certainly not to be considered as part of the necessary equipment for use in the next life is not questioned. What is suggested is that they had both a utilitarian and a sociotechnic function which must be inferred from the context of their occurrence. Certainly their context at the Eastport site does not suggest a sociotechnic function and the presence of Davis points, at least some specimens of which were manufactured Pomranky points, suggests a utilitarian function as blanks for future notching and hafting as projectile points.

Of the notched and stemmed projectile points present at the site three types and possibly a fourth have been recognized—Davis points, Dustin points, and Eastport "points," as well as a variety of other forms not assignable to any defined type. The differences between the small notched forms and the larger stemmed forms of Eastport points brings up the question of functional differences versus stylistic differences. Unfortunately, there is not sufficient data from the Eastport site to settle the interpretative problem of the meaning of the observed differences.

The asymmetry in blade shape, however, when taken in conjunction with information from the Andrews site, Saginaw County, Michigan, leads to the suggestion that the formal difference between Davis points and Eastport points is related to functional differences between the two forms. At the Andrews site a large "stemmed point" quite similar to the Eastport points was found in a grave along with Pomranky points and notched points similar to Davis points. For this reason it seems clear that both Davis and Eastport points were manufactured as part of the same complex. The differences in size and method of preparation for hafting suggest different intended functions. The convex working edge with marks of abrasion suggests a cutting motion. For this reason it is proposed that (*a*) Davis points are projectile points and Eastport points are knives, and (*b*) they both represent a single sociocultural entity.

The single diminutive specimen of Davis point is believed to be a projectile point but, because of observations made on other assemblages, it is interpreted as representative of a distinct form and not part of the range of variation within the defined type. At present the best hypothesis seems to be that the two forms are related to differing usage with respect to the game types exploited with each.

The Dustin point is interpreted as distinct and representative of a separate occupation. The meaning of the observed formal diversity within the unidentified class of projectile points cannot be assessed at present.

The cultural significance of the formal diversity observed among the scrapers is similarly difficult to assess. Whether the differences are stylistic and reflect multiple occupation of the site or whether the diversity is a result of alternative manufacturing techniques and/or different functions for the recognized forms is not known for certain. Those forms which suggest similar functions judging from the shape of the working edge are Types B and C, both sharing a less convex working edge and a steeper "snub nose" on the working edge. Thus, provisionally, these appear to have been utilized for the same purpose but the differences in mode of fashioning and in material utilized for production suggest that the two types are stylistically distinct representing different ethnosocial origins. On the other hand, Types A and D share pronounced convex working edges and the lack of a steep working edge, and differ primarily in the type of blank from which they were manufactured. Similarly, they both share a similarity in that the majority of specimens are manufactured of locally available Eastport chert. It seems likely that the differences between types A and D reflect alternative ways of scraper manufacture practiced by the same peoples responsible for the Davis points and the Pomranky points found at the site. This equation is made on the basis of numerical preponderance and the type of material utilized in manufacture.

Of the artifacts with lateral working edges only two forms are present suggestive of different functions. One specimen occurred with a pronounced polish on the internal face. The polish is of a form indicative of an accumulation on the surface of the specimen as opposed to the wearing down of the specimen. That is, the polish is very bright, occurs on the low spots as well as on the ridges, suggesting that the polish is not solely a function of abrasion, but may be the result of chemical action. Hide working is suggested as possibly the cause of this polish. The other specimens do not show this polish and yet do not differ in shape of the working edge from the polished specimen. All specimens are manufactured of Eastport chert and for this reason are attributed to the same complex as the Pomranky points.

The single drill fragment recovered is manufactured of exotic stone and no other traits can be utilized to postulate an association of the form.

The fragment of worked slate cannot be associated with any given grouping of materials. Its function is also unknown.

The four recognized groupings of hammerstones by weight are interpreted as representing different size requirements for different stone-working tasks. The entire assemblage of hammerstones is tentatively associated with material of which the Pomranky points are a part in view of the obvious flint-working activities of the groups responsible for the Pomranky points.

Interpretation of the Cultural Homogeneity and Functional Specificity of the Site

In order to eventually understand the nature of extinct cultural systems we must interpret each archaeological site in terms of (*a*) the cultural homogeneity and (*b*) the specificity of the occupation represented. The first problem is to determine whether the cultural material recovered from the site are the artifactual remains of a single cultural unit. The latter problem depends upon the solution of the former problem. Granted this, then we may try to determine (*a*) if the site is representative of the entire range of cultural activity carried on by a single sociocultural unit throughout a single subsistence cycle. If not, what specific activities are represented and to what part of the seasonal cycle do the represented activities apply?

In attempting to answer the first question the entire range of formal and special associations must be brought to bear. It has already been pointed out that the presence of the Dustin point at the site is taken as evidence for an occupation at the site both formally and temporally unrelated to the occupations responsible for the

Pomranky points. The status of the unnamed point forms as indications of other occupations cannot be determined. It may be stated, therefore, that the cultural materials from the site are representative of multiple occupations. The major occupation at the site is represented by the Pomranky points and associated artifact forms. On the basis of the formal analysis the following artifact classes can be attributed to a single cultural complex: block cores; triangular, fluted, lamellar, decortication, and ridged flakes; faceted and nonfaceted chips; all of the rejects in the manufacturing sequence of Pomranky point production; Blank Type A and pebble nuclei; Pomranky points; Davis points of both varieties; Eastport points; end scrapers of Type A and D; side scrapers of two types; and hammerstones. The Dustin point is the only recognized artifact representative of the Dustin occupation. Artifacts occurring at the site which can not be reasonably assigned to either of the above two archaeological complexes are: miscellaneous projectile point forms, end scrapers of Type B and C, drills, worked slate, and the truncated core. The latter artifacts may well be associated with one or the other of the recognized artifact complexes but available information does not provide a sufficient basis for assignation of these forms to either of the recognized components at the site. Similarly, some, or all, of the latter forms may represent other occupations at the site.

The problem of the functional specificity of the site can only be evaluated with respect to the major occupation represented by the Pomranky points and associated artifacts.

Quite obviously flint knapping was a major activity conducted at the site and the relative dearth of material representative of other activities suggests that the site was not primarily a site from which exploitation of the habitat for subsistence purposes was conducted. For instance, it has been found that Archaic hunting stations have a high proportion of broken projectile points represented only by bases. The obvious explanation is that hunters would retrieve the shafts of their projectiles and, back in the leisure of their camp, remove broken points, discarding the bases which still adhered to the shaft after breakage. No such high incidence of projectile point bases occurred at the Eastport site. Secondary tools are poorly represented, that is, tools that were utilized in the production of wooden and bone artifacts. Similarly, grinding stones known to have been utilized in the late Archaic period are also lacking. The impression one gains of the assemblage from the Eastport site is that the site was occupied repeatedly by small groups over a rather restricted period of time primarily for the purpose of roughing out artifacts from the Eastport chert nodules which were abundantly available at the site. Although no direct data is available to support the argument that occupations were seasonal it seems reasonable that the gathering and processing of stone at the "quarry" would be a warm weather activity. In summary, it is suggested that the Eastport site was occupied at least by two different social units at widely separated points in time represented by the Dustin point and the assemblage of materials associated with the Pomranky points. The occupations represented by the Pomranky points were short-term occupations associated with the specific task of gathering and processing the nodules of Eastport chert locally available in abundance. It is further suggested that these activities were probably restricted to the warm months, at least to the months when the ground was not covered with snow. This interpretation suggests a sociocultural system of rather simple type within which there are no highly specialized productive communities.

Sociohistorical Implications of the Analytical Conclusions

The only known analysis of industrial debris from the northeastern United States is that reported by John Witthoft from the Shoop site, a Paleo-Indian site in Pennsylvania. Naturally, there are certain similarities between the reports from the two sites because of a common concern with the same class of attributes. It is the opinion of the investigators, however, that the similarities go beyond the simple attributes common to flint debris in general. One obvious similarity is the presence of the truncated blade core at both sites. Witthoft has commented, in several instances, on the distinctive nature of this type of core (Witthoft, 1957, p. 43; 1952, p. 476). The block core present at the Eastport site, although not reported at the Shoop site, is believed by the authors to be a particular form of prepared core that is historically related to more conventional "blade" cores. At the Shoop site, Witthoft reports the presence of flakes similar to the "fluted flakes" from the Eastport site (Witthoft, 1952, p. 473). He also describes flakes that appear to be closely related formally to the triangular flakes described from the Eastport site (1952, p. 474). One striking difference in the debris from the two sites is the apparent absence of reticulately scarred flakes at the Shoop site. Witthoft commented that flakes derived incidentally from working bifacial tools at the Shoop site were invariably lamellar and were "consistent" with blade-making tradition represented there (1952, p. 475). Some of the differences between the debris from the two sites may reflect differences in the type of site described with respect to the processing of flint artifacts. For instance, Witthoft mentions that "less than three chips including tiny retouched flakes, per artifact" were found at the Shoop site (1952, p. 471). At the Eastport site there are, roughly, seven chips per artifact, which includes all rejects, and the like. This figure is only for the specimens that were classifiable as to form. There were an additional 51 pounds of flakes and broken rock that were not included in the reported tabulations because they lacked striking platforms and bulbs of percussion. That is, they were broken and could not be typed using the attributes selected for this study. There are an estimated six hundred flakes per pound for the combined material from the site. By adding the unclassified material, we have an estimate of approximately ninety-five flakes per artifact. Add to this figure the "five bushels" of rock that Gillis and Davis did not save from their original excavations and we should have a truly impressive ratio of flakes to artifacts. Certainly, this difference indicates that the two sites are different with respect to the processing stages carried out at each. If the blanks upon which the Shoop site projectile points were made had been manufactured at the site, would there be reticulately scarred chips present? About this we can only speculate, but, certainly, the fluted points at the Shoop site were not manufactured on the diminutive blades described by Witthoft.

The fluting stage in the processing of blank flakes at the Eastport site is a processing technique that is shared with the Paleo-Indian complexes. In a study of an early workshop site in Virginia, McCary (1951, pp. 9-17) provides us with further interesting similarities. McCary states (p. 13): "Eighteen implements (Figs. 9, 21-23, 27, 28), practically all of which are broken basal ends, should probably be called 'knives.' Their bases are usually wavy. This feature proves doubtless the previous existence of a platform from which the longitudinal flakes were struck. In all but three examples flutes were struck from each face to thin the basal portion . . . . It is evident that they were struck off after the flaking process had been practically completed because several of these implements (Figs. 9, 27, 28) show clearly that the flutes, instead of breaking upwards as the maker intended turned downward and broke completely through the blade forming an entirely smooth surface along the break." His discussion and illustrations of these rejected implements bear a startlingly close resemblance to the Stage No. 2 rejects pictured in Figure 4 of this report. These similarities are not pointed out as the basis for postulating a direct genetic relationship between the Paleo-Indian material as represented by the Enterline chert industry and the complex represented at the Eastport site which can be roughly classified as "Early Point Peninsula." What is intended is to emphasize a continuity between the flint-working technology of the Paleo-Indian cultures and the later cultures of the Great Lakes as represented by the Eastport material.

The usefulness of this type of analysis should be apparent. Flint-working techniques do not appear to exhibit the relatively rapid changes of style through time that are characteristic of artifact types as such. The analysis of flint-working techniques can provide us with a tool for tracing the general relationships between widely separated cultural complexes.

Since the Eastport site has been tentatively identified as a functionally specific site where quarry activities were carried out it is certainly not representative of the entire range of activities of the socio-cultural system represented. Judging from the typological similarities between the Pomranky points from the Eastport site and those from the Pomranky (Binford, pp. 149-92) and Kimmel (Papworth, 1958, pp. 51-56) sites it can be tentatively grouped with them as possibly representing another phase of the sociocultural systems represented at the latter two sites.

DATING THE SITE

Judging from the geologic context of the site and the typological similarities of the assemblage with materials from the Kimmel, Pomranky, and Hodges (Binford, pp. 124-48) sites it is estimated that the site was occupied by the peoples responsible for the production of the Pomranky points some time between 1300 B.C. and 500 B.C.

REFERENCES CITED

Davis, G. W., and Gillis, E. V.
1959. Grand Traverse Bay Archaic. The Coffinberry News Bull., Vol. 6, No. 6. Grand Rapids.

Dustin, Fred
1927. Materials of the Indian Lapidary in Saginaw District, Michigan. Papers of the Michigan Academy of Science, Arts, and Letters. Vol. 8, pp. 11-22.

1935. A Study of Bayport Chert. *Ibid.*, Vol. 20, pp. 465-75, Ann Arbor.

Ellis, H. Holmes
1960. Surface Exposures of Flint and Chert in Michigan. Michigan Archaeologist, Vol. 6, No. 4, pp. 56-67. Ann Arbor.

Holmes, William
1919. Handbook of Aboriginal American Antiquities. Smithsonian Institution, Bur. Amer. Ethnol. Bull., 60, pp. 276-329. Washington, D. C.

Hough, Jack L.
1958. Glacial Geology of the Great Lakes. Urbana: University of Illinois Press.

Leakey, L. S. B.
1960. Adam's Ancestors. Harper Torchbook. New York: Harper and Brothers.

McCary, Ben C.
1951. A Workshop Site of Early Man in Dinwiddie County, Virginia. American Antiquity, Vol. 17, No. 1.

Oakley, Kenneth P.
1958. Man the Tool Maker. British Museum, London.

Papworth, Mark L.
1958. Artifacts from the Kimmel Site, Berrien Springs, Michigan. Michigan Archaeologist, Vol. 4, No. 3. Ann Arbor.

Ritchie, William A.
1955. Recent Discoveries Suggesting an Early Woodland Burial Cult in the Northeast. New York State Museum and Science Service, Circular No. 40, State University of New York. Albany.

Witthoft, John A.
1957. The Art of Flint Chipping. Ohio Archaeologist, Vol. 6, No. 4,

pp. 138-42; Vol. 7, No. 1, pp. 17-20; Vol. 7, No. 2, pp. 42-46; Vol. 7, No. 3, pp. 80-87; Vol. 7, No. 4, pp. 122-27. The Archaeological Society of Ohio. Columbus.

1952. A Paleo-Indian Site in Eastern Pennsylvania. An Early Hunting Culture. Proc. Am. Philosoph. Soc., Vol. 96, No. 4, pp. 464-95. Philadelphia.

THE HODGES SITE
A LATE ARCHAIC BURIAL STATION

Lewis R. Binford

CONTENTS

Figures

Tables

ACKNOWLEDGMENTS

I wish to thank the owner of the materials, Jim Hunt, for his interest and co-operation, Anta White for the line drawings of artifacts, Charles Eyman for identification of human skeletal parts, Richard Yarnell for identification of the botanical materials, Charles Cleland for study of the nonhuman skeletal parts, and David Taggart for study of the types of stone.

As is quite obvious, most of the staff of the Museum of Anthropology, The University of Michigan, have been involved in the analysis of this material. The co-ordination and planning for such an efficient and well-staffed research institution has been largely through the efforts of Dr. James B. Griffin, Director of the Museum. The bringing together of the results of the staff's investigation have been the contributions of the author. Errors of both omission and commission are, of course, my responsibility entirely.

A part of the time devoted to this study was supported by funds provided by the National Science Foundation.

SITE DESCRIPTION AND DISCUSSION OF EXCAVATION

The Hodges site was brought to the attention of the staff of the Museum of Anthropology, The University of Michigan, by James Hunt of Saginaw, Michigan. Hunt was observing the removal of approximately 1.5 feet of sand from a sand knoll originally standing at an elevation of approximately 600 feet above sea level. The sand knoll is located on the property of Mr. Hodges of Saginaw County; the southeast quarter of the northwest quarter, section 35, township eleven north, range 4 east. During the course of the sand removal the bulldozer exposed an oval area approximately 6 feet long (north-south) and 4 feet wide (east-west). This area was defined by a heavy concentration of dark soil mixed with calcined bone fragments which contrasted sharply with the yellowish sand of the knoll. Mr. Hunt, together with Mr. Peacock, also of Saginaw, recognized the discolored area as an archaeological feature and proceeded to examine its contents, taking notes and measurements pertinent to the material they recovered. The area was cleaned, revealing the distinct outline of an intrusive pit 5 feet 6 inches

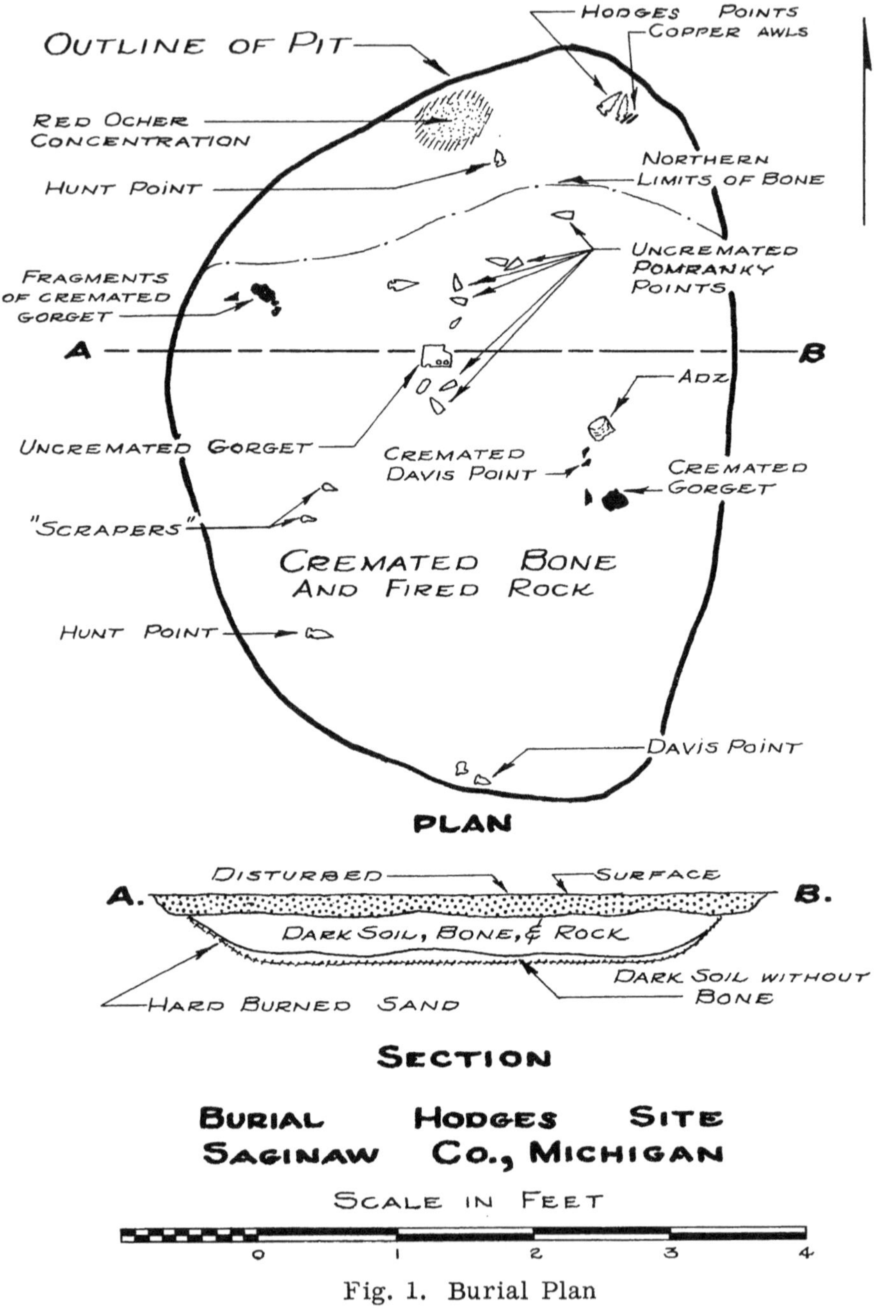

Fig. 1. Burial Plan

long and 4 feet 2 inches wide (Fig. 1). At the time of recognition, part of the feature had been destroyed by the bulldozer so that the point of origin of the pit could not be determined. Almost certainly, some of the cultural material had been removed. Only the very bottom of the feature remained, intruding into the sand 6 inches from the surface at the time of recognition. The most obvious soil unit in the feature contained fired rock, calcined human bone, and artifacts thinly scattered, and was composed of a very dark organic laden soil with identifiable charcoal fragments. This soil unit was distributed over the entire southern part of the feature, although it did not continue to the bottom of the pit. Over the entire bottom of the pit, and in the north quarter of the feature, was a brownish soil lacking bone and fired rock. This was heavily laden with organic material, and, in the north half of the feature, contained many of the uncremated artifacts. The third identifiable soil unit within the feature was a thin crust of fired sand which served to mark the bottom of the pit. Much of this crust was composed of sand and silt particles fused together so that it broke off and cleaved from the undisturbed sand in thin chunks. Finally, at the north end of the feature there was a small area in which was a concentration of powdered hematite or red ochre (Fig. 1). Hunt and Peacock excavated the feature and turned over the recovered artifacts to The University of Michigan Museum of Anthropology--a large lard tin of cremated bone and soil, together with their field notes. These materials serve as the basis of this report.

This site is by no means exhausted, for at the present time there are reported to be discolored areas visible on the surface as well as concentrations of red ochre. Aside from the material reported here and the indications of more material of a similar nature at the site, test excavations by a University of Michigan field party have shown that materials representing Middle and Late Woodland occupations also occur at the site. Whether there is a Late Archaic occupation of the site as opposed to utilization of the site as a burial area cannot be determined at the present time.

FORMAL ANALYSIS OF THE RECOVERED MATERIAL

Chipped-stone Material

Raw material.--As was done with the materials from the Pomranky site, the artifacts were analyzed according to the type of material from which they were manufactured. The raw materials have been given "type" designations by letter and will be described according to the same format as presented by Binford in A Proposed Attribute List . . . pp. 193-221). Seven different types of raw material were observed in the sample of chipped-stone material.

Type J is a reddish-brown chert with a dull surface, opaque diaphaneity, and of massive structure. Inclusions are lacking. The texture is generally uniform but occasionally narrow, irregular streaks occur. These are apparently elongated cavities lined with subtranslucent light gray to whitish chert. The distribution and sources of this material are unknown.

Type K is a mottled medium gray, yellowish-brown, reddish-brown chert with a slightly shiny (glimmering) surface, opaque diaphaneity, of massive structure and inclusions are lacking. The texture is very irregular, characterized by single bluish-gray narrow arced bands (concentric with the surface of the nodule) separating the various color bands, which are also apparently concentric with the nodular surface. Lined cavities are rare. The distribution and sources of this material are unknown.

Type L is a medium gray chert with a dull surface, opaque diaphaneity and of massive structure. Inclusions are lacking. The texture is irregular, characterized by elongated cavities lined with clear-to-dark gray chert in a broadly banded pattern. This material is known as "western Onondaga chert" and is distributed widely in western New York and in the Ontario peninsula.

Type M is a mottled, medium bluish-gray chert with a shiny surface, opaque diaphaneity and of massive structure. Inclusions are absent. The texture is irregular with narrow bands of brown alternating with narrow blue-gray bands constituting the broader of the bands. In the blue-gray bands there are elongated cavities lined with a dark brownish chert. The distribution and source of this material is unknown.

Type P is a yellowish-cream-colored massive chert with a shiny surface and opaque diaphaneity. The texture is very regular, lacking cavities, fossils, and banding. The distribution and sources of this material are unknown.

Type Q is a yellowish-brown to reddish-brown massive chert with a slightly shiny surface and opaque diaphaneity. Small white specks (fossils) are present, but not heavily concentrated. Cavities are absent, as in any definite banding. The distribution and sources of this material are unknown.

Comments. One fact should be pointed out that might be obscured in the typology of raw material: the majority of the material is brownish; a similar concentration upon brownish material for grave furniture was observed at the Pomranky site and is characteristic of Pomranky points from the Stroebel site in Saginaw County (to be reported in the future).

Pomranky points. Eight complete Pomranky points were recovered (Binford, *The Pomranky Site,* pp. 149-192). Seven of these points are clearly of the Saginaw variety, three of which are manufactured of Type Q stone and the remaining four of Type K stone. Metrical data on the points are given in Table I.

TABLE I

METRICAL DATA ON POMRANKY POINTS

Data	Length (In centimeters)	Maximum Width (In centimeters)	Base Width (In centimeters)	Thickness (In centimeters)
Sx . .	26.5	13.70	13.70	3.0
Sx^2 .	100.39	27.16	27.16	1.39
n. . .	7.00	7.00	7.00	7.00
x. . .	3.79	1.96	1.96	.43
s. . .	.10	.24	.24	.04

In addition to the Saginaw variety points, one cremated specimen of a Midland variety point was present. It was 5.9 cm long, 2.5 cm wide at the widest point, 2.3 cm wide at the base and .60 cm thick.

Notched projectile points.—A total of six complete notched projectile points were present. Within this small sample there is a great deal of formal diversity. Three types are clearly represented by two specimens each, while the seventh specimen is not clearly identifiable to any of the recognized types.

Hodges points (Fig. 2, A and B). This point type will be provisionally defined on the basis of two specimens. At present no variety designation will be offered in view of the fact that these specimens are not known in terms of their major range of variation.

Raw material. Both specimens are manufactured of Type L stone and are the only specimens from the site manufactured of

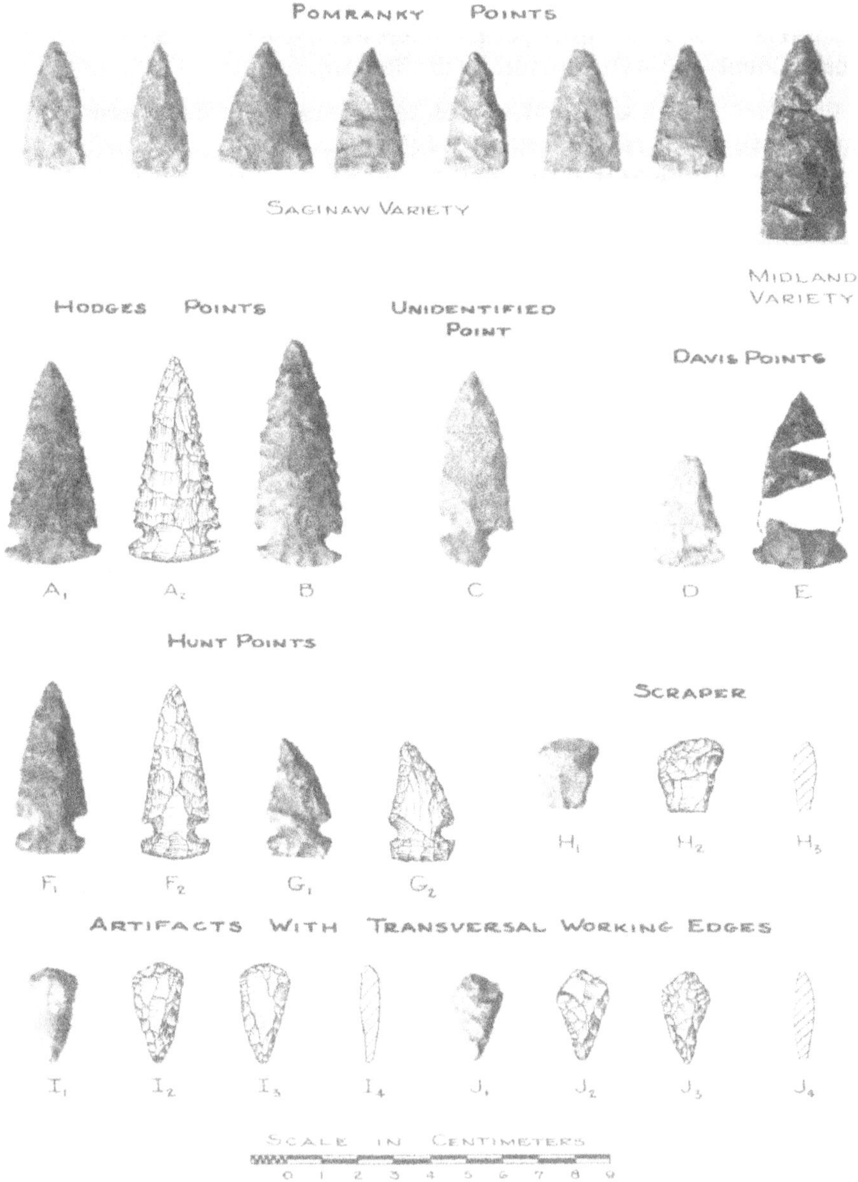

Fig. 2. Chipped-stone Artifacts

this material. This Type L stone was certainly obtained in either western New York or from the Ontario peninsula.

Blade element. Shape of the blade—both ovate and contracting ovate blade shapes are represented. Cross sections and longitudinal sections are biplano. The blade is symmetrical.

Chipping of the blade. Primary scars tend to be massive and expanding. Terminal diminutive hinge fractures are relatively common, yet the definition in terms of ridges between chip scars is not pronounced. Secondary retouch is continuous along both edges, composed of short expanding and conchoidal scars. There is no evidence of crushing, nibbling, or other signs of use. Secondary chips were removed so as to produce regular diminutive notches (serration) in the lateral edge.

Base element. Shape of the base—the base is subconvex.

Chipping of the base. The specimens have been chipped to the point that determination of the orientation of the finished specimen with respect to the original flake blank is impossible. The basal edge has been thinned to an even and delicate edge. There are no remnants of a striking platform at the base. Diminutive longitudinal primary scars originate at the basal edge and are present on both faces and continuous along the edge. Secondary chip scars are discontinuous in the form of small triangular and expanding scars. The basal edge is well defined and even.

Haft element. Juncture is lateral-lateral; however, the proximal point of juncture is almost coincidental with the lateral-basal point of juncture. The distal point of juncture is acute, right-angled, and obtuse, but is always angular. Acute appears to be the desired form, but breakage may result in other forms. Medial points of juncture are generally biright-angled with circular articulation. The proximal point of juncture is acute and circular and, as mentioned, almost coincidental with the lateral-basal point of juncture.

Notches were produced with diminutive primary and secondary chips. Scars originating in the haft element obscure longitudinal scars originating on the basal edge, as well as transverse scars originating along the lateral edge. These facts show that the production of the haft was the final step in the production of the finished product.

Grinding. Bases are well ground to a smooth edge while grinding is absent within the haft element and along the lateral edges.

TABLE II

METRICAL DATA ON HODGES POINTS

Specimen	Thickness (cm)	Base Width (cm)	Tang Width (cm)	Shoulder Width (cm)	Axial Length (cm)	Tang Length (cm)	Notch Length (cm)
Pl.I,A	. .	2.6	1.8	2.4	5.8	.8	.4
Pl.I,B	. .	2.4	1.5	2.5	6.4	.9	.4
Mean	. .	2.5	1.65	2.45	6.1	.85	.4

Comments. These appear to have been manufactured on Pomranky points of an undescribed variety more closely resembling those depicted by Ritchie (1955) from the Red Lake site in New York.

Hunt Point (Fig. 2, f and g). This point type is provisionally defined on the basis of two specimens. As in the case of the Hodges point, no designation of variety will be offered. It should be mentioned, however, that specimens believed to be representative of this type have been recovered from the Oberlander Number 2 site in New York State (Ritchie, 1944, Pl. 71, Figs. 5, 6, 11, and 12).

Raw material. One specimen is manufactured of Type K stone, and the other is the only representative of Type M stone.

Blade element. Shape of the blade—only a single specimen exhibits an un-reworked blade and it is contracting ovate in shape. The other specimen has been reworked, is asymmetrical, with one edge being incurvate and the other ovate in shape. Cross sections are both biconvex and biplano, while longitudinal sections are similarly biconvex and biplano.

Chipping of the blade. Primary scars tend to be massive and range from conchoidal to expanding in form. Terminal hinge fractures are relatively common and there is a distinct definition between separate chip scars. Secondary chip scars are generally ovate and conchoidal and are continuous along the entire edge. There is some evidence of use in the form of both crushing and nibbling. This tends to be restricted to a single edge. The definition of the lateral edges is fairly even and there is no serration.

Base element. Shape of the base—the base is straight or only slightly subconvex.

Chipping of the base—in both cases determination of the orientation of the finished specimen with respect to the original flake blank was impossible because of the complete reshaping of the flake blank. The basal edge has been thinned to an even but rather quickly expanding edge. There are no remnants of a striking platform or any form at the base. Diminutive longitudinal primary scars originate at the basal edge and are present on a single face only. Where present, they are continuous along the basal edge. Secondary chipping is discontinuous in the form of small oval scars. The basal edge is well defined, even and ground.

Haft element. Shape of the haft element—juncture is lateral-lateral, with a well-defined unmodified subelement of the tang below the haft element. The distal point of juncture is either right-angled or obtuse, with point articulation. Medial points of juncture are acute with circular articulation. The proximal point of juncture is obtuse and generally a point articulation.

Chipping of the haft element--diminutive primary conchoidal chips are common. Secondary chips are infrequent and, when present, are generally few. Scars originating in the haft element obscure both longitudinal scars and transverse scars originating along the lateral edge. From this it may be inferred that the preparation of the haft element was the final step in the manufacture of the artifact.

Unmodified subelement of the tang. This area may be either contracting or parallel with respect to the longitudinal axis of the specimen. Grinding is evident along the lateral edges. The point of juncture between the lateral edge and the basal edge exhibits right-angled point articulation.

Grinding. Present along the basal edge, lateral edges of the unmodified subelement of the tang and inside the haft element.

Size. Metrical attributes are given in Table III.

Comments. These specimens appear to have been manufactured on an undescribed variety of Pomranky point.

Davis Points (Fig. 2, D and E). Two specimens were identifiable as Davis points, originally defined from the Eastport site (Binford and Papworth, 1962). Both are manufactured of Type A stone which was a common type of raw material at the Pomranky site (Binford, pp. 149-92). Metrical data is given in Table IV.

TABLE III

METRICAL DATA ON HUNT POINTS

Specimen	Thickness (cm)	Base Width (cm)	Tang Width (cm)	Shoulder Width (cm)	Axial Length (cm)	Tang Length (cm)	Notch Length (cm)
Fig. F	. .	1.7	1.2	2.0	5.0	1.1	.55
Fig. G	. .	1.6	1.2	1.7	3.4	1.0	.45

TABLE IV

METRICAL DATA ON DAVIS POINTS

Specimen	Thickness (cm)	Base Width (cm)	Tang Width (cm)	Shoulder Width (cm)	Axial Length (cm)	Tang Length (cm)	Notch Length (cm)
Fig. D	. .	2.1	1.6	1.8	3.4	1.0	.40
Fig. E	. .	2.3	1.9	2.3	5.0	1.4	.40

Miscellaneous Point (Fig. 2, C). A single specimen occurred in the assemblage that was unassignable to any of the known types. This may be simply a function of a lack of knowledge of the variability of the described types. The specimen is 5.6 cm long, 1.8 cm wide at the base, 1.0 cm wide between the notches, 2.0 cm wide at the shoulder, with a tang length of 1.2 cm and is .45 cm thick. It is manufactured of Type J stone and is uncremated.

Artifacts with transversal working edges (Fig. 2, H, I, and J)-- Three artifacts of this general class occurred in the sample. One has a beveled working edge which makes it recognizable as what is normally designated as a scraper.

Scraper (Fig. 2, H). This specimen is the only specimen from the site manufactured of Type P stone. It is bifacially chipped, exhibiting expanding and conchoidal scars on both faces. The proximal end is an old hinge fracture, but does not appear to be a recent break in that longitudinal scars originate there. The working end (distal end) is slightly oblique to the longitudinal axis of the specimen. The shape of the working edge is subconvex and even. In the longitudinal section the distal end is beveled (Fig. 1, H_3) so that there is an acute angle articulated at the working edge. Crushing is evident on the working edge and along the one lateral edge. The specimen is slightly asymmetrical, in that a small "horn" or projection of the working edge extends out with a corresponding "notch" below. Crushing is evident within the "notch."

Unidentified forms. Two specimens occurred, quite similar in form to the scraper and manufactured of Type K and Type Q stone. Their general shape strongly suggests "triangular scrapers" in Ritchie's (1955) terminology. The form of the working edge, however, is not suggestive of a scraping function. It is beveled from both faces (Fig. 2, I_4 and J_4), is deeply crushed and, to some extent, ground. Both specimens are bifacially chipped, exhibiting conchoidal chip scars along the lateral edges. These are believed to have served as "strikers," which are part of a fire-making kit.

Artifacts with lateral working edges.—Two chips with unfaceted striking platforms, of the expanding type (Binford, 202-207) exhibited conchoidal chip scars on the internal face running continuously along the lateral edges. Judging from the absence of nibbling and the very acute edge, these two artifacts were utilized for cutting.

Fired rock.—Four large chunks of fine-grained rock that had obviously been exposed to intense heat accompanied the artifactual material. This material was otherwise unaltered and probably represents materials included in preparation of the crematory fire.

Polished-stone Material

Gorgets (Fig. 3)

Uncremated gorget fragment. This specimen is obviously one corner of a complete specimen. Two sides are evenly ground and polished, representing the original edges of the piece while the other two edges are broken and rough, but with polished ridges showing that after breakage the broken edges were polished and further use was made of the fragment. Two drilled holes (.35 cm in diameter), separated from one another by a distance of 1.60 cm, are aligned along one of the broken edges. These are believed to represent patching holes utilized prior to the complete breakage of the specimen. On this same edge are the remains of another drilled hole through which the break occurred. This is interpreted as one of the original central holes in the gorget. If it is assumed

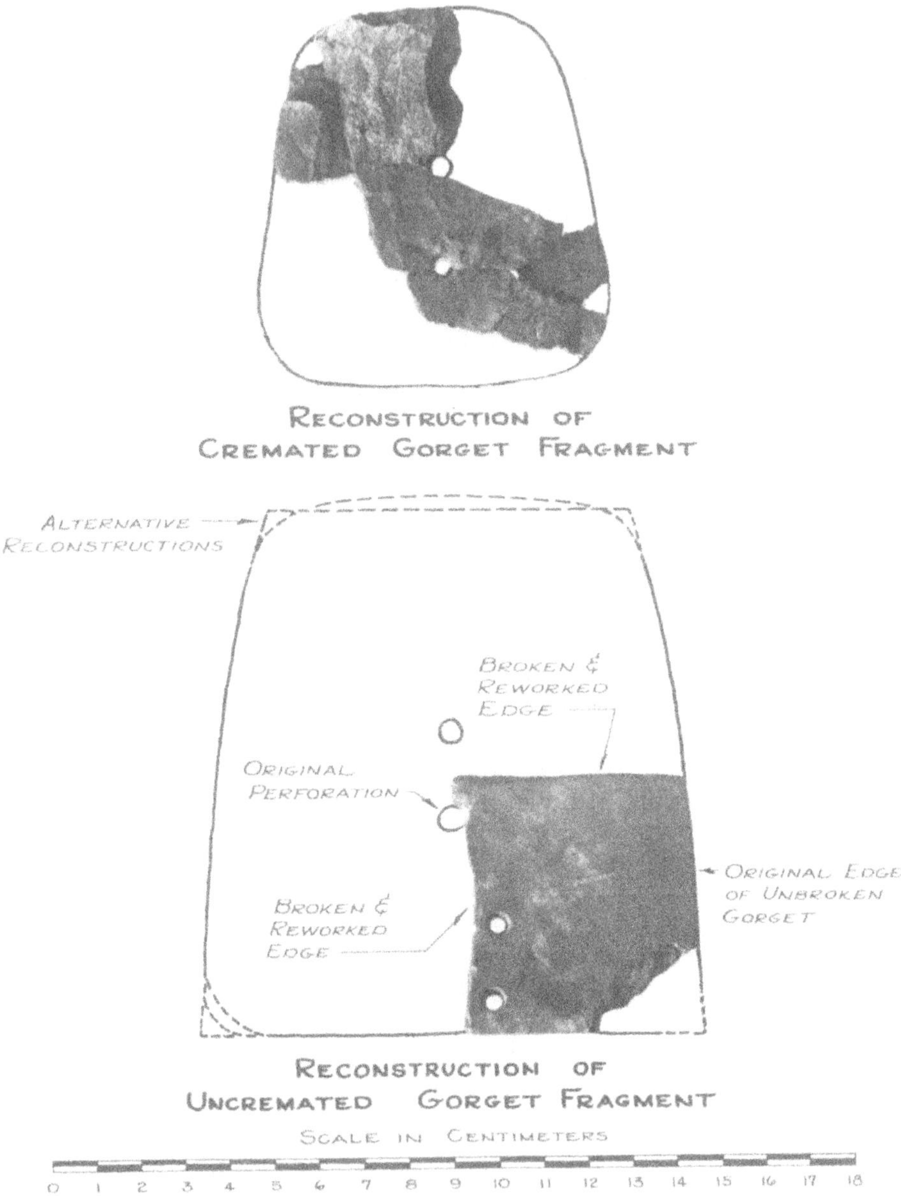

Fig. 3. Reconstructed Gorgets

that this is exactly one-quarter of a complete specimen, a reconstruction is possible as shown in Figure 3.

The shape of the reconstruction strongly suggests a gorget recovered from burial Number 2 at the Oberlander Number 2 component (Ritchie, 1944, Pl. 71, No. 15) and one from the Red Lake site, also in New York (Ritchie, 1955, Pl. 23, Fig. 15). Metrical data on the reconstructed gorget is compared to the two specimens mentioned above (Table V).

TABLE V

METRICAL DATA ON GORGETS

Specimen	Length (cm.)	Minimum Width (cm.)	Maximum Width (cm.)	Thickness (cm.)
Hodge's site . .	12.0	9.50	10.50	.45
Oberlander . . .	13.2	10.00	12.5	
Red Lake	12.0	9.40	11.00	.60

Cremated gorget fragment. Numerous fragments of a burned gorget were mixed with the bones. Enough of the specimen could be reconstructed to infer the original shape and dimensions. The length was 8.7 cm, the minimal width 5.4 cm, the maximum width 8.2 cm and the thickness .60 cm. The lateral edges are roughly straight while the distal and proximal ends are convex. The points of juncture between the lateral and terminal ends articulate with gradual short arcs.

Adz fragment. One fragment from the working end of a plano-convex adz was also included in the sample. It was made of a fine-grained stone. The working end was 4.80 cm wide and 2.5 cm thick. The bevel of the working end is bifacially symmetrical and extends back from the distal end 2.0 cm.

Copper Artifacts

Two copper awls were recovered, one with a triangular cross section and the other with a square cross section. They are identically the same length, 2.50 cm, and their maximum thickness is .30 cm and .25 cm, respectively. Neither shows any evidence of having been burned. There is only a slight tendency for one end to be more pointed than the other. These are very similar to specimens reported from burial Number 2 at the Oberlander site (Ritchie, 1944, Pl. 71, Fig. 21).

Limonites

Three rather large, decomposed chunks of iron pyrites were present. These no doubt originally composed part of a fire-making kit.

Human Skeletal Material

Three hundred and thirty-four grams of cremated human bone were turned over to the laboratory for analysis. The fragments were extremely small and ranged from partly cremated to completely calcined specimens. In general, the charred and blackened fragments predominated. Judging from the degree of warping, longitudinal cracking, and deep checking, the cremation had been of a body rather than of old dry bones. Of the very few identifiable fragments the following were recognized: 7 skull fragments, 3 vertebral fragments, 6 rib fragments, 3 lower arm fragments, 1 phalangeal fragment, 2 pelvic fragments, 1 femoral fragment, and 1 fibula fragment. Although only a very small fraction of the sample could be identified, the entire body is represented, indicating that a complete corpse was cremated. There is no duplication of parts, which suggests that it was one individual, and judging from the size of the bone and the epiphyseal closure the individual can be classed as a young adult. No sex determination was possible. It could not be determined from analysis of the bone whether the individual had been disarticulated at the time of cremation.

Faunal Material

Skeletal. Thirty-six fragments of animal bone were found mixed with the cremated human bone. In all cases the animal bone was cremated and could not be distinguished from the human bone in the degree of burning, etc. On the other hand, the deep longitudinal cracking, warping, etc., characteristic of cremation in the flesh, was not evident on some of the animal bone. Only a single specimen could be specifically identified and that was the distal end of the tibia of a racoon, *Procyon lotor*. This specimen exhibited only superficial checking and no warping or longitudinal cracking, suggesting the cremation of old dry bone. The remaining 35 specimens were identifiable in only the following classes: (*a*) small mammal—bones of this class were mostly rib and long bone fragments showing longitudinal cracking and warping indicative of cremation in the flesh (26 fragments), (*b*) small bird—five fragments of the long bone of birds of roughly songbird size showed only superficial checking suggesting cremation of old dry bone, and (*c*) turtle—five fragments of turtle carapace showed only superficial checking suggesting cremation of old dry bone.

Soft parts. Twelve dried and uncremated fragments of what is believed to be gut or sinew were found mixed with the soil from the cremation. Obviously this had been included after the crematory fire was extinguished.

Floral Material

Sixty-eight *Chenopodium* and three *Polygonum* seeds were recovered from the soil of the cremation. *Chenopodium* is variously called pigweed, goosefoot, or lamb's quarters. It is an economic plant in that the tender shoots and leaves are edible as vegetables and the seeds, which are available in the fall, were utilized aboriginally for making flour which was made into bread or mush (Yanovsky, 1936, p. 22). Various species of *Polygonum* were also utilized aboriginally, the roots, leaves, and seeds being exploited (Yanovsky, 1936, p. 20). The presence of these seeds in the fill of the burial pit is indicative of placement in the burial after the crematory fires were extinguished, either as accidental inclusions in the fill, or as part of the mortuary goods. Regardless of the context of their inclusion, it is quite likely that the burial was made in the fall, for it is in that period of the year when seeds of both *Chenopodium* and *Polygonum* are abundant, either for exploitation or are likely to be on the surface of the ground where they might be accidentally included in the fill. Several identifiable charcoal fragments were all from Red Maple (*Acer rubrum*).

FORMAL-SPACIAL CORRELATIONS: ANALYSIS AND INTERPRETATION

At this level of analysis we are concerned with determining whether there is any tendency for one artifact form to be associated with another and what, if any, pattern of distribution exists between various artifact forms. Stated another way, what, if any, indications are there that a given set of artifacts represents a unit as opposed to any other group of artifacts. Two obvious attribute classes suggest themselves as useful in segregating groups of artifacts as to whether they were cremated and the types of raw material from which they were manufactured. Table VI presents the comparative information on the recognized artifact forms in terms of the above-mentioned criteria.

TABLE VI

ARTIFACTS BY CLUSTER AND STONE TYPE

	Stone Type								Condition	
	J	K	L	M	P	Q	A	Unidentified	Cremated	Uncremated
Pomranky points										
Saginaw variety.	3	4	..	..	..	..	..	...	...	7
Midland variety.	..	..	..	..	..	..	..	1	1	..
Unidentified ..	..	..	..	..	..	..	..	6 frag.	6 frag.	..
Hodges points ...	..	..	2	..	..	..	..	...	...	2
Hunt points	..	1	..	1	..	..	..	...	...	2
Davis points	..	..	..	..	..	..	2	...	1	1
Misc. points	1	..	..	..	..	..	..	...	...	1
Scraper	..	..	..	..	1	..	..	...	...	1
Scraper-like object	..	1	..	..	..	1	..	...	...	2
Artifacts with lateral working edges	1	..	..	..	..	..	1	...	...	2
Gorgets	..	..	..	..	..	..	..	2	1	1
Adz	..	..	..	..	..	..	..	1	...	1
Copper awls	..	..	..	..	..	..	..	...	...	2

Turning now to the distributional information (Fig. 1), it can be observed that there are two clusters of cremated artifacts, one represented by fragments of the cremated gorget and fragments of a cremated Davis point in the east-central part of the feature. A second concentration of cremated material is located along the northwestern edge of the pit containing fragments of the same cremated gorget and fragments of several cremated Pomranky points. Distributed lineally between these two clusters were all the uncremated artifacts. The Hodges points and copper awls clustered tightly together at the north and a less tight cluster in the central area made up of the uncremated gorget, all the uncremated Pomranky points, the miscellaneous projectile point, a "scraper" of Type K stone, and a worked chip of Type K stone and limonites. A southwestern cluster was composed of a "scraper" of Type Q stone and a scraper of Type P stone. At the south end of the pit was a fourth cluster composed of a Davis point and a worked chip of Type A stone. The Hunt points and adz appear to have been individually placed in the burial. Thus far it can be reasonably inferred that: (*a*) the cremated goods were included in the pit along with the body that was cremated, and (*b*) the uncremated goods were added after the fires had been extinguished. Further support for the inference that the four clusters of materials described above actually represent discrete units in terms of placement in the burial pit is found in the high internal consistency of each recognized cluster in terms of raw material from which the included artifacts were manufactured.

TABLE VII

ARTIFACTS BY CLUSTER AND STONE TYPE

Cluster	Number of Chipped-stone Artifacts	Stone Type						
		J	K	L	M	P	Q	A
North. . . .	2	. .	. .	2	. .	. .	. .	. .
Central. . .	10	3	7	. .	. .	. .	. .	. .
South West	2	. .	. .	. .	. .	1	1	. .
South	2	. .	. .	. .	. .	. .	. .	2

It should be observed that in no case does one cluster have artifacts manufactured from the same type of stone present in any other cluster, yet within each cluster there is a great deal of homogeneity in the raw material utilized for their manufacture. These observations are interpreted as indicative of: (*a*) the validity of the recognized clusters as discrete units in terms of placement of grave furniture in the burial pit and (*b*) that more than one individual, and/or group contributed to the mortuary goods.

Finally, it remains to make some observations regarding the artifacts and their position with respect to the recognized soil units within the burial feature. First, all the cremated artifacts were included in the soil unit containing the cremated human bone, fired rock, and charcoal. This is consistent with the inference that the cremated artifacts actually accompanied the corpse into the crematory fire. On the other hand, it should be noted that the northern cluster of uncremated artifacts, the ochre concentration and central cluster of artifacts were included in the dark soil zone which lacked bone and fired rock. The bone and fired rock soil actually covered the central cluster of artifacts. The southwestern cluster, southern cluster, adz, and southern Hunt point were within the bone-bearing soil. The only hypothesis that can be offered to account for this distribution and remain consistent with previous interpretation, is that the cremated bone was raked into a pile at the south end of the pit prior to the placement, in the pit, of the uncremated burial goods. The absence of bone in the lower soil lens in the pit is the result of the ash from the funeral pyre making a thick accumulation prior to the breakdown of the burning body. In raking the cremated bone to the south end some of this ash layer was left undisturbed at the north end of the pit. It was on this ash layer that the uncremated artifacts in the north end were placed. Later, during the filling of the pit, the bone pile was pushed down covering the uncremated material in the north end of the pit.

INTERPRETATION OF THE RECOVERED MATERIAL

Interpretation of the Cultural Significance of the Formal Diversity Observed Among the Artifacts

The presence, in the burial, of Pomranky points of two varieties, one cremated and the other uncremated, suggests that the cremated specimens were personal belongings of the cremated individual, while the uncremated specimens constituted mortuary offerings included at the time of interment. As suggested by Binford, in *The Pomranky Site* (pp. 149-92), there is nothing in the form of the Pomranky points suggestive of anything but a techno-exploitative function. The context of their occurrence, however, is indicative of a social, rather than a technonomic function, for the form as a whole.

The variety of unburned projectile point forms, including Hodges points, Hunt points, Davis points, and an unnamed form, in addition to the burned Davis point forms, can be interpreted to support the inferences made with respect to the Pomranky points. The cremated specimens represent objects which were the property of the deceased, while the uncremated specimens represent the mortuary offerings contributed at the time of interment. The variety in form and raw material of the uncremated projectile points suggest that different contributors were responsible for the mortuary offerings. There were no formal characteristics of the various projectile point forms suggestive of differential functions for the several types. Similarly, there was nothing formally suggestive of anything but a technoexploitative function. Whether there were differences in form between specimens actually utilized technoexploitatively and those utilized ritually is not known at present because of the lack of correlation between burial and habitation sites attributable to the same archaeological complex.

Of those artifacts present exhibiting a working edge orientated to the longitudinal axis of the specimen, only one can reasonably be described as a scraper. The other two specimens must have served a different and unknown function. The shape of the working edge does not indicate a scraping motion, rather some form of pushing or pounding motion was necessary to produce the crushed and beveled edge observed. This is commensurate with their inferred function as strikers. All of these were uncremated and as such they are interpreted as part of the mortuary offering distinct from the personalia of the interred individual.

The gorgets, one cremated and one uncremated, may be classified as personal and contributed goods respectively. It is interesting that the cremated specimen probably represented a complete artifact, while the uncremated specimen was obviously only one-fourth of a complete gorget. The fact that the latter specimen had been reworked after breakage with no apparent modification in its function, suggests that it had a social rather than a technoexploitative usage. This view is further supported by the frequent occurrence of unmodified, but reworked, broken specimens from other sites, that is, burials 4, 6, and 14 at the Oberlander Number 2 site and Features 1 and 3 at the Red Lake site (Ritchie, 1944: 152-60 and Ritchie, 1955: 59). The general absence of indications of use, either in the form of polish within the perforations or wear on the surface of the specimens themselves, is further support for a nonutilitarian functional interpretation (Peabody and Moorehead, 1906: 48). The relatively infrequent occurrence of gorgets in assemblages argues against their function solely as ornaments of personal adornment or as amulets, articles which generally have a relatively high frequency of occurrence within any given population. It is suggested that gorgets functioned as a material accompaniment of a system of ranking, being available only to those occupying certain defined positions within the system and subsequently deriving "ritual value" from their history of ownership. This interpretation is offered as best fitting the observed formal, quantitative, and qualitative data. Alternative interpretations suggesting a utilitarian function in coping directly with the physical environment, or simply ornamental or magical usage not integrated into a system of ranking, do not account for the formal data in the former case, nor the quantitative data in the latter. It is believed that gorgets functioned in societies, as represented by the examples from the Hodges site, Oberlander Number 2, and the Red Lake site, as symbols of social position to which certain ritual and, possibly, economic prerogatives accrued. Gorgets extant at any one time were probably known individually in terms of their ownership history and were valued accordingly. At social events where reciprocal obligations were an integral part of the occasion, gorgets may have been given away or destroyed together with the accruing social-ritual prerogatives. Similarly, they were broken up and parts distributed to several social segments. The actual alteration in the form of the implement did not impair its function nor value within the social system. In fact, if an analogy may be drawn with the coppers of the Northwest coast, broken and repaired items may have been of greater social significance because of the particular history of the events leading to breakage, distribution of parts, and the eventual acquisition of two or more parts by a given individual. Such an interpretation accounts for: (*a*) the frequency of occurrence of repaired specimens, (*b*) the frequency of occurrence of broken and reworked specimens, (*c*) the general absence of any indication of wear from usage, (*d*) their relatively infrequent occurrence within any given assemblage, and (*e*) their frequent multiple occurrence in a single burial or association with other articles believed to be nontechnonomic, that is, possessing ritual value rather than value as a utilitarian article, for example, Hodges site, 2 gorgets; Oberlander Number 2 site, burial Number 6, 2 gorgets and a birdstone; burial Number 4, several gorgets; burial 14, 2 gorgets, birdstone and tubular pipe; Red Lake site, feature Number 3, gorget and quartz crystals; feature Number 1, 3 gorgets (Ritchie, 1944 and 1955).

The formal characteristics of the adz are commensurate with its widely accepted functional interpretation. The fact that it was uncremated and broken can be taken as evidence for its being a mortuary offering and being symbolic rather than completely functional as an adz, in that it was broken and the other parts were not present. The copper awls were probably hafted in antler or bone and utilized as perforators. The limonites are no doubt decomposed iron pyrites which probably formed part of a fire-making kit.

Reconstruction of the Interment Procedure

A crematory and burial pit of undetermined depth was dug into the sand knoll. A crematory pyre was prepared of red maple wood in the crematory basin, which measured roughly 5 feet 6 inches long and 4 feet 6 inches wide and was roughly orientated north and south. Following the ignition of the fire and the production of a bed of hot coals which functioned to fuse the sand particles in the bottom of the pit, more maple wood, together with several stones, was placed on the bed of coals in preparation for placement of the corpse on the crematory fire. Subsequent to this, a complete corpse of a young adult, together with the corpse, or corpses, of small mammals, was placed on the fire. Accompanying the individual were the dried bones of racoon, turtle, and small birds. These were possibly part of a headdress, medicine bag, or personal adornments. A broad rectangular gorget, several Pomranky points, and a Davis point also accompanied the corpse into the crematory fire-- probably the individual's personal belongings. Judging from the small size of the bone fragments, the burning remains must have been frequently raked and stirred during the process of cremation. Once the body had been cremated the remains were raked to the south end of the crematory basin and contributed grave goods were placed in two discrete clusters in the north end of the pit, as well as a small amount of red ochre, possibly in a container. One cluster contained two Hodges points and two copper awls, while the other contained a fragment of a broad rectangular gorget, seven Pomranky points, one projectile point of an undefined type, one scraper-like object, a worked chip, and iron pyrites, which were probably part of a fire-making kit. These two clusters are believed to have been contributed by different individuals. Similarly, along the edges of the pile of bone other contributors placed clusters of grave furniture. One cluster on the east contained a scraper and a scraper-like object, while a similar cluster on the south contained a Davis point and a worked chip. Other included materials consisted of two Hunt points, a plano-convex adz fragment and some item composed of gut or sinew. Whether these were all the contributed goods cannot be determined, for it will be remembered that part of the feature had been removed by a bulldozer. Following the placement of the contributed goods into the burial pit, it was filled and the pile of bone at the south end of the pit was pushed down so that it covered some of the contributed goods at the north end of the pit. Judging from the seeds in the fill of the pit, the interment occurred in the late summer or early fall.

The mortuary practices may be summarized as *in situ* cremations of a complete corpse accompanied by personal effects and, apparently, food, followed by the inclusion in the crematory basin of grave furniture placed and grouped so as to suggest contributions from a number of different individuals. After the ritual, which no doubt accompanied the placement of the grave furniture in the pit, the crematory-burial pit was filled.

Sociocultural Implications of the Archaeological Remains

Of the recovered artifactual material, the only items that, on the basis of their form, can be interpreted as having solely a sociotechnic function, are the gorgets. All other items appear to be clearly technonomic. The small number of Pomranky points present, as compared with the Pomranky site, may be indicative of a slightly different function of the same form at the two sites. The Pomranky points at the Hodges site, being simply "blanks" for future notching, and as such, constituting a standard part of the supply of items for use in the afterlife. This interpretation is commensurate with the largely utilitarian nature of the kinds and quantities of included material at the Hodges site. The contributed goods appear simply to represent a supply of the necessary equipment to carry on life in the next world. The presence of both cremated and uncremated gorgets in the burial may be indicative of a form of internal ranking within the social unit represented. Regardless of this, the composition of the grave goods is largely suggestive of a supply of personal equipment both owned in life and contributed at the time of interment. This is in contrast to the inclusion in the burial pit of large quantities of materials obviously in excess of any requirements as necessary equipment for carrying on life in the next world, as characterized the grave furniture at the Pomranky site. Whether these differences reflect: (*a*) differential treatment of individuals according to their status in similar sociocultural systems, (*b*) different types of sociocultural system, (*c*) simple stylistic differences in burial procedure between differing sociopolitical units, or (*d*) noncontemporaniety of the sites but socioethnic continuity with style change through time, cannot be adequately determined on the basis of the available information.

DATING THE SITE

The absolute age of the site has not been determined and an inadequate sample of organic material for use in carbon-14 age determination makes future dating of the site unlikely. The best estimate of the age of the site is obtained from a comparison with dated sites exhibiting a similar artifact assemblage. Two sites are of aid here--the Oberlander Number 2 station in New York and the Morrow site in New York (Guthe, 1958, p. 11). Both share a number of characteristics in common with the Hodges site, including specific artifact forms and burial practices. The former is carbon-14 dated at 998 ± 170 B.C. and the latter at 561 ± 250 B.C. On the basis of this information, I estimate the date of the Hodges site at approximately 650 B.C.

REFERENCES CITED

Guthe, A. K.
1958. The Morrow Site. Eastern States Archaeological Fed. Bull., No. 17

Moorehead, Warren K.
1917. Stone Ornaments Used by Indians in the United States and Canada. Andover, Mass.: Andover Press.

Peabody, Charles, and Moorehead, W. K.
1906. The So-Called "Gorgets." Phillips Academy, Department of Archaeology Bulletin II. Andover, Mass.: Andover Press.

Ritchie, William A.
1944. The Pre-Iroquoian Occupations of New York State. Rochester Museum of Arts and Sciences, Rochester.

1955. Recent Discoveries Suggesting an Early Woodland Burial Cult in the Northeast. N. Y. State Mus. and Sci. Service, Circular No. 40. University of the State of New York. Albany.

Yanovsky, Elias.
1936. Food Plants of the North American Indians. U. S. Dept. of Agriculture Misc. Publ. No. 237. Washington, D. C.

THE POMRANKY SITE
A LATE ARCHAIC BURIAL STATION

Lewis R. Binford

CONTENTS

Figures

Tables

DESCRIPTION OF SITE AND EXCAVATION[1]

The Pomranky site is located in the state of Michigan, Midland County, Midland township, the northwest quarter of the northeast quarter of section 18, township 14 north, range 2 east. The site is on the western tip of a sand ridge which approaches the south bank of the Tittabawasse River from the east. The original elevation of the sand ridge was approximately 610 feet above sea level, probably representing a fluvial terrace dating to the Nippissing stage of the ancestral great lakes, approximately 4,200 years ago.

The presence of the site was brought to the attention of the Museum of Anthropology by Mr. Harold W. Moll of Midland. Mr. Moll had been contacted by the property owner, Mr. Clive Pomranky, who was aware of Moll's interest in Michigan prehistory. While plowing at a 10-inch depth, 2 inches deeper than in previous years, Mr. Pomranky uncovered what was later identified as a burial. The plow lifted eighty-six chipped-stone artifacts in association with a heavy concentration of red ocher. On the advice of Moll, further investigation of the find was delayed. On the following day, May 24, 1960, a party from The University of Michigan, Mark Papworth, and Malcomb Webb excavated the burial.

The present condition of the sand ridge in which the burial was located does not reflect the original topography of the site. Most of the ridge was removed for construction purposes in 1954. At that time the top soil was removed and stored. Then the sand was removed down to the underlying clay by bulldozers, and later the top soil was replaced. On the extreme western end of the sand ridge approximately 10 inches of sand had been left undisturbed, and it was in this remaining sand that the burial was discovered.

When The University of Michigan party, assisted by Harold Moll, arrived at the site, an area approximately 8 feet east-west and 9.5 feet north-south around the exposed red ocher and projectile points was cleared to a depth of about 8 inches. At this level the

[1]As is true in most scientific investigations it is not a one-man job. This investigation is no exception. I should like to thank Anta White for the excellent illustrations, Henry Wright for assistance in the analysis of the data, Richard Yarnell for inspection of the recovered material for seeds and macrofossils, and Mark L. Papworth for aid in the analysis of the human remains, and David Taggart for aid in the description of the raw materials. The analysis of these materials was largely supported by funds from the National Science Foundation.

A.

B.

Fig. 1. Excavation at the Pomranky Site: A—eight inch level; B—outline of pit.

only detectable trace of a feature was the ocher-stained sand around the area disturbed by the plow. The marks of old furrows running north and south were clearly visible (Fig. 1, A). A second cut was made which leveled the entire area to the bottom of the original plow furrow from which the artifacts had been derived, and here, approximately 10 inches below the surface, the outline of a pit was clearly visible (Fig. 1, B). The pit was defined by discolorations of a mottled gray to russet-colored sand forming an oval 45 inches wide (east and west) and 54 inches long (north and south). Scattered throughout the mottled area were zones of differential concentrations of red ocher. While bringing the floor level down to this point the first artifacts not removed by the plow were observed. From this point on, the excavation procedure was altered to assure the association of all artifacts with other included materials. This is the datum floor for Figure 2. Specific elements in the pit were isolated and removed as units for transport to The University of Michigan for more controlled laboratory-type excavation and eventual analysis. Such areas recognized in the field included three concentrations of cremated human remains, one area of uncremated human remains, one concentration of stemmed projectile points, and several concentrated areas of unstemmed "cache blades." The spatial distribution of all removed units as well as associations with such things as the intensity of red ocher concentration and the like were carefully noted. Removal of all included material showed that the pit in which the materials had been placed had intruded into the sand strata from an undetermined point of origin on the original sand ridge. The pit had been roughly oval-shaped with gently sloping sides penetrating to a slightly bowl-shaped bottom (Fig. 3). Actual distribution and interpretation of positioning of the recovered material within the pit are more fruitfully discussed after the artifact analysis has been presented, and after certain observations have been made concerning the distribution of varieties of artifacts within the burial, thus adding appreciably to any interpretation. The excavation, as well as the note-taking in the Museum of Anthropology, was done by Malcomb Webb.

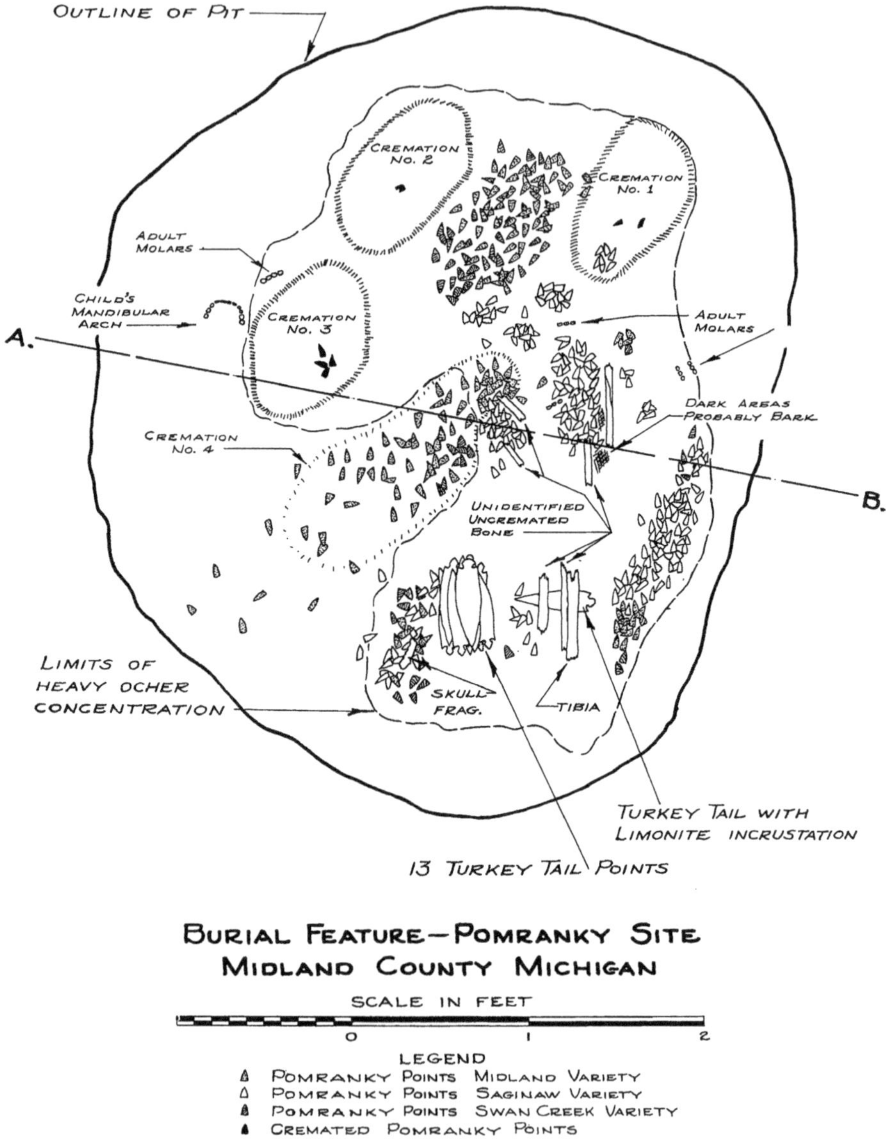

Fig. 2. Plan of Burial Feature

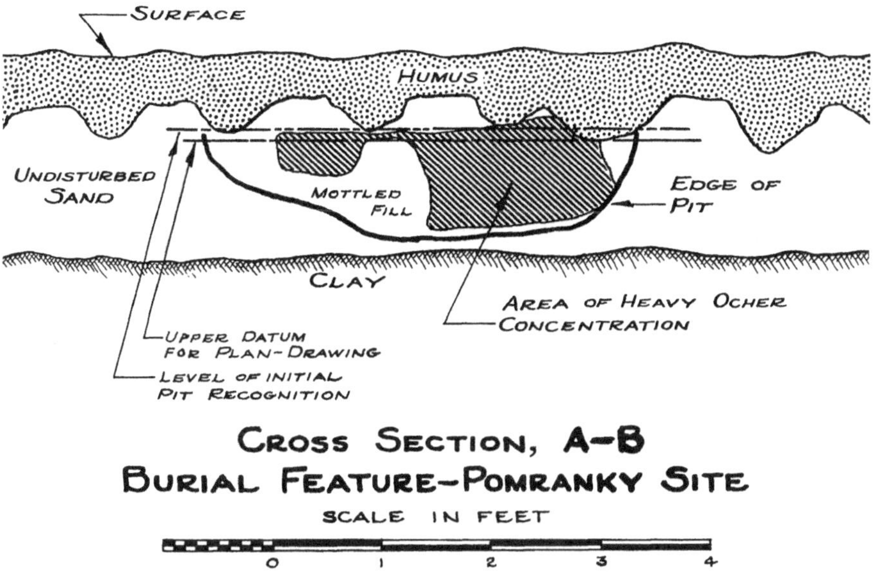

Fig. 3. Cross Section of Burial Feature

FORMAL ANALYSIS OF RECOVERED MATERIAL

Chipped-stone Artifacts

Raw Material.—A total of 516 subtriangular "cache blades" and 14 "turkey tails" were recovered and constituted the sample studied. Nine different types of stone were represented within the sample; that is, blades had been manufactured on stone derived from at least 9 different sources.

Type A is a white-to-cream chert with a dull surface, opaque diaphaneity, massive structure (rarely banded) and with few inclusions or cavities. When the latter occur, they are lined with fine quartz crystals. Minor mottling of a waxy subtranslucent light gray chert, the surface of which shines more than the dominant material, is fairly common. At present the distribution and the origin of this material is unknown. The only other reported site from which artifacts manufactured from this material are known is the Kimmel site in Berrien County.

Type B is a dark-gray-to-brownish chert with a dull surface, opaque diaphaneity, broadly banded structure of light-to-bluish-gray bands. Fine, irregular cavities are frequent and may be lined with a white opaque chert or a gray-to-cream subtranslucent waxy chert, both of which exhibit quartz crystals internally. Minor mottling is of a light-to-bluish-gray. A further observation is that cavities tend to occur in the dark gray bands. At present, this type of raw material is known to have a wide distribution in the central part of the lower peninsula of Michigan and to occur on sites in Ontario, Canada. The sources of the material are unknown. Several sites in the Saginaw area are known to yield artifacts of this material.

Type C is a medium-to-light-gray chert with a dull surface, opaque diaphaneity, of massive structure. Inclusions of fine white calcareous fossils (Crinoides) are numerous. These are easily weathered and are generally replaced by fine quartz crystals. Banding is absent and color and texture are uniform. The distribution and source of this material is unknown.

Type D is a dark gray chert with a slightly shiny surface, opaque diaphaneity, and of massive structure. Inclusions are numerous and are very fine white specks, presumably fossils. There is no banding and texture is uniform. The distribution and source of this material is unknown.

Type E is a dark gray chert with a dull surface, opaque diaphaneity, and of finely banded structure (light gray bands). Cavities, when present, are spherical to elongated, with subtranslucent waxy-whitish chert, lined with quartz crystals. The cavities tend to occur in the darker bands. The distribution and source of this material is unknown.

Type F is a medium gray chert with a dull surface, opaque diaphaneity, and of massive structure. Cavities are rare, and very fine specks of white (presumably fossils) are present. Banding is absent; color and texture are uniform. The distribution and source of this material is unknown.

Type G is a cream-white to light-and-medium-gray chert with a dull surface, opaque diaphaneity, and of massive structure. Inclusions are numerous in the form of fine white calcareous fossils. The texture is mildly mottled with large buff splotches. The distribution and source of this material is unknown. One other site is known to have yielded artifacts of this material, the Kimmel site in Berrien County.

Type H is a medium blue-gray chert with a slightly shiny surface, opaque diaphaneity and of massive structure. There are no inclusions. The texture tends to be uniform but, occasionally, faint bands of light gray are discernible. The cortex of the nodule is white-to-dull-brownish. This material has a very wide distribution throughout Ohio, Indiana, and into Michigan. It is known in the literature as Harrison County "flint" named after the area from which it is derived in Indiana (Fowke, 1928: 522-28; Fowke, 1894: 328-35). Other sites in Michigan known to yield artifacts of this material are the Andrews site, Saginaw County, and the Kimmel site, Berrien County, Michigan.

Type I is a dark-to-medium-gray chert with a slightly shiny surface, opaque diaphaneity and a broadly bonded structure alternating with medium-gray bands. Cavities are frequent, being subspherical in shape with light gray subtranslucent waxy chert linings and frequent internal clusters of fine quartz crystals. The cavities occur predominantly in the dark bands. The distribution and source of this material is unknown.

Formal Analysis of the Cache Blades.—Unsystematic examination of the sample suggested the presence of formal differences correlated with the various types of raw material utilized. Thus, it was decided to observe and examine each specimen for a total of seven discrete attribute classes and six continuous attributes in addition to recording the type of raw material from which the artifact was manufactured. All of these observations were recorded in edge punch cards together with the catalogue numbers which designated the various provenience units within the burial. The use of punch cards facilitated the easy tabulation of the data and also provided a permanent record by specimen of the observations for future comparison.

The following attribute classes were utilized in the observations: blade shape, base shape, flaking of the base, basal primary

TABLE I

ARTIFACT CLASSES BY TYPES OF RAW MATERIAL

Class	Raw Material								
	A	B	C	D	E	F	G	H	I
Cache blades	231	139	15	8	0	29	69	6	. . .
Turkey tails	. . .	. . .	. . .	. . .	2	. . .	. . .	12	. . .

retouch, placement of the basal scars, type of base preparation, flake blank orientation, and placement of grinding. All of the above attribute classes are defined and the possible variations described by Binford in *A Proposed Attribute List for the Description and Classification of Projectile Points*, pp. 193-221. Five separate metrical attributes were observed: maximum length, maximum width, width of base, thickness, and index of the angle of basal orientation.[2]

TABLE II

ATTRIBUTE FREQUENCY BY STONE TYPE WITHIN CLASSES ESTABLISHED ON THE BASIS OF THE TYPE OF RAW MATERIAL

Class	Stone Type								
Blade shape	A	B	C	D	E	F	G	H	I
Expanding ovate . . .	23	. .	. .	. .	. .	2	1	1	. .
Excurvate	86	50	5	2	2	10	36	1	4
Ovate	108	81	10	6	7	12	26	2	6
Parallel ovate	12	6	. .	. .	. .	2	1	. .	. .
Contracting ovate . .	2	2	. .	. .	. .	3	5	2	. .
Base shape									
Convex	2	4	. .	. .	. .	. .	. .	. .	. .
Subconvex	101	78	8	4	4	18	27	1	5
Straight	60	28	5	3	2	7	19	1	3
Subconcave	61	29	2	1	3	9	23	4	2
Concave	7	. .	. .	. .	. .	. .	. .	. .	. .
Flaking of the base									
1. Primary retouch									
Longitudinal scars	99	21	5	3	2	7	46	2	3
Transverse scars	. .	8	. .	. .	. .	1	. .	. .	. .
Long. & trans. scars	116	14	1	. .	. .	2	13	. .	1
Dimin. scars only.	16	96	9	5	7	19	10	4	6
2. Placement of scars									
Bifacial of 2 types	109	97	10	5	6	20	19	4	6
Unifacial	6	1	. .	. .	. .	. .	2	. .	. .
Bifacial of 1 type.	116	41	5	3	3	9	48	2	4
3. Preparation type									
Striking platform.	6	6	1	. .	1	2	. .	. .	. .
Transverse scar .	32	48	3	2	2	. .	7	. .	5
Thinned only . . .	193	85	11	6	6	32	65	6	5
Flake-blank orientation									
Distal	3	12	2	1	. .	3	14	. .	1
Oblique	6	23	3	1	3	6	. .	1	2
Obscured	222	104	10	6	6	25	55	5	7
Grinding									
Tip	41	. .	. .	. .	. .	. .	. .	. .	. .
Lateral edge	11	. .	. .	. .	. .	. .	. .	. .	. .
Base	14	. .	. .	. .	. .	. .	. .	. .	. .

[2] Descriptive terms utilized in this report are consistent with the definitions presented by Anta White, pp. 1-71.

Tabulated information on the discrete and metrical attributes is given in Tables II and VIII.

Blade shape. Five different forms of blade shape were observed in the sample (Table II) and the central question was whether there were any differences in the relative frequencies with which a given form was represented among specimens manufactured of different stone materials. In order to answer this question chi square calculations were carried out for the following sample combinations: (1) stone type A with stone type B; (2) stone type A with stone type G; (3) stone type B with stone type G; (4) stone type B with stone type F; (5) stone types B, C, D, and E taken together. Other combinations were not calculated specifically, for it was obvious from inspection that such calculations were unnecessary. The resulting values of chi square and the expected values at stated levels of probability are given in Table III.

TABLE III

CHI-SQUARE CALCULATIONS FOR FORMS OF BLADE SHAPE COMPARED TO STONE TYPE

Stone Type Combinations	A & B	A & G	A & F	B & G	B & F	B,C,D,E
Level of probability	.01	.05	.05	.02	.02	.70
Expected chi-square value	11.34	7.82	7.82	7.82	7.82	3.83
Degrees of freedom	3.0	3.0	3.0	2.0	2.0	6.0
Observed chi-square value	16.13	9.26	8.86	7.96	8.07	3.45

It will be noted in Table III that comparisons of the relative frequencies of form of blade shows that specimens of stone type A, B, G, and F each represent samples from different populations. Stated another way they each, in all probability, exhibit real differences with respect to blade shape, while specimens made of stone types B, C, D, and E could all have easily been drawn from the same population of "cache blades." Specimens made from stone types H and I appear to differ from all the above groups with respect to blade shape (Table II), although the samples are small and the numbers are not consistent with other recognized samples. The best conclusion seems to reflect that, in all probability, they do represent different populations.

Base shape. Five different forms of base were represented in the total sample (Table II). As in the previous case we are concerned with determining whether differences, observed in the occurrence of any particular form of base among the specimens manufactured of different materials, represent real differences in the populations from which the samples were drawn or whether they are merely the result of sampling error. Chi square calculations were made for the following combinations: (1) stone type A with stone type B; (2) stone type A with stone type G; (3) stone type B with stone type G; (4) stone type B with stone type F; and (5) stone types B, C, D, and E taken together.

TABLE IV

CHI-SQUARE CALCULATIONS FOR FORMS OF BLADE SHAPE COMPARED BY STONE TYPE

Stone Type Combinations	A & B	A & G	A & F	B & G	B & F	B,C,D,E
Level of probability	.10	.30	.50	.05	.80	.70
Expected chi-square value	6.25	2.41	2.36	5.99	.446	3.83
Degrees of freedom	3.0	2.0	3.0	2.0	2.0	6.0
Observed chi-square value	5.33	1.12	2.22	6.51	.41	3.44

It is apparent that only in the case of the comparison of specimens manufactured of B- and G-type stone does the observed value exceed the expected value at a probability level of 5 per cent of higher. In view of the fact that A and B samples are not observed to differ more than would be expected from sampling error, and that A and G do not differ, it is likely that the observed difference between B and G is also the result of sampling error. Accepting this argument, it can be concluded that there is no difference between any of the samples with respect to base shape.

Chipping of the base. This attribute class records observations that are indicative of the steps in the manufacture of a projectile point. Attribute classes of this nature are particularly useful in distinguishing between different populations. Although there are many observations that can be made under this attribute class, only four were made, and it is believed that they are broad enough to distinguish between different manufacturing processes. Comparisons were made by means of chi-square calculations between: (1) stone type A with stone type B; (2) stone type A with stone type G; (3) stone type B with stone type G; (4) stone type B with stone type F; and (5) stone types B, C, D and E taken together.

TABLE V

CHI-SQUARE CALCULATIONS FOR FORM OF BASE SHAPE COMPARED BY STONE TYPE

Stone Type Combinations	A & B	A & G	A & F	B & G	B & F	B,C,D,E
Level of probability	.001	.001	.05	.001	.50	.30
Expected chi-square value	16.27	13.81	13.81	13.81	3.36	7.23
Degrees of freedom	3.0	2.0	2.0	2.0	3.0	6.0
Observed chi-square value	184.43	21.91	76.95	16.71	1.68	5.59

The comparisons between A, B, and G show differences between each exceeding the degree that could be accounted for by sampling error while samples B, F, C, D, and E could easily have been drawn from the same population. From this observation it may be concluded that with respect to this attribute, three separate populations are represented in the total sample.

Placement of primary scars on the base. This class deals with attributes that reflect stone-knapping techniques, and, as in the above attribute class three major positions of placement were recognized. As in the previous cases comparisons were made between samples defined by the various recognized flint types.

TABLE VI

CHI-SQUARE CALCULATIONS FOR FORMS OF PLACEMENT OF SCARS ON THE BASE COMPARED BY STONE TYPE

Stone Type Combinations	A & B	A & G	A & F	B & G	B & F	B,C,D,E,I
Level of probability	.001	.02	.05	.001	.80	.95
Expected chi-square value	13.82	7.82	3.84	13.82	.06	.71
Degrees of freedom	2.0	2.0	1.0	2.0	1.0	4.0
Observed chi-square value	18.36	8.64	4.33	33.57	.02	.69

The observed values exceed the expected value at the 5 per cent level of probability for all combinations between A, B, and G, while observed differences between B, C, D, E, and F could all easily arise as a result of sampling error. It must be concluded that in all probability three separate populations are represented in the total sample.

Basal preparation. This attribute class records the presence of specifically prepared striking platforms for the removal of longitudinal flakes (striking platform), the presence of a ready-made striking platform in the form of a remnant edge of the original flake blank from which the specimen was fashioned (transverse scar), and the complete absence of an observable striking platform in the form of bifacially thinned base showing no bevel. Comparisons were made as with the previous attribute classes (Table VII).

Obviously there are two major populations represented with regard to this attribute, one composed of specimens of A- and G-type stone while the other is composed of specimens of B, C, D, E, F, and I-type stone.

TABLE VII

CHI-SQUARE CALCULATIONS FOR FORMS OF CHIPPING ON THE BASE COMPARED BY STONE TYPE

Stone Type Combinations	A & B	A & G	A & F	B & G	B & F	B,C,D,E,I
Level of probability	.001	.20	.001	.001	.05	.70
Expected chi-square value	13.82	3.22	13.82	13.82	5.99	5.53
Degrees of freedom	2.0	2.00	2.00	2.00	2.00	8.00
Observed chi-square value	23.73	2.90	128.80	19.98	1.20	3.21

Flake blank orientation. This attribute class records the orientation of the longitudinal axis of the finished specimen with respect to the axis of percussion of the original flake blank from which the artifact was fashioned. Three differing attributes of orientation were recognized within the sample: distal, oblique, and obscured. There are three populations represented with regard to this attribute: type A stone, type G stone and types B, C, D, E, F, and I stone.

TABLE VIII

CHI-SQUARE CALCULATIONS FOR FORMS OF BASAL PREPARATION COMPARED BY STONE TYPE

Stone Type Combinations	A & B	A & G	A & F	B & G	B & F	B,C,D,E,I
Level of probability	.05	.05	.05	.05	.05	.05
Expected chi-square value	5.99	5.99	5.99	5.99	5.99	15.51
Degrees of freedom	2	2	2	2	2	8
Observed chi-square value	37.48	37.16	23.84	16.59	.03	3.145

Grinding. No calculations were necessary to determine that there are two major populations with respect to this attribute. The one represented by specimens of type A stone, exhibiting grinding, and the other represented by all the other specimens of different raw material, exhibiting no grinding.

Metrical attributes. Summary data on the metrical observations is given in Table IX. This data was analyzed as in the case of the discrete attributes; that is, comparisons were made to determine whether the observed differences between the samples grouped according to stone type could reflect sampling error, or whether they were sufficiently great to suggest that the samples had been drawn from different populations. An analysis of within and among sample variance was carried out for a number of sample combinations. The results are given in Table X. When the observed value of (F) exceeds the expected value at the 5 per cent level of probability it indicates that the differences between the samples compared are likely to arise as a result of sampling error (less than 5 out of 100 samples drawn from the same population). Therefore, it is highly probable that the samples compared were, in fact, drawn from different populations. It will be noted that specimens of stone types B, C, D, E, F, and I do not differ in any metrical attribute except thickness. On the other hand specimens of stone type A and G differ consistently between themselves and from the grouped sample of B, C, D, E, F, and I. From this it is concluded that there are three distinct populations represented in the "cache blades" recovered at the Pomranky site with respect to metrical attributes.

Summary of the formal analysis. Table X presents the summary data for the between-sample comparisons of both the discrete and metrical attributes. It is obvious that there are at least three distinct populations represented in the total sample: (1) a population represented by the specimens manufactured of stone type A; (2) a population represented by specimens manufactured of stone type G; and (3) a population represented by specimens manufactured of stone types B, C, D, E, and I. Whether specimens manufactured of stone type F represent a different population is difficult to assess; however, in view of the fact that dissimilarity in thickness is one of the differentiating attributes and the behavior of this attribute is erratic, the single differentium showing that the relative proportions of observed blade shape vary is not considered to be sufficient basis for the recognition of a separate population. It seems likely that thickness may vary according to the nature of the

TABLE IX

METRICAL DATA FOR GROUPINGS OF POMRANKY POINTS BY STONE TYPE

Attribute Class	Stone Type								
	A	B	C	D	E	F	G	H	I
Length									
Sx	1102.00	555.90	54.55	31.60	37.35	139.15	287.75	25.00	37.85
Sx^2	5356.18	2327.43	230.25	125.28	158.83	578.26	1229.10	105.98	144.45
n	230.00	135.00	13.00	8.00	9.00	34.00	68.00	6.00	10.00
$\bar{x}$	4.79	4.12	4.20	3.95	4.15	4.09	4.23	4.17	3.78
s	.57	.53	.33	.25	.70	.52	.41	.60	.36
Maximum Width									
Sx	576.95	289.70	27.70	15.80	18.35	67.30	177.09	15.75	21.25
Sx^2	1462.07	612.79	60.07	31.87	38.94	135.52	468.70	41.83	47.55
n	231.00	140.00	13.00	8.00	9.00	34.00	68.00	6.00	10.00
$\bar{x}$	2.50	2.07	2.13	1.97	2.04	1.98	2.60	2.63	2.12
s	.30	.30	.26	.31	.44	.84	.33	.31	.41
Basal Width									
Sx	554.80	278.20	25.98	15.40	17.95	63.40	168.60	15.05	21.25
Sx^2	1339.61	564.88	54.46	30.44	37.60	122.78	420.57	38.48	47.45
n	231.00	140.00	13.00	8.00	9.00	34.00	69.00	6.00	10.00
$\bar{x}$	2.40	1.99	2.00	1.93	1.99	1.86	2.44	2.51	2.12
s	.17	.30	.60	.33	.48	.37	.36	.38	.50
Thickness									
Sx	132.40	74.95	8.40	5.35	5.60	20.20	41.45	3.05	5.15
Sx^2	81.22	40.83	5.52	3.70	3.51	12.35	25.83	1.65	2.77
n	228.00	141.00	13.00	8.00	9.00	34.00	69.00	6.00	10.00
$\bar{x}$	.58	.53	.65	.67	.62	.59	.60	.51	.52
s	.14	.08	.08	.13	.06	.10	.12	.14	.12
Angle of basal orientation									
90- 92 . . .	87.0	44.0	5.0	3.0	5.0	16.0	28.0	5.0	5.0
92- 94 . . .	50.0	23.0	2.0	2.0	2.0	10.0	17.0	. . .	1.0
94- 96 . . .	33.0	18.0	2.0	2.0	1.0	4.0	11.0	. . .	2.0
96- 98 . . .	28.0	17.0	2.0	1.0	. . .	1.0	9.0	1.0	2.0
98-100 . . .	16.0	12.0	2.0	. . .	. . .	2.0	5.0	. . .	. . .
100-102 . . .	12.0	9.0	. . .	. . .	. . .	1.0	1.0	. . .	. . .
102-104 . . .	4.0	4.0	. . .	. . .	. . .	. . .	1.0	. . .	. . .
104-106 . . .	2.0	2.0	. . .	. . .	. . .	. . .	. . .	. . .	. . .
Total .	232.0	129.0	13.0	8.0	8.0	34.0	72.0	6.0	10.0

raw material itself and may record fortuitous differences: differences in the relative proportions of blade forms may simply reflect individual chipping habits. For these reasons specimens manufactured of stone type F will be included in the population represented by specimens manufactured of type B, C, D, E, and I stone. Because of the small sample specimens manufactured of type H stone have not been included in this analysis.

Typology of the "Cache Blades."--Following the principles of classification that have been suggested for projectile point classification (Binford, 194-221) it is obvious that the observed differences in the specimens from the Pomranky site are at the variety level of differentiation. For this reason a type name and description for the total sample will be offered. Specimens of very similar nature have been excavated from a number of sites in the Great Lakes region. Among the more recently discovered and described sites are the Red Lake and Muskalonge sites in New York (Ritchie, 1955). Ritchie has compared these finds to a number of other sites among which are the Oberlander Number 2, and Wray sites. Since there are demonstrable differences, at least with respect to size between the samples from the Red Lake and Muskalonge sites, that are indicative of possible differentiation at the variety level, I feel that the use of "Pomranky Point" as a type name or "generic" term will be profitable. Thus, "Pomranky Point" will be used as the type designator for the points recovered in New York as well as for those recovered in other areas, such as the site reported here.

Pomranky Points (Fig. 4)

Blade shape. A variety of blade shapes may occur including ovate, excurvate, contracting ovate, expanding ovate, and parallel ovate; triangular blade shapes are unknown as are incurvate, incurvate-excurvate, and excurvate-incurvate forms.

Chipping of the blade. Primary chipping results in flat expanding scars frequently merging with scars originating on the opposite edge to leave ill-defined transitions between separate scars. When definition is pronounced, shallow hinge fractures generally constitute the defining elements. Deep massive conchoidal scars are never observed, and lamellar scars are not characteristic. Orientation of the primary scars with respect to the longitudinal axis of the specimen is primarily a function of the shape of the lateral edges so that the scar orientation varies with the position on the specimen.

Secondary chipping may be present and is generally of the stepped lamellar, conchoidal, or contracting varieties. When

TABLE X

DATA ON COMPARISONS BY MEANS OF VARIANCE ANALYSIS BETWEEN STONE TYPE GROUPS

Attributes	Sample Combinations					
Length	A & B	A & G	A & F	B & F	B & G	B,C,D,E,I
Among sample variance......	38.58	16.52	14.44	.01	.68	.13
Within sample variance......	.32	.29	.32	.28	.25	.60
Expected F value at .05 level of P	3.85	3.89	3.89	3.91	3.89	2.67
Observed value of F	120.56	57.96	45.13	.03	2.72	.22
Maximum width						
Among sample variance	15.99	.60	7.95	.22	11.78	.04
Within sample variance	.09	.10	.09	.09	.10	.10
Expected F value at .05 level of P	3.85	3.89	3.89	3.89	3.89	2.65
Observed value of F	177.66	6.00	88.30	2.44	117.80	.40
Basal width						
Among sample variance	14.98	.09	6.55	.40	9.62	.007
Within sample variance	.05	.05	.05	.10	.10	.092
Expected F value at .05 level of P	3.86	3.89	3.89	3.89	3.89	2.67
Observed value of F	288.08	1.70	125.00	.41	96.20	.07
Thickness						
Among sample variance	.20	.005	.01	.12	.22	.11
Within sample variance	.014	.018	.18	.008	.009	.007
Expected F value at .05 level of P	3.86	3.89	3.89	3.91	3.89	3.91
Observed value of F	13.79	.28	.06	15.00	24.44	15.70

Note: Observed values that exceed the expected values are underlined.

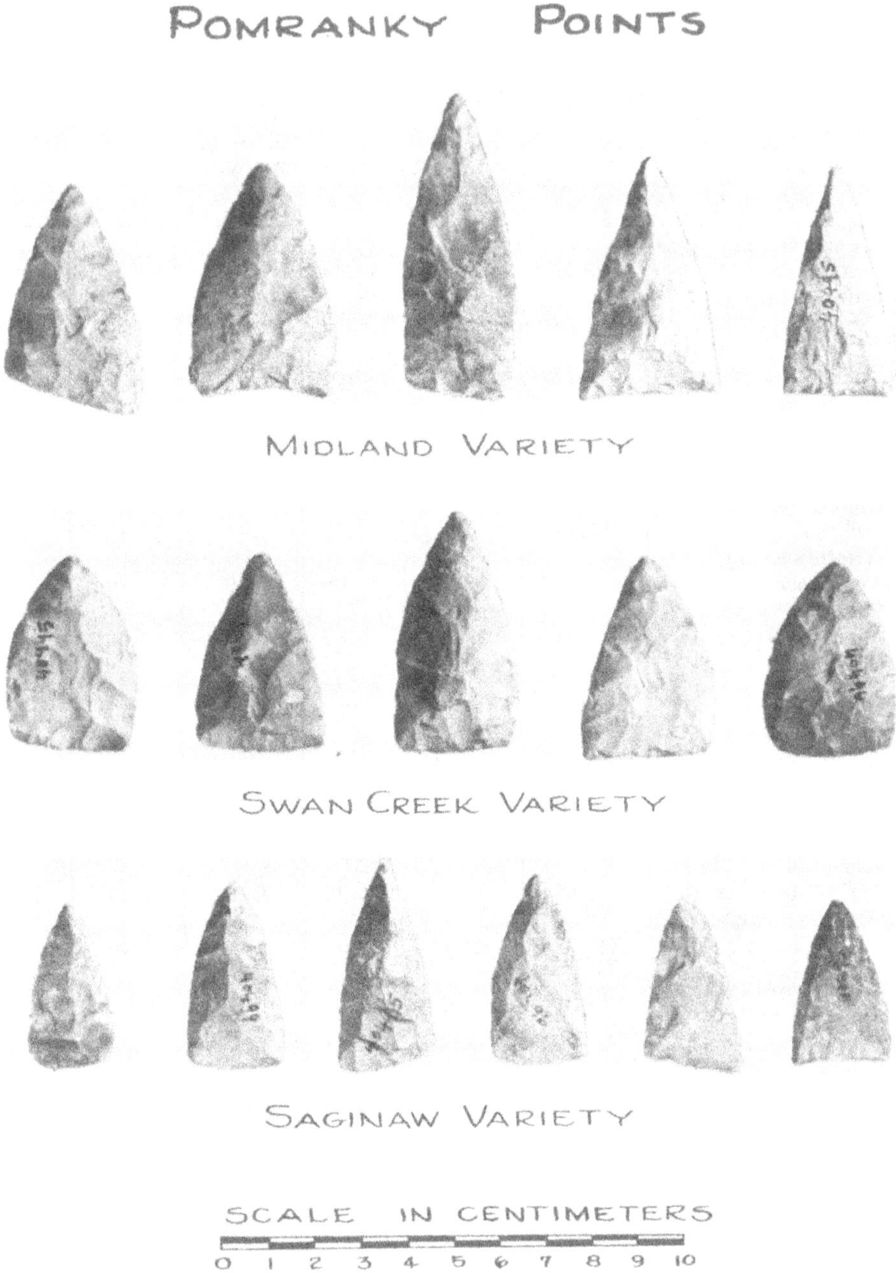

Fig. 4. Varieties of the Pomranky Point.

TABLE XI

COMPARISONS BETWEEN CACHE BLADE SAMPLES

Attribute Classes	Sample Combinations					
	A & B	A & G	A & F	B & F	B & G	B,C,D,E,I
Blade shape	Different	Different	Different	Different	Different	Same
Base shape	Same	Same	Same	Same	Different	Same
Nature of basal primary flaking	Different	Different	Different	Same	Different	Same
Placement of primary basal scars	Different	Different	Different	Same	Different	Same
Type of basal preparation	Different	Same	Different	Same	Different	Same
Flake blank orientation	Different	Different	Different	Same	Different	Same
Grinding	Different	Different	Different	Same	Same	Same
Length	Different	Different	Different	Same	Same	Same
Maximum width	Different	Different	Different	Same	Different	Same
Basal width	Different	Same	Different	Same	Different	Same
Thickness	Different	Same	Same	Different	Different	Different
Basal orientation	Same	Same	Same	Same	Same	Same
Totals						
Different	10	8	9	2	8	1
Same	2	4	3	10	4	11

present it is continuous along the retouched edge and never completely obscures the primary scars on the face of the piece.

Shape of the base. Specimens are observed with convex, slightly convex, straight, (and infrequently) slightly concave bases; concave bases are never observed unless there is a flaw in the raw material or the specimen is broken.

Chipping of the base. Primary scars originating on the basal edge frequently extend along the longitudinal axis for over a centimeter (Fig. 5). Such longitudinal chip scars may occur on a single face or on both faces but are always multiple and continuous along the edge. When longitudinal chipping is present on only one face the opposite face may exhibit a transverse scar, smooth and unaltered, completely across the basal edge (Fig. 5, D_1, D_3, E_2, E_4, F_2, F_4). This scar is the remnant of the lateral edge of the original flake blank from which the specimen was fabricated (Fig. 5, B). Diminutive retouching or secondary retouching, when present, is continuous along the entire edge or partial segment of the edge.

Orientation of the base (Fig. 5, C). Frequently the base is not orientated at right angles to the longitudinal axis of the specimen. The angle between the basal edge and the longitudinal axis may be as high as 106 degrees although the modal tendency is between 90 and 96 degrees.

Point of juncture between the basal edge and the lateral edge. Right angles and obtuse angles are the only recognized form of edge articulation. The actual transition from basal edge to lateral edge is either accomplished by a very short arc or as a point of intersection between two straight lines.

Haft element. No haft element is present; that is, there has been no alteration along the lateral edge or the basal edge to facilitate hafting. This is one of the defining attributes of the type.

Cross section. Symmetry and irregularity is the rule, that is, cross sections may be biconvex, biplano, and only occasionally asymmetrically convex, plano-convex, etc. Although there is a general symmetry, a convex curvature is not a perfect arc and there may be small irregularities in the described arc. Biplano cross sections are frequent and in these cases irregularities in the described lines are not as pronounced. This is in contrast to certain forms of spear points of a general "lanceolate" form where irregularity is not noticeable.

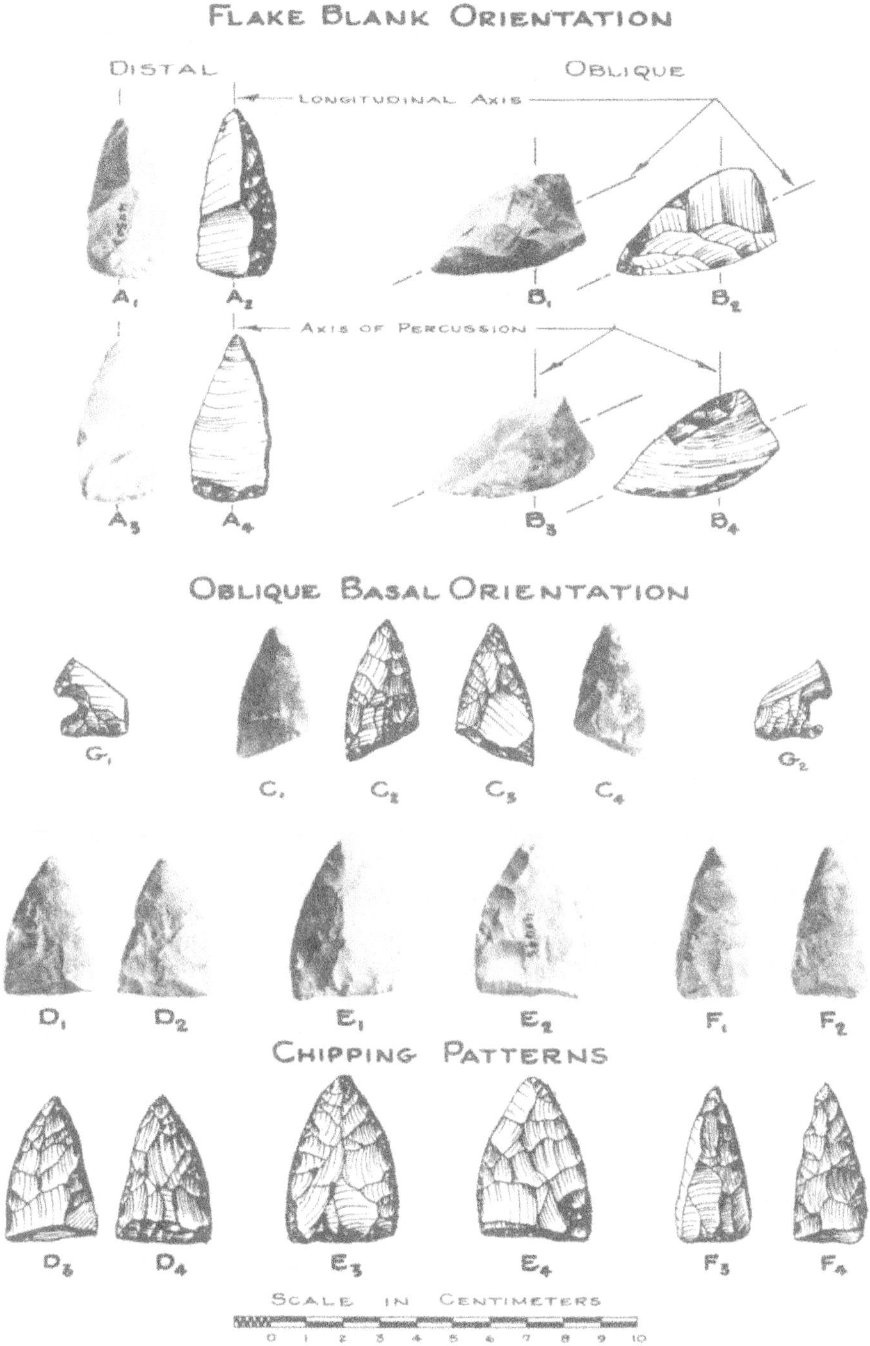

Fig. 5. Technical Attributes of the Pomranky Point

Varieties of the Pomranky Point

Three varieties of the Pomranky point have been recognized primarily on the basis of variation in the treatment and preparation of the base and on differences in size. It should be kept in mind that this level of differentiation requires the analysis and comparison of a sample: determination of the variety of single specimens provides only a low degree of accuracy.

Midland variety (Fig. 4)

This variety was recognized because of demonstrable differences between specimens manufactured of A-type stone and those manufactured of other materials. Two hundred and thirty-two specimens constituted the sample upon which the variety has been described. Two major attribute classes serve to differentiate specimens of the Midland variety from those of other recognized varieties: size, and the nature of basal preparation.

Blade shape. Five different forms of blade shape were observed: expanding ovate (9.96 per cent); excurvate (37.23 per cent); ovate (46.75 per cent); parallel ovate (5.19 per cent); and contracting ovate (.86 per cent). Although the same variety of forms is represented in the Midland materials they differ from the other recognized varieties in the frequency of occurrence of the various forms.

Chipping of the blade. No variation was recognized between the varieties with respect to the form of the chip scars on the blade. (See type description for definition.)

Shape of the base. No appreciable variation was recognized among the varieties. Five basal forms were observed in the sample: convex (.87 per cent); subconvex (43.72 per cent); straight (25.98 per cent); subconcave (26.98 per cent); and concave (3.03 per cent).

Chipping of the base. Primary scars originating on the basal edge are of two forms: (1) relatively long lamellar or expanding scars, or (2) diminutive conchoidal or expanding scars. Single specimens rarely exhibit both forms. Specimens with long lamellar or expanding scars may be retouched only on a single face (2.06 per cent), while those exhibiting longitudinal scars may be retouched bifacially (42.86 per cent), or retouched on a single face, the opposite of which face was shaped by chips originating along the lateral edge only (50.22 per cent). In addition to the nature and placement of chip scars originating along the basal edge the basal form was observed to vary according to the presence or absence of a distinct striking platform from which longitudinal chips had been struck. No such striking platform occurred on 83.55 per cent of the specimens, while 13.85 per cent of the specimens exhibited a striking platform formed by a remnant of the original angled edge of the flake blank from which the finished piece was fabricated. Only 2.60 per cent exhibited a prepared striking platform produced by the removal of short chips resulting in a slight bevel on the basal edge.

Longitudinal chipping, when present, generally consists of from two to four contiguous chip scars while diminutive conchoidal scars, when present, are generally continuous along the basal edge.

Orientation of the base. There was no variation observed among the varieties in the orientation of the base with respect to the longitudinal axis of the point. Observed angles range from 90 to 106 degrees with the following distribution by class: (1) 90-92 degrees, 38.14 per cent; (2) 92-94 degrees, 21.15 per cent; (3) 94-96 degrees, 14.43 per cent; (4) 96-98 degrees, 11.86 per cent; (5) 98-100 degrees, 7.31 per cent; (6) 100-102 degrees, 4.54 per cent; (7) 102-104 degrees, 1.78 per cent; (8) 104-106 degrees, .79 per cent.

Flake blank orientation. 96.10 per cent of the specimens have been retouched to the point that the determination of the original orientation of the flake with respect to the finished specimen is impossible. 1.30 per cent of the samples exhibited a distal orientation; that is, the bulb of percussion on the original flake blank was located at what became the tip of the finished specimen (Fig. 4, A). 2.60 per cent exhibited an oblique orientation, the bulb of percussion of the original flake blank located near the point of juncture between the lateral edge and the base along the lateral edge (Fig. 5, B). No specimens were observed with the original bulb of percussion located at the base of the finished specimen.

Grinding. One of the important distinctive attributes of this variety is the presence of grinding either on the base of the lateral edge, or tip. 28 per cent of the samples exhibited grinding on one or more of the above-mentioned edges.

Size. This variety is by far the largest recognized, although it does not exceed the Swan Creek variety in width measurements. For summary information see Table X.

Swan Creek Variety (Fig. 4, Row 2)

This variety was recognized because of demonstrable differences between specimens manufactured of G-type stone and those manufactured of other materials. Seventy-two specimens constituted the sample upon which the variety has been described.

Blade shape. The same forms of blade were observed in this sample as in the sample of the Midland variety but a much higher proportion of the Swan Creek specimens exhibited an excurvate blade shape. The observed frequencies are as follows: expanding ovate, 1.45 per cent; excurvate, 52.17 per cent; ovate, 37.68 per cent; parallel ovate, 1.45 per cent; and contracting ovate, 7.25 per cent.

Chipping of the blade. Primary scars are the same as the Midland variety except that there tends to be less terminal hinge fractures and a generally smoother surface, that is, less definition between chip scars. There is also a tendency for the primary scars to be smaller than on the Midland variety points. Secondary scars, unlike Midland variety points, tend to be clustered together at the points where primary chip scar ridges meet the lateral edge. In form, secondary scars are of the diminutive expanding and lamellar form. In this characteristic the Swan Creek variety shares common characteristics with the Turkey Tail points recovered from the site.

Shape of the base. Same as the Midland variety.

Chipping of the base. Basal treatment is much more homogeneous on the Swan Creek specimens, in that there is a higher proportion of the specimens exhibiting preparation by the removal of longitudinal chips originating along the basal edge. Of the total sample, 66.67 per cent exhibited longitudinal scars on both faces, while 18.84 per cent exhibited longitudinal scars on a single face with either transverse or diminutive scars on the opposite face. The remaining 14.49 per cent exhibited either transverse and/or diminutive scars only. There was a total absence of specimens with the bases prepared specifically as a striking platform, while 9.72 per cent exhibited an acute striking platform formed by the remnant edge of the original flake blank from which the specimen was fabricated. The remaining 90.28 per cent showed no specific acute angular striking platforms.

Orientation of the base. Same as Midland variety.

Flake blank orientation. A very marked difference was noted between the Swan Creek variety and the Midland variety in this attribute. 20.29 per cent of the total sample exhibited a distal orientation, the bulbar end of the original flake blank coinciding with the distal end of the finished specimen (Fig. 5, A). The remaining 79.71 per cent of the specimens had been retouched to the point that determination of the flake blank orientation was obscured. No specimens were observed with an oblique orientation.

Grinding. No grinding was observed along any edge.

Size. In size the Swan Creek variety is closest to the Midland variety, but there are real differences between the populations. (See Table IX for summary data on the metrical data.)

Saginaw Variety (Fig. 4, Row Number 3)

This variety was recognized because of demonstrable differences between specimens manufactured of types A and G stone as opposed to those manufactured of stone types B, C, D, E, F, and I. The sample consisted of 214 specimens upon which the variety has been described.

Blade shape. As with the other varieties five different blade shapes were observed in the sample but the relative frequencies with which the various forms occurred differed between the varieties. The following frequencies occurred: expanding ovate, (.95 per cent); ovate, (58.09 per cent); excurvate, (34.76 per cent); contracting ovate, (2.38 per cent); and parallel ovate, (3.18 per cent).

Chipping of the blade. The flat expanding scars characteristic of the Midland variety, and the fine, ill-defined primary scars of the Swan Creek variety are never seen on the Saginaw variety. Primary scars are frequently largely obscured by secondary flaking. When primary scars are present they tend to be irregularly shaped and some approach the conchoidal form. Ridges between separate chip scars tend to be pronounced and terminal hinge fractures are frequent. Secondary chipping is common, being continuous along the lateral edges. Scar forms range from conchoidal to fine lamellar.

Shape of the base. Same as the Midland variety, but with less subconcave forms than is characteristic of the Swan Creek variety.

Chipping of the base. One striking difference between the Saginaw variety points and the other varieties is the overwhelming proportion of specimens exhibiting diminutive conchoidal, and expanding scars along the basal edge (Fig. 5, C_3). Longitudinal scars so common on the other varieties only account for 19.52 per cent of the specimens while 67.62 per cent exhibit diminutive scars only; 8.57 per cent have longitudinal scars only on a single face with the typical transverse scars on the opposite face, while 4.28 per cent show only transverse scars with no primary scars originating along the basal edge. In terms of basal preparation a much lower proportion of the specimens have been worked so that there is no remnant of a striking platform at the base (67.13 per cent). 27.78 per cent of the specimens exhibit the unobscured remnant of the edge of the flake blank on one surface of the basal edge and 5.90 per cent have specifically prepared striking platforms. Both primary and secondary scars, when present, tend to be sporadic in occurrence along the basal edge.

Orientation of the base. Same as the Midland variety.

Flake blank orientation (Fig. 5, A, B). By far the majority of specimens exhibiting unobscured segments of the flake blank reflect an oblique orientation (17.67 per cent) while only 8.84 per cent exhibit a distal orientation. The remaining 73.49 per cent are obscured with respect to this attribute.

Grinding. No grinding was observed along any edge.

Size. This is by far the smallest variety. (See Table IX for summary data on the metrical attributes.)

Turkey Tail Points (Fig. 6)

Blade shape. Excurvate blade shape is the most frequently observed (13 out of 14 specimens) while a single specimen exhibited a parallel ovate blade shape.

Chipping of the blade. Primary chipping invariably results in massive flat expanding chip scars which normally terminate in very shallow hinge fractures not sufficiently deep to result in pronounced ridges between chip scars. Chipping is uniform over the entire blade and the scars are orientated with respect to the shape of the lateral edge. Secondary chipping was observed on all specimens. Secondary chip scars are of the diminutive expanding and lamellar form, generally clustered at the points where primary chip scar ridges meet the lateral edge. Continuous secondary chipping

TABLE XII

DATA ON THE METRICAL ATTRIBUTES OF THE THREE RECOGNIZED VARIETIES
(In centimeters)

Data	Midland Variety	Swan Creek Variety	Saginaw Variety
Length			
Sx	1102.00	287.75	856.55
Sx^2	5356.18	1229.10	3564.50
n	230.00	68.00	209.00
$\bar{x}$	4.79	4.23	4.10
s	.57	.41	.51
Maximum width			
Sx	576.95	177.09	440.10
Sx^2	1462.07	468.70	926.74
n	231.00	68.00	214.00
$\bar{x}$	2.50	2.60	2.08
s	.30	.33	.32
Basal width			
Sx	554.80	168.40	422.18
Sx^2	1339.61	420.57	857.61
n	231.00	69.00	214.00
$\bar{x}$	2.40	2.44	1.97
s	.17	.36	.34
Thickness			
Sx	132.40	41.45	119.65
Sx^2	81.22	25.83	68.68
n	228.00	69.00	215.00
$\bar{x}$	.58	.60	.56
s	.14	.12	.10

uninterrupted along the entire lateral edge was only observed on 2 specimens.

Shape of the base. Two forms of base were observed: bivectoral and convex. A bivectoral base is defined as the proximal edges of a tang which is described to the 2 lateral edges which meet at a point on the longitudinal axis of the specimen, extending distally to the proximal points of juncture of the haft element. Nine out of 14 specimens exhibited bivectoral bases. The remainder were deeply convex.

Fig. 6. Turkey Tail Points.

Chipping of the base. Primary chip scars occurring on the tang did not originate along the basal edge as defined on the finished specimen. Secondary chip scars originate along the basal edge and their removal is responsible for the finished form.

Secondary scars are diminutive, expanding, or triangular in shape, are orientated relative to the shape of the basal edge, and are not continuous on either face or along any edge. They are placed solely with regard to the varying thickness of the tang. Frequently the basal point in the case of bivectorally shaped specimens will be a thin section of the cortex of the original flint nodule (9 of the 14 specimens).

Haft element. All specimens exhibit lateral basal juncture, with 9 specimens having acute and circular distal points of juncture, and the remainder having right-angled and circular distal points. Medial points of juncture of the haft element are all circular in their articulation with 6 examples of right angles, 6 examples of acute angles, and 2 examples of obtuse angles described internally. Distal points of juncture are all obtuse and circular. The haft element was produced by the removal of massive primary chips, normally on a single face with the subsequent shaping being accomplished by diminutive secondary chip removal within the haft element. Production of the haft element was certainly one phase of the final step in the manufacture of the artifact, for scars originating in the haft element obscure primary scars originating on both the base and the lateral edge. Occasionally, secondary scars originating along the edge of the haft element are continuous with secondary scars along the basal edge showing that final shaping of the base was part of the same operation as the production of the haft element.

TABLE XIII

METRICAL ATTRIBUTES OF TURKEY TAIL POINTS

Data	Total Length	Maximum Width	Shoulder Width	Base Width	Haft Width	Tang Length
Sx . . .	192.3	51.4	44.2	23.8	23.2	22.9
Sx^2 . .	2647.19	189.74	140.30	41.16	38.84	38.15
n . . .	14.0	14.0	14.0	14.0	14.0	14.0
$\bar{x}$ . . .	13.74	3.67	3.16	1.70	1.66	1.64
s . . .	.85	.28	.24	.22	.17	.22

Other observations. All specimens exhibited a slight polish along the high ridges of the flake scars on the blade. There was no polish at the tip or on the base. This suggests that the specimens may have been carried around so that the polish resulted from their having rubbed together.

Comments. In view of the well-known nature of these artifacts further detailed description was considered unnecessary.

Notched Projectile Point (Fig. 5, G).—One small basal fragment of a notched projectile point was recovered from the mass of cremated bone designated "Cremation Number 2." The fragment had also been cremated. Very little can be said about the specimen. It has a slightly concave base, lateral-coincidental juncture of the haft element, absence of secondary chipping within the haft element. The distal point of juncture of the haft element is right angled while the proximal point of juncture is acute and circular. The medial point of juncture is circular and acute. Haft width is 1.4 cm, basal width is estimated at 2.2 cm.

Formal Analysis of the Samples of Human Skeletal Material

Within the burial pit were 3 obvious concentrations of cremated human bone together with charcoal fragments giving each mass a much darker color than the surrounding soil. Within the masses of bone and charcoal there was no red ocher, although red ocher had been spread over the top of the cremations. These were designated cremations Number 1, 2, and 3 (Fig. 2).

Cremation Number 1. Included within the area designated "Cremation Number 1" were 36.2 gm of cremated human bone among which were the following identifiable fragments: 37 skull fragments, mostly from the parietal/occipital region; 1 fragment of cervicle vertebra; 4 tooth caps, 3 mandibular molars, 1 mandibular premolar; 2 rib fragments; 38 humerus fragments; 4 fragments of the radius; 4 fragments of the ulna; making 90 identifiable fragments.

On the basis of these fragments, suture closure, size of bones, and dentition an identification was made of an individual of undetermined sex between eight and twelve years old at death. It is interesting to note that there is a complete absence of identified remains from the thoracic, or lumbar regions of the vertebra, pelvic area, and lower limbs. This suggests that the individual was either partly disarticulated prior to cremation or that only part of the cremated remains were recovered from the crematory basin.

All of the cremated bone fragments exhibit deep transverse fractures, frequently curved, much warping, and deep checking. These are all traits associated with the cremation of bodies in the flesh as opposed to the cremation of old dry bones (Baby, 1954; Binford, n.d., *a*). In addition to the cremated human remains there were 2 fragments of cremated Pomranky points of undetermined variety (probably Saginaw) included in Cremation Number 1.

Obviously the cremation had been contained in some receptacle (possibly a skin bag) prior to placement in the grave, for the lines of demarcation between the cremation and the surrounding soil, which was obviously fill, heavily stained with red ocher, was very clear. There was no ocher between the bottom of the cremation and the floor of the pit showing that the cremation had been placed in the pit prior to the filling with ocher and sand.

Cremation Number 2. Cremation Number 2 contained 109.5 gm of human bone representing the cremated remains of at least one individual of undetermined sex judged to have been between 12 and 15 years old at death. The following anatomical parts were identifiable: 26 skull fragments, mostly from the facial region and the parietal/occipital region; 1 fragment of mandibular condyle; 2 cervical vertebra; 2 fragments of thoracic vertebra; 5 rib fragments; 2 humeral fragments; 5 radial fragments; 5 fragments of ulna; and 1 phalangeal fragment.

As was the case with Cremation Number 1 there is a complete lack of identifiable remains from the pelvic area, and the lower limbs. The central vertebral column is represented, which was not true in Cremation Number 1. The lack of teeth is interesting in view of the presence of skull fragments from the facial region. The bones are judged to have been cremated in the flesh. A single cremated fragment of a notched projectile point was the only additional material included in the mass of cremated remains. The inferred container and placement directly on the floor of the pit prior to filling with red ocher and sand is also suggested by this cremation.

Cremation Number 3. The individual represented in Cremation Number 3 is judged to have been approximately 10 to 13 years old at death. The sex of the individual is undetermined. The following anatomical parts were identifiable among the 93.5 gm of bone: 35 skull fragments representing the entire skull; 2 cervical vertebra; 2 thoracic vertebra; 5 fragments of ribs; 13 fragments of humerus; 4 fragments of radius; 4 fragments of ulna; 1 phalangeal fragment; 7 femoral fragments; and 18 fragments of long bones.

The represented remains differ from the other two cremations only in the presence of femoral fragments and long bone fragments believed to be from the lower limbs. The lack of teeth is similar to Cremation Number 2. Again the bones are judged to have been cremated in the flesh.

In addition to the cremated remains, Cremation Number 3 contained the uncremated and poorly preserved fragments of an antler. The preservation was so poor that it could not be determined whether the antler had been worked into some type of tool. A small section of antler directly on the bottom of the cremation resting on the floor of the pit was covered with an even layer of material tentatively identified as carbonized skin. This is further support for the hypothesis that the cremations had been placed in the burial pit in skin bags. Burned fragments of at least four Pomranky points were also included within the mass of cremated bone.

Cremated Remains not Clustered in Discrete Masses

Cremation Number 4. A concentration of cremated remains occurred in the very center of the burial pit mixed with uncremated Pomranky points of the Midland variety; scattered out to the southwest following the scattered distribution of Midland variety points were similar cremated bone fragments. These represent the cremated remains of an individual of undetermined sex whose age at death was approximately five to seven years old. The following anatomical parts were identifiable among the 46.2 gm of bone: 14 skull fragments representing the entire skull; 8 teeth—incisors, premolars, and molars—all milk teeth; 3 cervical vertebra; 7 rib fragments; 6 fragments of humerus; 5 fragments of radius; 6 fragments of ulna; 20 phalanges; and 28 unidentified long bone fragments (probably humerus).

The inventory of identified parts is very similar to the other cremations and shares the general lack of lower limbs and pelvic fragments. It differs from the other cremations in that there was an absence of a differentiated concentration, being identifiable by difference in soil color, presence of charcoal fragments and absence of red ocher within the mass of cremated bone. Red ocher was present throughout the concentration of bone. The difference suggests this individual had not been placed in a skin bag and deposited in the burial pit; rather, the cremated remains had been mixed with red ocher and Midland variety points, and dumped into the pit in the central area. There were no cremated artifacts found in association with this material.

Uncremated Human Remains (Fig. 2)

Tooth caps. Five separate clusters of tooth caps were discovered. All were clusters of adult molars except one, which represented the complete mandibular arch of a child (all milk teeth). The clusters of adult molars were not associated with other bony remains and do not appear to have been part of complete mandibles. They were also not located in a consistent fashion with either the cremations or the uncremated bone fragments. Suspecting that they may represent cut human jaw fragments similar to those frequently found in Hopewell burials (McGregor, 1952, p. 90), they were examined to determine whether there was any evidence of cutting along the lateral edges of the teeth. No such evidence was observed. It seems likely, however, that the occurrence of these isolated adult tooth caps in a burial of children and adolescents probably represent inclusion of human mandibular sections as part of the grave furniture.

Long bone fragments. Seven large, long, bone fragments together with five very small fragments were identified from the southeast quarter of the burial pit. Exact identification of the bones was not possible in most cases because of the poor preservation; however, a tibia was identifiable from the extreme south end of the pit. Five of the long bone fragments were orientated parallel to one another in a north-south direction. If the northern fragments represent fragments of humerus then it is possible that there was a flexed burial in this area; yet, in view of the absence of lower limb bones in the cremations it is possible that they had been severed from the bodies prior to cremation and included in the flesh in the southeastern quarter of the burial pit. In view of the lack of identification it is impossible to accurately interpret these remains.

Botanical Remains

Charcoal recovered from the three cremations has been identified by Volney Jones of The University of Michigan as Red Maple (*Acer rubrum*). Identifiable specimens were not numerous due to the extremely small size of the majority of charcoal fragments. It is believed, however, that all the charcoal represented *Acer*. Also recovered from the cremations were three seeds, two unidentified and the third identified as *Chenopodium*.

ANALYSIS AND INTERPRETATION OF THE DISTRIBUTION OF ARTIFACTUAL MATERIAL WITH RESPECT TO THE SKELETAL REMAINS

Two major clusters of Pomranky points of the Midland variety are clearly discernible (Fig. 1). One cluster occurred between Cremations 1 through 3. In this cluster the points were not stacked in a compact pile. They appear to have been included together with powdered hematite and sand as a unit, possibly dumped in from a single container. Another cluster of Pomranky points of the Midland variety occurred in the central portion of the burial and the burial and the cluster thinned out to the southwest. These points were mixed with red ocher, sand, and the cremated bones designated "Cremation Number 4." As in the previous case the entire grouping of materials appears to have been dumped into the burial pit from a container holding originally all of the clustered elements, points, bone, hematite, and sand. Within both of the above clusters there occurred a small number of Pomranky points of the Swan Creek variety.

On the southeastern side of the burial pit surrounding the uncremated remains were several clusters of Pomranky points of the Saginaw variety. These clusters obviously represent placement in the burial pit specifically as clusters of points, either as handfuls or in small containers. They certainly had been placed in the pit as piles of points and were subsequently covered with ocher and sand. In all cases the points were resting directly on the floor of the burial pit, stacked and interbedded, not thinly scattered as with the clusters of Midland variety points. Treated in a similar manner were the Turkey Tail points which were stacked one on top of the other, alternately, with the bases and tips in opposite directions. Possibly originally associated with the Turkey Tail points were pyrites, which is inferred from the presence of limonite stains on the surface of one point. The latter point was broken and not included in the stacked cluster of unbroken points. Within the burial pit there was a central area of heavy ocher concentration. This, in general, surrounded the cremations, and clusters of Saginaw variety points as well as uncremated bone. The exception to this rule was Cremation Number 4 and the associated cluster of Midland variety points. Judging from the position of this material with respect to the area of heavy ocher concentration, Cremation Number 4 must have been dumped into the burial pit after the other cremations. The uncremated bone and the clusters of Saginaw and Turkey Tail points had been partly covered by highly concentrated powdered ocher. Outside of the area of heavy ocher concentration were a disassociated child's mandibular arch, and two clusters of adult molars. These appear to have been included after the major concentration of bone and artifacts had been covered with ocher and sand.

Overlying the entire distribution of materials as shown in Fig. 2, there was a layer of sand and ocher which was removed as a unit during excavation (Fig. 3), and which constituted the soil between the level of initial recognition of the pit feature and the upper datum plain for Figure 3. The specimens removed from this level included the following numbers of artifacts: Midland variety, 58; Swan Creek variety, 18; and Saginaw variety, 10. The relative proportions of varieties in this area is greatly different from the relative proportions in the pit feature as shown in Figure 2. There are many more Midland variety points in the upper fill relative to the number of Saginaw variety points. These were scattered and not clustered, suggesting that they were spread over the pit during filling and that they were specifically placed in the pit.

It should be noted that in no case were Midland or Swan Creek variety points observed to have been placed in the burial pit as handfuls or in containers. All the clusters of predominantly Midland and Swan Creek specimens appear to have been dumped into the pit. It should be noted that there is a much higher frequency of Midland and Swan Creek variety points outside the area of heavy ocher concentration, while the great majority of Saginaw variety points are inside the area of heavy ocher concentration.

INTERPRETATION OF THE RECOVERED MATERIALS

Interpretation of the Observed Formal Diversity Among Chipped-stone Artifacts

The observed formal diversity among the described forms must be considered within four major frames of reference: (1) what specific flint-working habits resulted in the observed differences; (2) what differences can be attributed solely to stylistic variability conceived as the differences in the conceptions as to what a particular artifact form should be current among different groups of people; (3) what functional differences if any, are suggested by the formal diversity; and (4) what does the observed diversity mean in terms of sociocultural relationships.

Pomranky points. Certainly some of the observed differences can be accounted for on the basis of differences in habits of flint-working. For instance, the demonstrable differences between the varieties in the orientation of flake blanks shows that the manufacturers differ in the types of blanks selected for use in point manufacture. The absence of obliquely orientated specimens within the Swan Creek variety suggests that the stages of manufacture outlined for the Eastport site (Binford and Papworth, pp. 81-98) were probably followed by the manufacturers of the Swan Creek specimens. A single exception is notable—at the Eastport site, where bulbar ends of flake blanks were frequently worked into the basal end of finished specimens, the opposite was true of the Swan Creek materials, where bulbar ends of blanks were located at the tip of finished specimens. Aside from this the basic stone-working techniques involved were the same—the removal of the flake blank from prepared cores so that the resulting flakes were parallel-sided or expanding. On the other hand, the high percentage of obliquely orientated specimens in the Saginaw variety sample suggests a different mode of flake blank selection and similarly a different mode of detaching flakes from prepared cores. A true "blade" technique is not indicated for the production of flake blanks from which the Saginaw specimens were manufactured. Going hand-in-hand with the suggested differences in the manner of working primary stone material are the differences in chipping observed on the finished specimens, particularly in the basal area and, to some extent, on the blade faces themselves. These differences suggest slightly different motor habits in the removal of chips during the modification of the blank, and possibly a different sequence in steps of production. The presence of grinding on the edges of the Midland variety points and the complete absence on the Saginaw and Swan Creek varieties also shows that different techniques were being employed by the manufacturers of the several varieties.

With regard to stylistic variability it seems reasonable that differences in size are about the only characteristics that reflect differing concepts concerning the "desired" form of a Pomranky point. It should be mentioned that these differences could reflect variable adaptations to the utilization of differing types of raw material, but such a position is made less tenable by the wide variety of stone types represented in the Saginaw variety sample with no appreciable variability in size among the specimens of different material.

It should be emphasized that the formal diversity among the several varieties of Pomranky point does not suggest functional differences for the various forms. Nothing in the form of the Pomranky points suggests anything other than a technoeconomic function for the specimens. Analysis of similar material from the Eastport site (Binford and Papworth, pp. 114-16), lead to the suggestion that the specific function of Pomranky points was as blanks which were later notched for hafting.

What are the sociocultural implications of the observed diversity? This is a more difficult question to assess. The fact that there is a one-to-one correlation between the form and material of the Midland and Swan Creek varieties, and a great variety of materials were utilized in the manufacture of the Saginaw variety points is believed to reflect sociocultural phenomena. It is proposed that the Saginaw variety points represent locally manufactured forms while the Midland and Swan Creek varieties originated in other regions. Such an interpretation is logically supportable if we assume that it is more likely that an individual, obtaining artifacts from some distance away, is likely to have obtained them from a single individual and the probability is high that, at any one time, an individual is likely to have manufactured specimens out of a single type of raw material. This interpretation would be more tenable if it could be demonstrated that type A and G stone was not local. It must be kept in mind that all three varieties were recovered from a single burial and therefore they were all probably in use contemporaneously. In view of this it is likely that observed differences between varieties reflect regional differences between contemporary sociocultural units in the stylistic and technical basis of point manufacture.

Turkey Tail points. The fact that the Turkey Tail points differ widely in form from the Pomranky points suggests a different function for the two forms. The very narrow dimension between the haft elements of the Turkey Tails suggests that if they were hafted so that the haft was parallel to the longitudinal axis of the specimen that vigorous usage would quickly result in blade breakage just above the haft element. No other technique of hafting is suggested by the form of the specimen; therefore, it seems logical to postulate a limited intended usage for the specimens. In view of the context in which they are normally found some social function rather than a technoeconomic function is suggested. This is further supported by the polish on the faces of the specimens suggesting that they had been carried around for some time and had been rubbing together. The exotic material from which they are made also suggests some ritual function or significance attached to these specimens.

Notched projectile points fragment. The form of this specimen suggests a technoeconomic function. Whether or not it is a modified form of Pomranky point could not be determined.

Summary. Formal differences between the three classes of chipped-stone material suggest a ritual function for the Turkey Tails, technoeconomic function for the notched point, and certainly there is nothing about the form of the Pomranky points that suggests anything other than a technoeconomic function for that form. The observed diversity among varieties of Pomranky point were interpreted as representing regional differences between contemporary sociocultural units in the stylistic and technical basis of point manufacture.

Reconstruction of Interment Procedure

The fill dirt from the cremations was inspected microscopically by Richard Yarnell of the Museum of Anthropology, The University of Michigan. He reports that: "Contents: mostly dirty sand with many charred and some uncharred bone fragments, some wood charcoal, three tiny seeds (one identified as *Chenopodium*), probably all the seeds are fortuitous inclusions, and a very small amount of red ocher. There is no evidence of copper and no flint chips or other cultural remains."

Yarnell, who has inspected the dirt from a number of late archaic burials, has observed that very small flint chips, etc. are frequent in the backfill of pits excavated in habitational areas. The absence of this material in the fill of the Pomranky burial is interpreted by Yarnell as follows: "The burial was apparently located in a culturally barren stratum, apart from the area of habitation." An alternative interpretation might be that the pit was filled with soil obtained in another place; however, there is no evidence in support of this position. It seems that the locus of the burial pit was away from the habitation area. Following the selection of the burial location the pit was dug into the ground, and the floor was probably lined with bark. Cremations Number 1 through 3 were placed in the pit contained in skin bags. Uncremated bones, either a complete skeleton or disarticulated lower limbs, were placed on the floor of the pit and surrounded by small piles of Saginaw variety points, a pile of Turkey Tail points, possibly contained in a skin bag, and probably some pyrites. Powdered red ocher was dumped over the uncremated bones. A container of both Midland variety points and hematite was dumped between the cremations Number 1 through 3 and the entire area of included materials was covered with heavy concentrations of red ocher possibly mounded up over the remains on the bottom of the pit. After this, Cremation Number 4, together with a number of Pomranky points of the Midland variety, was dumped on the edge of the mounded up pile near the center of the pit. The pit was filled with sand and smaller amounts of red ocher. Several sections of adult mandible and one complete subadult mandible were included in the fill. After the pit had been filled level with the mounded pile of red ocher and included material, containers of Pomranky points, primarily of the Midland variety, and ocher were spread over the entire pit. Filling continued until the pit was completely filled.

Reconstruction of the Mortuary Practices

Bodies were cremated in crematoriums away from the interment area, the fires being built of maplewood. At the time of cremation of the bodies the lower limbs and pelvic area were severed from the trunk and upper torso or there was an attempt made, when recovering the cremated remains from the crematorium, to recover the bones from the upper torso as units. Individuals appear to have been treated as such, that is, there was not a mass cremation in which there was no attempt made to keep separate the remains of different individuals. Calcined bone from the crematorium was apparently stored in containers, probably skin bags, and later included in subsurface burial pits accompanying the uncremated remains of a different individual or the uncremated lower limbs of the individual represented by the cremated bone. Within any one bag of cremated remains was only a small proportion of the bone from any given individual. Some measure of the "token" nature of the cremated remains is offered by comparing the weight of the bone from each cremation to the 1750.00 gm estimated weight of a complete cremated skeleton, cremated and interred in conditions identical fo the soil at the Pomranky site. Personalties in the form of Pomranky points and notched points were cremated with the individuals.

The second phase of mortuary practice is represented by interment in subsurface burial pits. This phase is characterized by the interment of more than one individual in a single burial placement of cremated remains, placed peripherally in the pit with respect to the placement of uncremated remains. Offertory goods in the form of Pomranky points of three varieties, Turkey Tail points, sections of human mandible, and possibly fire-making kits represented by pyrites were arranged around the human remains. That these materials were offertory and not personalties is attested to by the differential treatment of the varieties of Pomranky point with respect to the entire burial—differential treatment in the form of cremated and noncremated artifacts, and the large numbers of Pomranky points included.

Sociocultural Implications of the Mortuary Practices

The fact that all the identified human remains that could be considered as objects of interment and not grave furniture were adolescents or children, together with the fact that a large quantity of artifacts believed to be mortuary offerings were included in the burial, suggests that some status accrued to individuals of this particular age group, or at least social importance was attached to children and adolescents that was not simply a function of the acquired status positions of the interred individual. The presence among the mortuary offerings of at least three varieties of Pomranky point and the inference that the varieties reflect regional differences between contemporary sociocultural units in the stylistic and technical basis of point manufacture raises the question of the nature of the contributors to the mortuary goods. It has been suggested that the Saginaw variety points were locally manufactured. It is observed that the great majority of this variety were placed around the uncremated bones in small clusters resembling handfuls or small containers full of points. Also, the vast majority of this variety were included within the area of concentrated red ocher. This "primary" placement of the Saginaw variety points suggests that they may have been contributed by a special class of close relatives. On the other hand, the Midland and Swan Creek varieties, when clustered, were believed to have been dumped into the pit rather than placed in a tight cluster, and the majority were located outside the area of heavy ocher concentration. These facts, together with the suggestion that they were of nonlocal origin, may reflect contribution to the mortuary goods by individuals of a slightly different order of relationship than were the contributors of the Saginaw variety points.

The presence among the mortuary goods of artifacts manufactured of materials obtained as far away as Harrison County, Indiana, is certainly indicative of wide-spread logistics networks for the transference of goods and materials.

The inferred ritual function of the Turkey Tail points and the context of occurrence of the large numbers of Pomranky points, infrequently constituting large proportions of the materials from surface collections in the area, suggests that the uncremated grave furniture was functionally specific with respect to a ritual usage.

A large body of goods was obtained and manufactured specifically for utilization in mortuary rites and possibly for other social ritual. These materials do not appear to have been part of the technological-exploitative aspect of the cultural system represented.

Elaboration in the quality and quantity of nontechno-exploitative artifacts which are not identifiable as personalties generally is suggestive of increasing sociocultural complexity. Certainly the late archaic burial practices as represented at the Pomranky site indicate a trend in this direction.

DATING OF THE POMRANKY MATERIAL

Material for "carbon fourteen" age determination has been submitted to The University of Michigan Radiocarbon Laboratory for analysis, but as yet the results have not been obtained. In spite of this lack of information it is my opinion that the Pomranky burial dates approximately 800 B.C. This estimate is based on comparison with other sites of similar nature which have been dated by "carbon fourteen" analysis.

SUMMARY

A burial pit containing the remains of at least four adolescents and children, together with the included artifacts, has been described and taxonomically studied. Three varieties of Pomranky points were recognized in the sample of 516 such points recovered from the burial. Fourteen Turkey Tail points, one notched projectile point fragment, red ocher, and the inferred presence of pyrites suggesting fire-making kits have been described. Interpretation of the formal properties of the included material, as well as their relative placement within the burial, has served as the basis for the reconstruction of the interment procedures and mortuary practices of the sociocultural system represented. Further interpretation has been offered as to the functions of the included artifactual materials within the sociocultural system represented and the socioimplications of these interpretations have been pointed out. Finally, a date of 800 B.C. has been suggested for the age of the site.

REFERENCES CITED

Baby, Raymond S.

1954. Hopewell Cremation Practices. The Ohio Historical Society, Papers in Archaeology No. 1. Columbus.

Binford, Lewis R.

N.D.*a* Crematory Practices at the Andrews Site, Saginaw County, Michigan.

N.D.*b* The Lamoka Point: A Study in Typology.

Fowke, Gerard

1894. Material for Aboriginal Stone Implements. The Archaeologist, Vol. II, Waterloo, Ind.

1928. Archeological Investigations -II, 44th Annual Report, Bureau of American Ethnology, 1926-27, Washington, D.C., 1928. pp. 401-555.

McGregor, John C.

1952. The Havana Site. *In*: Hopewellian Communities in Illinois, ed. Thorne Deuel. Illinois State Museum, Scientific Papers, Vol. V., pp. 43-94. Springfield.

Ritchie, William A.

1952. Recent Discoveries Suggesting an Early Woodland Burial Cult in the Northeast. New York State Museum and Science Service. Circular No. 40, State Univ. of New York. Albany.

A PROPOSED ATTRIBUTE LIST FOR THE DESCRIPTION AND CLASSIFICATION OF PROJECTILE POINTS

Lewis R. Binford

CONTENTS

INTRODUCTION

For many years American archaeologists have shown great interest and concern with ceramic typology. This same concern with standardization of descriptive terms for projectile-point studies has been the focal point of innumerable efforts particularly by young archaeologists eager to deal with a large temporal hiatus in American prehistory represented by archaic remains. In view of these many attempts, it is surprising that there is as yet no accepted terminology and certainly no standardized attribute list for the comparison of projectile point forms. When dealing with preceramic assemblages, chipped-stone material is about all we have, and we must develop adequate techniques for analyzing these assemblages. It is with this in mind that the scheme presented in this paper has been designed.

Before a typological scheme can be presented, we must specify what meaning is intended when the word "typology" is employed. A "type" is a demonstrable clustering of attributes observed among specimens of a given class of phenomena. This paper is not concerned primarily with techniques involved in demonstrating clusters of attributes, or with such pseudoproblems as the "reality" of types. What concerns us here are the problems the archaeologist must face before typological studies can be conducted. What attributes will be used in conducting cluster analysis? Any object has an infinite number of attributes. A projectile point may be studied by the geologist with regard to the attributes of the stone from which it is made or the patina that has altered its face. The student of tool evolution may consider only those attributes that contribute to the efficiency of the point as a piercing tool. Both of these studies could result in the establishment of types of projectile points. When we conduct typological studies, we must select a limited number of attributes, and only with respect to those will we analyze the projectile points. Once we have selected the attributes and established a typology its efficacy depends upon; (1) the relevance and completeness of the selected attributes to the specific problem of the typologist, and (2) the skill of the investigator in the use of statistical techniques for the isolation of attribute clusters. I should say at this point that valid types can be defined without the explicit use of formal statistics, but statistics are always used, though they may be called "common sense," experience or "familiarity with the data."

The *relevance of an attribute* to a typological study depends upon the problems with which the typology is expected to deal. Traditionally archaeologists have considered problems of local chronologies, culture histories, evolutionary sequences, morphological distinctions implying functional or use differences, and of course, the definition of culture types. Thus we might say that the relevance of an attribute for inclusion in typological studies by archaeologists depends on its recognition as a culturally dependent quality. This is not always possible to determine initially, and preliminary studies to test the cultural significance of the questionable attributes may be required.

The *completeness* of an attribute list is not easy to assess. Certain general statements are applicable, but no real rule of thumb can be used. In general, types defined upon larger numbers of attributes will be pertinent to a greater number of problems. For instance, if Eastern United States ceramic typologies had been established only on the basis of temper and vessel shape they would be much less useful in studies of stylistic change, diffusion, and the like, than would existing types defined on the basis of many more attribute classes.

Aside from the general problems of establishing attribute lists and considering them from both the standpoints of relevance and completeness, a good typology should be established on the basis of attributes that are completely objective. They should all be defined explicitly by the typologist and should be understandable and recognizable by other investigators so that comparative typological studies can be conducted with as little dependence upon individual opinions as possible. A published typology which uses vague or general terms, or does not make explicit the attributes upon which the typology is based, is of limited utility. It is also a waste of potentially valuable information.

Guided by these general considerations, an attribute list for use in the study of projectile points has been devised. There are numerous published schemes but, in most cases, these were found inadequate in view of the above discussion of relevance and completeness. Few of the projectile point studies that were consulted gave attention in any systematic way to attributes that are the result of different technical processes used in the manufacture of the point or differences in motor habits employed by the manufacturers. In an attempt to recognize attributes of this nature, as well as to reduce to less gross categories certain attributes dealing with the geometrical form of projectile points, various descriptive concepts current in American archaeology have been abandoned.

As would be expected, a number of different attribute lists were devised and tested before one was found that seemed adequate to describe projectile points regardless of their diverse form. The list that has been worked out at The University of Michigan has been found very useful and quite adequate for the description of projectile points in a very objective and quantifiable manner.

Because the attribute list was designed to be used with punch cards, automatically introducing certain coding difficulties, projectile points were considered to be of three classes: tanged, untanged, and multinotched classes. Tanged points are all those that have an edge or base modification to facilitate hafting. Untanged points are all those that lack such a modification, or in the case of fluted points have a single alteration along the longitudinal axis of the point. Multinotched forms are all points having more than a pair of edge modifications. The attribute system described here was designed for the formal analysis of tanged points.

The principles underlying the attribute scheme are simple. First the projectile point is broken down into morphological elements defined either as areas or edges. Second, each element is then described in terms of its geometrical and technical attributes. Geometrical attributes are of two classes, those that are descriptive of the element itself, and those that describe the articulation of the given element with other elements. Technical attributes are those that reflect either manufacturing techniques and/or motor habits of chipping stone.

PROJECTILE POINT MORPHOLOGY

Points of Juncture (Fig. 1)

The term "points of juncture" refers to the points where one element of a projectile point can be said to join with other elements. These points will be referred to in terms of their relation to the longitudinal axis and its point of intersection with the proximal end of the projectile point. They may be named by using the terms of the two elements that can be said to come together at the given point; for instance, the lateral-basal point of juncture would be the point at which the lateral sides of the projectile point intersect with the basal edge of the point.

Proximal point of juncture (Fig. 1).—This is a relative term that refers to the defining point of juncture of any element that is nearest the point where the longitudinal axis of the point intersects the basal edge.

Distal point of juncture (Fig. 1).—Like the above term, this is relative and may be used with reference to any element, but it always indicates the defining point of the element most distant from the point of intersection between the longitudinal axis and the basal edge of the projectile point.

Medial points of juncture (Fig. 1).—These are the points at which any major directional change occurs along the edge of a defined element. In the event that there are more than one such directional change the separate medial points may be designated as proximal or distal medial points depending upon their position relative to the point of intersection between the longitudinal axis and the basal edge of the point.

Tip (Fig. 1).--This is the only permanently defined point of juncture on the projectile point. It is coincidental with the most distal point of the projectile and is defined as the point of juncture between the two lateral edges of the distal segment of the projectile.

Elements of the Projectile Point

Elements are those morphologically differentiated edges or areas of the projectile points that are definable in terms of points of juncture.

Haft element (Fig. 1).—The haft element is defined as the edges between any two points of interruption in the projected symmetry of the proximal segment of the projectile point. This includes the lateral edges, or basal point as the case may be.

Blade element (Fig. 2).—The blade is defined as the area delimited by the distal points of juncture of the haft element and the tip.

Base element (Fig. 2).--The base element is the edge between the two points that serve to mark the transition between the proximal transverse edge and the lateral longitudinal edges of the projectile point.

Tang element (Fig. 3).--The tang element is the area of the projectile point defined by a line drawn through the two most distal

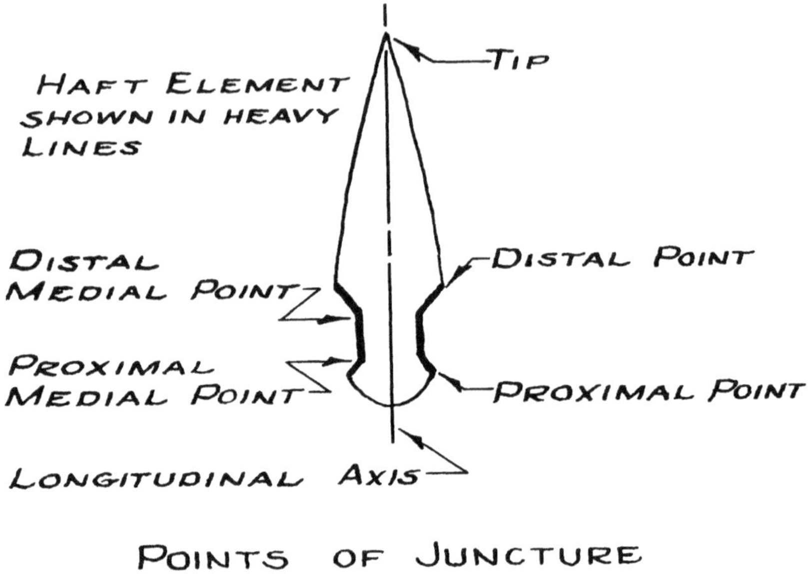

Figure 1

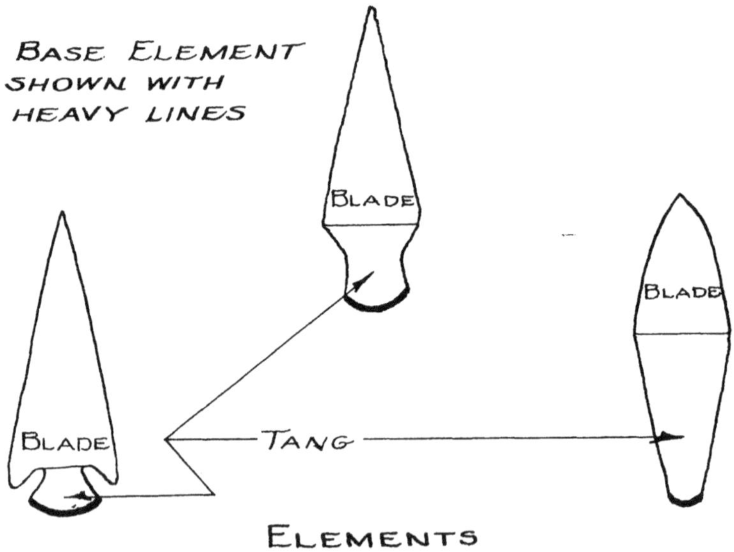

Figure 2

points of the haft element, regardless of whether they are points of juncture or medial points, and taking in all the area below this line to the proximal limits to the projectile point. In the absence of a haft element the point can be said to lack a tang.

Subelements of the Projectile Point (Fig. 3)

It has been found useful for descriptive purposes to break down some of the elements into subelements. A subelement is any edge between the defining points of an element that can be defined in terms of medial points only or a medial point and a point of juncture.

Modified Subelement of the tang (Fig. 3).—There are the edges of the haft element between the distal medial points and the proximal points of juncture of the haft element. In some cases there will be an absence of medial points, when this is the case, the modified subelement will be considered absent.

Unmodified subelement of the tang (Fig. 3).—The unmodified subelements are those edges between the proximal point of juncture of the haft element and the point of juncture for the lateral edge and the basal edge of the projectile point. This may or may not be present.

Longitudinal Axis (Fig. 1.)

The logitudinal axis is located by the construction of a line from the tip through a point midway between the medial points or the apex of the arc of the haft element as the case may be.

ATTRIBUTE LIST

Discrete Attributes

The following list is arranged in outline form presenting all of the recognized variations for any given attribute class. The utility of such a scheme is that if, in the future, new variations are observed they can always be added under the appropriate class.

1. Blade element—the area delimited by the distal points of juncture of the haft element and the tip.

1.1 Geometric attributes of the blade

1.11 Outline

1.111 Triangular (Fig. 4A) blades are defined as those whose edges describe a straight line between the proximal defining points of the blade and the tip. The widest part of the blade is between the proximal defining points.

1.112 Excurvate (Fig. 4B) blades are defined as those whose edges describe convex lines between the proximal defining points of the blade and the tip. The widest part of the blade is not between the proximal defining points.

1.113 Incurvate (Fig. 4C) blades are defined as those whose edges describe concave lines between the proximal defining points of the blade and the tip. The widest part of the blade is between the proximal defining points.

1.114 Ovate (Fig. 4D) blades are defined as those whose lateral edges describe convex lines between the proximal defining points of the blade and the tip. The widest part of the blade is between the proximal defining points.

1.115 Excurvate-incurvate (Fig. 4E) blades are defined as those whose edges describe concave-convex reverse arcs between the proximal defining points of the blade and the tip. The widest part of the blade is between the proximal defining points.

1.116 Parallel-ovate (Fig. 4F) blades are defined as those whose edges describe convex lines diverging from the tip to intersect straight parallel lines along the lateral edge. The straight lines then pass through the proximal defining points of the blade. The widest part of the blade is between the parallel straight lines.

1.117 Expanding-ovate (Fig. 4G) blades are defined as those whose edges describe convex lines diverging from the tip to intersect straight edges expanding from the proximal defining points to the point of intersection with the convex lines. The widest part of the blade is at the point of intersection between the straight and convex lines.

1.118 Contracting-ovate (Fig. 4H) blades are defined as those whose edges define convex lines diverging from the tip to intersect straight lines along the lateral edge of the projectile. The straight lines then continue to the proximal defining points of the blade. The widest part of the blade is between the proximal defining points of the blade.

1.119 etc. To be filled in as new variants are observed.

1.12 Transverses section of the blade—observed at the midpoint of the blade.

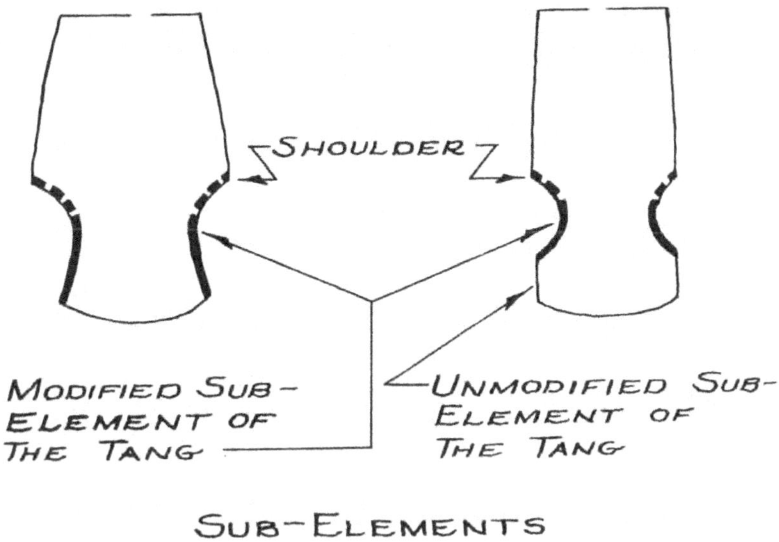

Figure 3

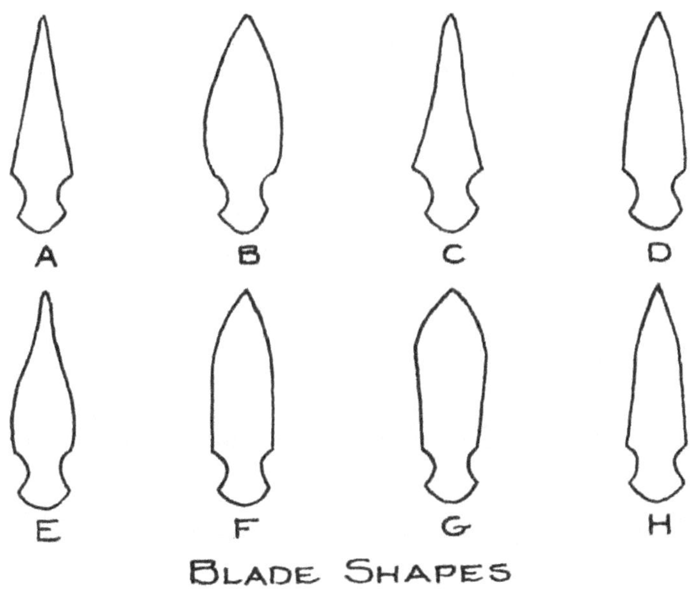

Figure 4

1.121 Plano-convex (Fig. 5A)

1.122 Plano-triangular (Fig. 5B)

1.123 Biplano (Fig. 5C)

1.124 Biconvex (Fig. 5D)

1.125 Bitriangular (Fig. 5E)

1.126 Asymmetrically biconvex, (Fig. 5F)

1.127 Asymmetrically bitriangular (Fig. 5G)

1.128 Convexo-triangular (Fig. 5H)

1.13 Longitudinal section of the projectile—observed on the longitudinal axis of the point orientated vertically.

1.131 Plano-convex (Fig. 6A)

1.132 Biplano (Fig. 6B)

1.133 Biconvex (Fig. 6C)

1.134 Asymmetrically biconvex (Fig. 6D)

1.135 Concavo-convex (Fig. 6E)

1.136 Excurvate (Fig. 6F)

1.137 Ovate or triangular (Fig. 6G)

1.138 Assymetrically ovate (Fig. 6H)

1.139 Asymmetrically excurvate (Fig. 6I)

1.1391 Assymmetrically concavo-convex (Fig. 6J)

1.14 Symmetry of the blade

1.141 Symmetrical—both of the lateral edges are geometrically complementary.

1.142 Asymmetrical—the two lateral edges are not geometrically complementary, e.g. one edge ovate, one excurvate, etc.

Note: When asymmetrical specimens are observed the section under 1.11 should be described in terms of the most geometrically consistent edge. Most asymmetrical specimens are the result of reuse or imperfect fracture of the material.

1.2 Technical attributes of the blade

Attributes of this class describe the formal attributes that are believed to reflect the motor habits of the manufacturers as well as the sequence of steps in the manufacturing process.

1.21 Primary chipping—chip scars that are believed to be the initial alterations made on the "blank" to achieve the desired shape, are considered primary chips. All chip scars not obscured or partly obscured by others made in a distinctly different manner will be described as primary chip scars.

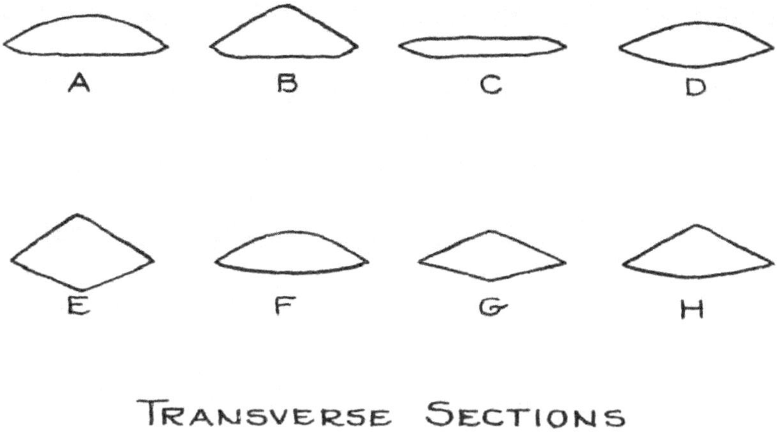

Figure 5

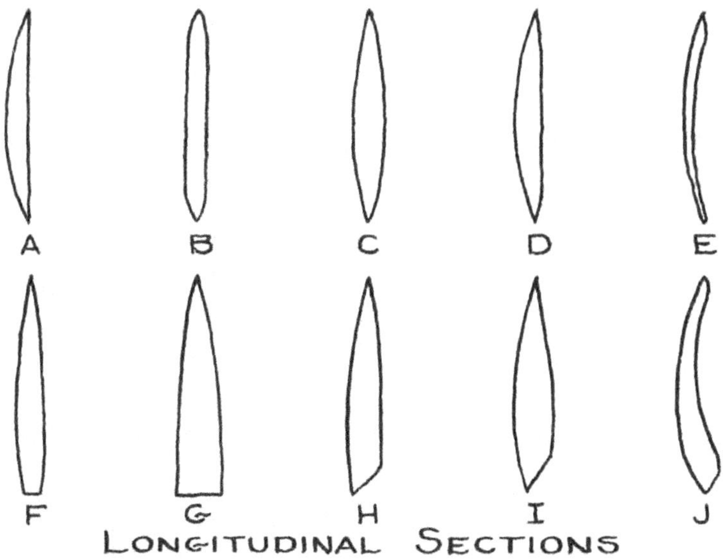

Figure 6

1.211 Size of scars

1.2111 Plan View

1.21111 Massive—scars are those that generally extend more than half way across the projectile point and have a modal width at the widest point at right angles to the longitudinal axis of the scar, of greater than one-half inch.

1.21112 Dimunitive—scars are those that generally do not extend more than half way across the projectile point and have a modal width at the widest point at right angles to the longitudinal axis of the scar, of less than one-half inch.

1.21113 Obscured—records the case where primary scars are present but they cannot be identified because of obscuring secondary scars.

1.2112 Depth

1.21121 Deep—scars are those exhibiting a well-defined negative bulb of percussion with pronounced ridges separating individual scars.

1.21121 Flat—scars are those exhibiting ill-defined negative bulbs of percussion together with ill-defined ridges separating individual scars.

1.212 Type of scars

1.2121 Expanding scars (Fig. 7B) expand rather markedly as the distance from the lateral edge increases and usually terminate in a random, ill-defined manner.

1.2122 Conchoidal scars (Fig. 7A) contract as the distance from the lateral edge increases and generally terminate in a regular convex ridge scar.

1.2123 Lamellar scars (Fig. 7C) have parallel lateral edges and generally terminate in angular fashion.

1.213 Placement of scars

1.2131 Bifacial—primary scars present on both faces of the projectile point.

1.2132 Internal face only—primary scars present on the internal face of the point only. The internal face is the face that was the cleavage face of the original flake blank.

1.2133 External face only—primary scars present on the external face of the point only. The external face is the outer core surface or nonbulbar face of the original flake blank.

1.2134 Unifacial indetermined face—primary scars present on only one face of the point but the particular face with respect to the original flake blank is not known.

1.22 Secondary chip scars—these scars originate along the lateral edge and tend to obscure the points of origin of primary scars. These represent a separate step in the manufacturing process of the finished artifact.

1.221 Type of scars

1.2212 Smooth lamellar scars (Fig. 8A) have parallel lateral edges and generally terminate in smooth angular ridges.

1.2212 Stepped lamellar scars (Fig. 8B) have parallel lateral edges and generally terminate in deep angular scars. (hinge fractures)

1.2213 Conchoidal scars (Fig. 8C) contract as the distance from the lateral edge increases and terminate in regular convex ridges a short distance from the lateral edge.

1.2214 Triangular scars (Fig. 8D) contract as the distance from the lateral edge increases and terminate at a point a short distance from the lateral edge.

1.2215 Expanding scars (Fig. 8E) expand as the distance from the lateral edge increases and generally terminate in an ill-defined edge.

1.2216 Angular expanding scars (Fig. 8F) expand rapidly from the point of origin and terminate quickly in deep transverse fracture scars.

1.2217 Ovate scars (Fig. 8G) exhibit convex lateral edges and terminate in regular convex scars.

1.222 Placement of scars

1.2221 Bifacial-bilateral—secondary scars present on both faces of both lateral edges.

1.2222 Bifacial-unilateral—secondary scars present on both faces of one lateral edge, and absent completely from either face of the opposing lateral edge.

1.2223 Unifacial-bilateral—secondary scars present on both lateral edges of a single face.

1.2224 Unifacial-unilateral—secondary scars present on one face and one edge only.

1.2225 Alternating faces-bilateral—secondary scars present on opposite faces at opposite edges.

1.223 Pattern of occurrence of secondary scars

1.2231 Continuous (Fig. 9A) secondary scars occur sequentially along the entire lateral edge.

1.2232 Discontinuous (Fig. 9B) secondary scars occur nonsequentially arranged as a function of the thickness irregularities resulting from primary flaking.

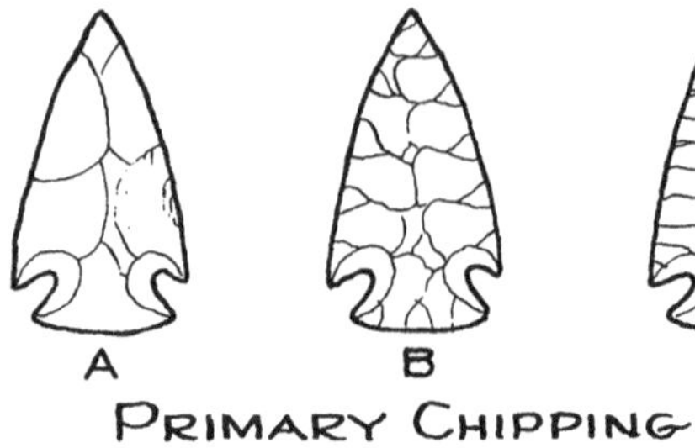

Figure 7

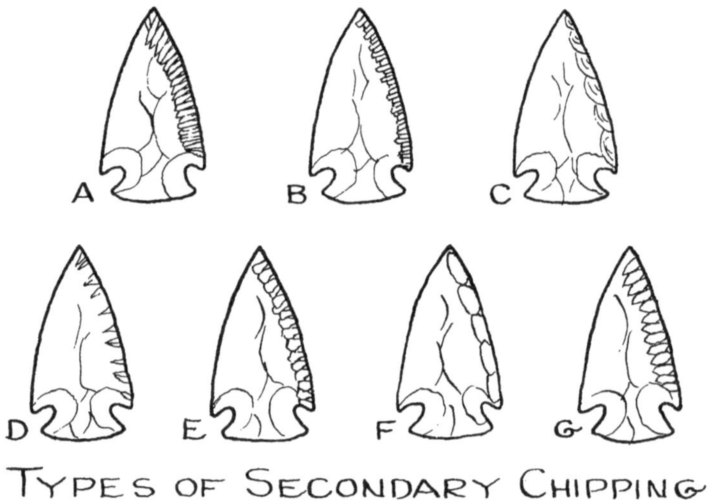

Figure 8

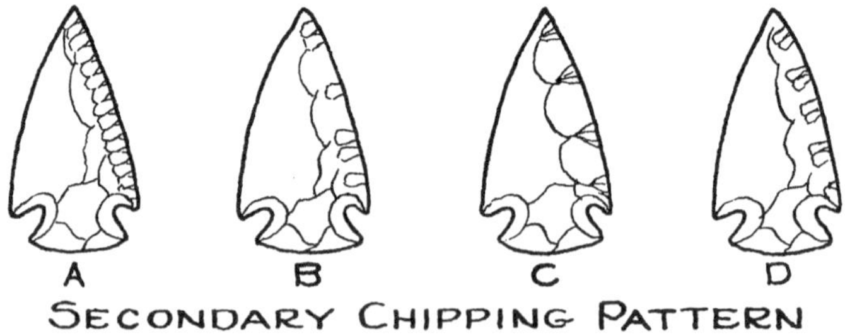

Figure 9

1.2233 Patterned scar clusters (Fig. 9C) secondary scars occur contiguously in clusters arranged at points where the ridges between primary scars approach the lateral edge.

1.2234 Fortuitous scar clusters (Fig. 9D) secondary scars occur as contiguous scar clusters arranged only with regard to shaping requirements, e.g. frequently at tip, or near proximal end of blade.

1.224 Use or tertiary flaking (specify placement)

1.2241 Crushing--steep shallow fracture scars lacking distinct definition. Produced by mashing the projectile point against an anvil. Scar types are of the angular expanding type.

1.2242 Nibbling—very dimunitive ovate scars produced generally by use on such materials as wood.

1.2243 Polish—occurs as a smoothing of the scar ridges frequently accompanied by a high gloss.

1.225 Form of the lateral edge

1.2251 Serration--chips removed so as to produce regular notches in the lateral edge of the piece.

1.2252 Even (chipped)—chips removed so as to produce a regular smooth definition of the lateral edge.

1.2253 Even (ground)—lateral edge ground to produce a regular smooth definition.

1.2254 Irregular—lateral edge lacks a clear even definition. Many scar notches occurring in a nonsymmetrical pattern.

1.226 Reworking—when the blade has been reshaped either as a function of breakage or remodification into another style of implement.

1.2261 Present

1.2262 Absent

2. Base element—The edge between the two points that serve to mark the transition between the proximal transverse edge and the lateral longitudinal edges of the projectile point.

2.1 Geometric attributes of the base

2.11 Outline

2.111 Straight base (Fig. 10A)—is defined as an edge which describes a straight line between the two defining points of the base.

2.112 Subconvex base (Fig 10B) is defined as an edge which describes a convex line between the two defining points of the base. The length of a perpendicular line constructed from the cord to the apex of the arc does not exceed one-fourth the length of the cord which is drawn through the defining points of the base.

2.113 Convex base (Fig. 10C)—is defined as an edge which describes a convex line between the two defining points of the base. The length of a perpendicular line constructed from the cord to the apex of the arc does exceed one-fourth the length of the cord which is drawn through the defining points of the base.

2.114 Subconcave base (Fig. 10D)—is defined as an edge which describes a convex line between the two defining points of the base. The length of a perpendicular line constructed from the cord to the apex of the arc does not exceed one-fourth the length of the cord which is drawn through the defining points of the base.

2.115 Concave base (Fig. 10E)—is defined as an edge which describes a concave line between the two defining points of the base. The length of a perpendicular line constructed from the cord to the apex of the arc does exceed one-fourth the length of the cord which is drawn through the defining points of the base.

2.116 Triangulo-concave base (Fig. 10F)—is defined as an edge which describes a bivectorally concave line between the two defining points of the base. The vectors are relatively straight and are connected by a short arc.

2.117 Bivectoral base (Fig. 10G)—is defined as the proximal segment of a tang which is described by the two lateral edges and a line drawn across the point from the proximal points of juncture of the haft element.

2.118 Trivectoral base (Fig. 10H)

2.12 Symmetry of the base

2.121 Transverse—A cord constructed between the defining points of the base would cross the longitudinal axis forming roughly a ninety degree angle.

2.122 Oblique—A cord constructed between the defining points of the base would cross the longitudinal axis forming complementary angles of roughly 112 degrees and 68 degrees.

2.123 Suboblique—A cord constructed between the defining points of the base would cross the longitudinal axis forming complementary angles of roughly 100 degrees and 80 degrees.

2.2 Technical attributes of the base

2.21 Orientation—This section describes the basal attributes that are indicative of the orientation of the flake nucleus to the form of the finished projectile point.

2.211 Distal orientation (Fig. 11A) the finished projectile is orientated to the original flake-blank so that the axis of percussion of the flake and the longitudinal axis of the projectile point are parallel.

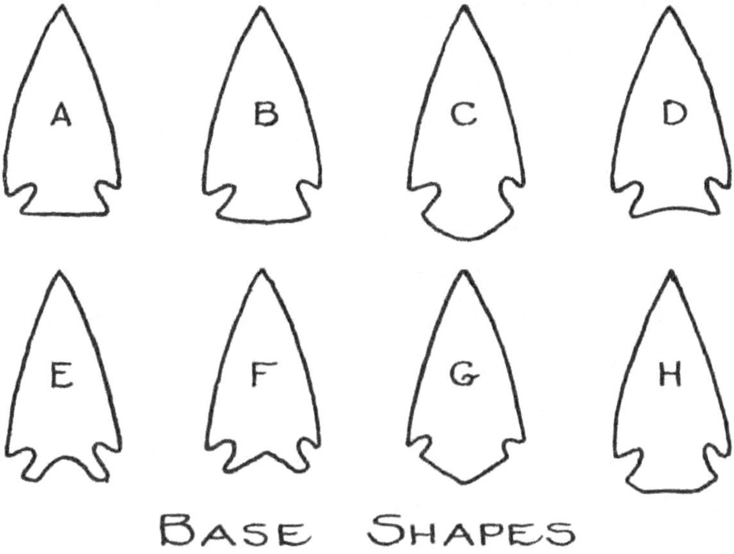

Figure 10

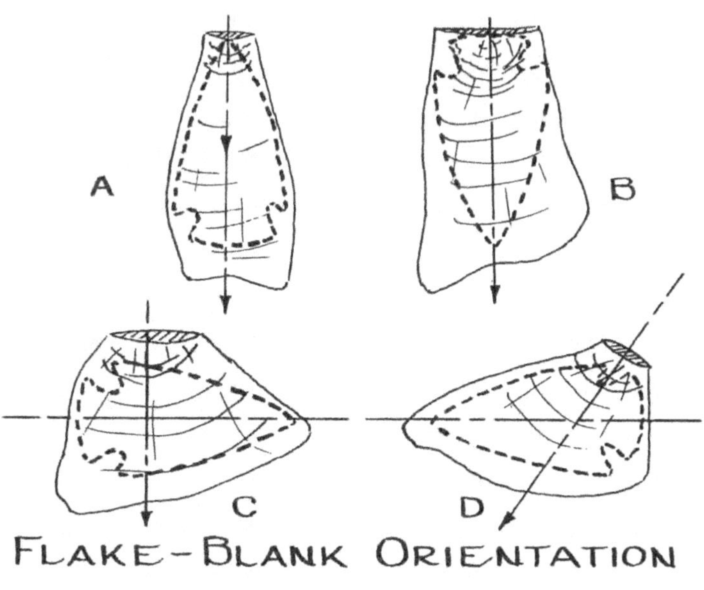

Figure 11

The nonbulbar end of the flake forms the base of the implement. This may take three general forms, (a) a hinge fracture, (b) a tapered edge, and (c) an abrupt end where the flake ran through the core leaving on the base a faceted or cortextual end.

2.212 Proximal orientation (Fig. 11B)—the finished projectile is orientated to the original flake blank so that the axis of percussion of the flake and the longitudinal axis of the projectile point are parallel. The positive bulb of percussion is at the base of the projectile.

2.213 Lateral orientation (Fig. 11C) the finished projectile is orientated to the original flake blank so that the axis of percussion of the flake crosses the longitudinal axis of the projectile at roughly a ninety degree angle.

2.214 Oblique orientation (Fig. 11D) the finished projectile is orientated to the original flake blank so that the axis of percussion crosses the longitudinal axis of the projectile at an oblique angle.

2.215 Obscured—the above identifying characteristics have been removed.

2.22 Preparation of the base

2.221 Unprepared base—lacks preparation specifically as a base, beyond the attributes of the flake from which the projectile point was made.

2.222 Striking platform preparation—a striking platform has been prepared at the base for the removal of longitudinal chips.

2.223 Thinning only—base prepared by thinning and shaping but utilizing the basal edge only as a striking platform.

2.23 Primary retouch—chip scars that are believed to be the initial alteration of the flake blank in achieving the desired shape are classified as primary retouching. All chip scars not obscured or partly obscured by others made in a distinctly different manner will be described as primary retouch flake scars.

2.231 Size and type of scars

2.2311 Longitudinal scars—lamellar or expanding scars originating at the base and paralleling the longitudinal axis of the finished artifact.

2.2312 Transverse scars—lamellar or expanding scars originating along the lateral edge of the tang.

2.2313 Transverse and longitudinal scars—scars of both the above types.

2.2314 Dimunitive scars—scars of either, ovate, triangular, conchoidal, or angular expanding type originating along the basal edge, exclusive of the above types.

2.232 Placement of scars

2.2321 Bifacial scars of mutually exclusive type—scars of either longitudinal, transverse, or dimunitive form occurring exclusively on opposite faces.

2.2322 Unifacial—primary scars occur on only one face.

2.2323 Bifacial—primary scars of the same type occur on both faces.

2.24 Secondary retouching scars—originate along the basal edge and tend to obscure the points of origin of primary retouching scars. They represent a separate step in the manufacturing process of the production of the finished artifact.

2.241 Placement of scars

2.2411 Absent

2.2412 Unifacial

2.2413 Bifacial

2.242 Pattern of occurrence

2.2421 Continuous—secondary scars occur sequentially along the entire basal edge.

2.2422 Discontinuous—secondary scars occur nonsequentially arranged as a function of the irregularities in thickness resulting from primary flaking.

2.2423 Patterned scar clusters—secondary scars occur contiguously in clusters arranged at points where the ridges between primary scars approach the lateral edge.

2.2424 Fortuitous scar clusters—secondary scars occur as contiguous scar clusters arranged only with regard to shaping requirements, e.g. frequently at the tip or around points of juncture.

2.25 Shape of basal edge

2.251 Even (chipped)—chips removed so as to produce a regular smooth definition of the basal edge.

2.252 Even (ground)—base ground to produce a regular smooth definition of the basal edge.

2.253 Irregular—basal edge lacks a clear even definition—many scar notches occurring in nonsymmetrical patterns.

3. Haft element—defined as the edges between any two points of interruption in the projected symmetry of the proximal segment of the projectile point. This includes the lateral edges or basal point as the case may be.

3.1 Geometrical attributes

3.12 Juncture—describes the points of transition between the haft elements and other elements or subelements of the projectile point.

3.121 Lateral-lateral juncture (Fig. 12A) both the proximal and distal points of juncture of the haft element are codefined by the lateral edges of the projectile point.

3.122 Lateral-basal juncture (Fig. 12B) the distal point is co-defined by the lateral edge of the projectile point and the proximal points are codefined by the basal edge.

3.123 Lateral-coincidental juncture (Fig. 12C) the distal point of the juncture is codefined by the lateral edge of the projectile and the proximal points are codefined by the basal edge. The latter point is coincidental with the projected point of juncture of the lateral edge and the basal edge.

3.124 Lateral-base defining juncture (Fig. 12D) the distal point of juncture is codefined by the lateral edge and the proximal point of juncture of the haft element serves to define the base. This is only possible in the case of specimens exhibiting no point of juncture between the projected symmetry of the basal edge and the lateral edge.

3.125 Coincidental-basal juncture (Fig. 12E) the distal point of juncture is codefined by the lateral edges but is coincidental with the point of juncture between the projected symmetry of the lateral edge and the base. The proximal point of juncture is codefined by the basal edge.

3.126 Basal-basal juncture (Fig. 12F) where both the distal and proximal points of juncture are codefined by the basal edge.

3.127 Lateral-axial juncture (Fig. 12G) the distal point of juncture is codefined by the lateral edge of the projectile and the proximal point is codefined by the other edge of the haft modification. This point of juncture is generally on the longitudinal axis of the projectile point.

3.128 Absent—no definable haft element present.

3.13 Configuration of the points of juncture

3.131 Distal point of juncture of the haft element

3.1311 Acute-angular--describes the point of juncture whose defining vectors form an acute angle and intersect at a point.

3.1312 Acute-circular—describes the point of juncture whose defining vectors form an acute angle and are articulated by a short arc.

3.1313 Obtuse-angular—describes the point of juncture whose defining vectors form an obtuse angle and intersect at a point.

3.1314 Obtuse-circular--describes the point of juncture whose defining vectors form an obtuse angle and are articulated by a short arc.

3.1315 Right-angled-angular—describes the point of juncture whose defining vectors form a right angle, and intersect at a point.

3.1316 Right-angled-circular—describes the point of juncture whose defining vectors form a right angle, and are articulated by a short arc.

3.132 Medial points of juncture of the haft element

3.1321 Internal angles formed at the points

3.13211 Absent (Fig. 13A)—there are no intervening points between the proximal and distal points of juncture of the haft element.

3.13212 Obtuse (Fig. 13B)—there is a single obtuse-angled point intervening between the defining points of the haft element.

3.13213 Biobtuse (Fig. 13C)—there are two obtuse-angled points intervening between the defining points of the haft element.

3.13214 Right-angled (Fig. 13D)—there is a single right-angled point intervening between the defining points of the haft element.

3.13215 Biright-angled (Fig. 13E)—there are two right-angled points intervening between the defining points to the haft element.

3.13216 Acute (Fig. 13F)—there is one acute-angled point intervening between the defining points of the haft element.

3.13217 Biacute (Fig. 13G)—there are two acute-angled points intervening between the defining points of the haft element.

3.13218 Obtuse-right-angled (Fig. 13H)—there are two medial points intervening between the defining points of the haft element. The distal medial point is obtuse and the proximal medial point is right-angled.

3.13218 Right-angled-obtuse (Fig. 13 I)—there are two medial points intervening between the defining points of the haft element. The distal medial point is right-angled and the proximal medial point is obtuse.

3.132110 Acute-obtuse—there are two medial points intervening between the defining points of the haft element. The distal medial point is acute and the proximal medial point is obtuse.

3.132111 Multijuncture Fig. 13J) describes the case where there are more than two points intervening between the distal and proximal defining points of the haft element.

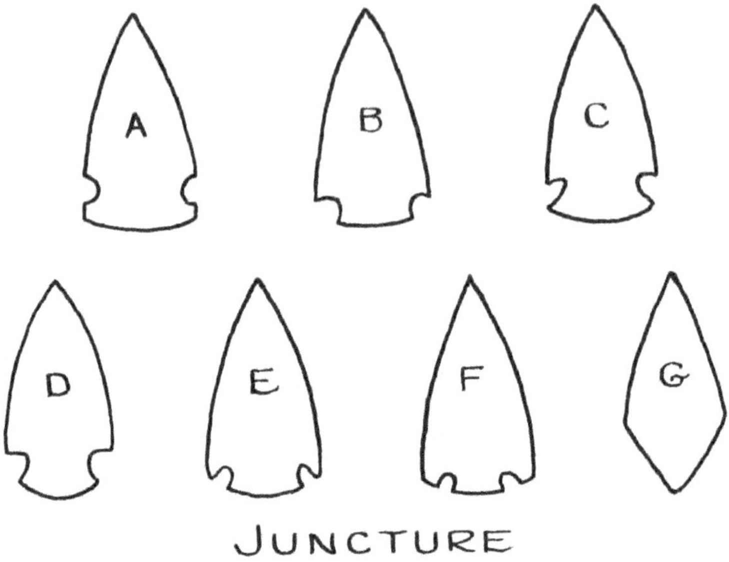

Figure 12

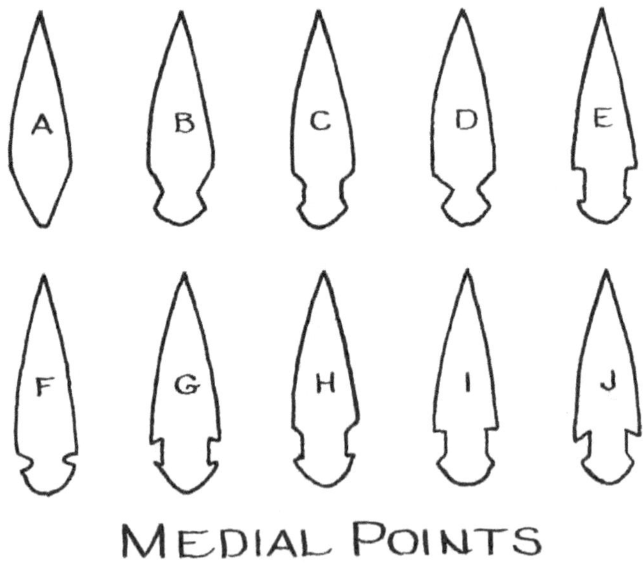

Figure 13

3.1322 Articulation of the vectors

3.13221 *Angular*—when the vectors intersect at a point.

3.13222 *Circular*—when the vectors are articulated by a short arc.

3.133 Proximal point of juncture of the haft element

3.1331 *Acute-angular*—describes the point of juncture where vectors form an acute angle and intersect at a point.

3.1332 *Acute-circular*—describes the point of juncture where vectors form an acute angle and are articulated by a short arc.

3.1333 *Obtuse-angular*—describes the point of juncture where vectors form an obtuse angle and intersect at a point.

3.1334 *Obtuse-circular*—describes the point of juncture where vectors form an obtuse angle and are articulated by a short arc.

3.1335 *Right-angled-angular*—describes the point of juncture where vectors form a right angle and intersect at a point.

3.1336 *Right-angled-circular*—describes the point of juncture where vectors form a right angle and are articulated by a short arc.

3.2 Technical attributes of the haft element

3.21 Type of retouch scars

3.211 Massive primary scars--scars extending more than half way across the projectile point. They have a modal width at the widest point at right angles to the longitudinal axis of the scar or greater than one-half inch.

3.212 Dimunitive primary scars--scars not extending more than half way across the projectile point. They have a modal width at the widest point at right angles to the longitudinal axis of the scar of less than one-half inch.

3.213 Massive primary scars and secondary scars—same as 3.211 above, but with the addition of secondary retouching obscuring the points of origin of the primary scars.

3.214 Dimunitive primary scars and secondary scars—same as 3.212 above but with the addition of secondary retouching obscuring the points of origin of the primary scars.

3.22 Placement of haft element scars

3.221 Obscuring lateral and basal originating scars—chips removed in the production of the haft element obscure chip scars from previously removed chips originating at both the lateral edges and the basal edge.

3.222 Obscuring laterally originating scars only—chips removed in the production of the haft element obscure chip scars from previously removed chips originating on the lateral edge only.

3.223 Obscuring basally originating scars only—chips removed in the production of the haft element obscure chip scars from previously removed chips originating on the basal edge only.

3.224 None—chips removed in the production of the haft element do not obscure chip scars originating on any other edge.

3.225 Haft element scars obscured by basally originating scars—chips removed in the production of the haft element are obscured by chip scars originating on the basal edge.

3.226 Haft element scars obscured by laterally originating scars—chips removed in the production of the haft element are obscured by chip scars originating on the lateral edge.

3.227 Haft element scars obscured by both laterally and basally originating scars—chips removed in the production of the haft element are obscured by chip scars originating from both the lateral and basal edges.

3.23 Grinding

3.231 Present inside the haft element

3.232 Absent inside the haft element

3.24 Symmetry of the haft element refers to whether or not both of the haft elements are formally alike. The described side is the side considered to be the most difficult to chip.

3.241 Symmetrical

3.242 Asymmetrical

4. Subelements

4.1 Shoulder—geometrical form

4.11 Presence or absence of shoulder and/or barb

4.111 Shoulder absent

4.112 Barbed—the distal point of juncture of the haft element is more proximal than the distal medial point of the haft element.

4.113 Nonbarbed—the distal point of juncture of the haft element is more distal than is the distal medial point of the haft element.

4.12 Outline of the shoulder segment

4.121 Straight—the edge between the distal medial point and the distal point of juncture of the haft element describes a straight line.

4.122 Concave—the edge between the distal medial point and the distal point of juncture of the haft element describes a concave line.

4.123 Convex—the edge between the distal medial point and the distal point of juncture of the haft element describes a convex line.

4.2 Modified Subelement of the tang

4.21 Geometrical form of the tang

4.211 Expanding—the edge is uninterrupted and expands proximally away from the longitudinal axis of the specimen.

4.212 Contracting—the edge is uninterrupted and contracts proximally toward the longitudinal axis of the specimen.

4.213 Parallel—the edge is uninterrupted and extends proximally paralleling the longitudinal axis of the specimen.

4.214 Parallel-expanding—the edge is interrupted by a proximal medial point and the edge between the medial points parallels the longitudinal axis of the specimen but the edge from the proximal medial point to the proximal lateral point is expanding proximally away from the longitudinal axis of the specimen.

4.215 Biexpanding—the edge is interrupted by the proximal medial point but both edges of the element expand differentially away from the longitudinal axis of the specimen.

4.216 Contracting-expanding--the edge is interrupted by the proximal medial point and the edge between the medial points is contracting proximally toward the longitudinal axis but the edge between the proximal medial point and the proximal lateral point is expanding proximally away from the longitudinal axis of the specimen.

4.22 Outline—the most proximal segment only

4.221 Straight—an edge defined by the most proximal medial point and the proximal point of juncture of the haft element that describes a straight line.

4.222 Convex—an edge defined by the most proximal medial point and the proximal point of juncture of the haft element that describes a convex line.

4.223 Concave—an edge defined by the most proximal medial point and the proximal point of juncture of the haft element that describes a concave line.

4.3 Unmodified subelement of the tang—those edges between the proximal point of juncture of the haft element and the point of juncture between the lateral and basal edges of the specimen.

4.31 Presence and form of articulation

4.311 Absent—absence of any extension of the lateral blade edge below the proximal point of juncture of the haft element.

4.312 Lateral-basal juncture—the proximal point of juncture is of unmodified subelement of the tang is co-defined by the basal edge.

4.313 Lateral-lateral juncture—the proximal point of juncture of the unmodified subelement of the tang is co-defined by the corresponding lateral edge of the unmodified subelement of the tang.

4.32 Symmetry of the tang segment

4.321 Contracting—the lateral edges of the unmodified subelement of the tang contract proximally toward the longitudinal axis of the specimen.

4.322 Expanding—the lateral edges of the unmodified subelement of the tang expand proximally away from the longitudinal axis of the specimen.

4.323 Parallel—the lateral edges of the unmodified subelement of the tang parallel the longitudinal axis of the specimen.

4.33 Grinding

4.331 Present

4.332 Absent

5. Point of maximum thickness

5.1 Longitudinal dimension

5.11 Proximal placement--point of maximum thickness occurs at a point located proximally of the distal point of juncture of the haft element.

5.12 Medial placement—point of maximum thickness occurs at a point located opposite the distal point of juncture of the haft element or more distally up to one-third the length of the blade.

5.13 Distal placement—point of maximum thickness occurs at a point located on the blade in the most distal two-thirds of the blade length.

5.2 Lateral dimension

5.21 Medial placement--point of maximum thickness occurs along the longitudinal axis of the specimen.

5.22 Lateral placement—point of maximum thickness occurs along the most lateral two-thirds of the area between the longitudinal axis and the lateral edge of the specimen.

6. Metrical attributes

Aside from the discrete attributes defined in the previous section it has been found that certain measurements are necessary to adequately describe a projectile point. The continuous attributes, in some cases, are restatements in metrical terms of some of the discrete attributes while in others they are mutually exclusive of the discrete attributes.

6.1 Widths

6.11 Width of base—this measurement is taken between the two defining points of juncture for the base. In the case of bivectoral bases this measurement is not applicable.

6.12 Width of tang—this measurement is taken between the two symmetrically opposing medial points of the haft element. The two medial points closest to the longitudinal axis of the specimen. In cases where medial points are not present this measurement is not applicable.

6.13 Width at shoulder—this measurement is taken between the two distal points of juncture of the haft element. In cases where there is no definable haft element this measurement is not applicable.

6.14 Point of maximum width—if the axis of maximum width is not located at any of the above areas, it will be measured and its location recorded.

6.2 Lengths

6.21 Axial length—this measurement is taken on the longitudinal axis of the specimen between the tip and the basal edge.

6.22 Tang length—this measurement is taken on the longitudinal axis of the specimen. It is made between the point where the longitudinal axis crosses the most proximal transverse edge of the specimen and a constructed line between the two most distal points of the haft element regardless of whether the points mentioned correspond to a point of juncture or not.

6.23 Blade length—this measurement is taken on the longitudinal axis of the specimen. It is made between the tip of the specimen and the point where the longitudinal axis crosses a line constructed between the two distal points of juncture of the haft element.

6.24 Notch length—this measurement is taken between the proximal and distal points of juncture of the haft element.

6.3 Thickness—taken at point of maximum thickness

6.4 Measures of symmetry

6.41 Index of the angle of basal orientation—this is the measurement of the orientation of the base with respect to the longitudinal axis of the specimen. It is taken by aligning the base of the specimen parallel and adjacent to the intersection of a 90 degree angle. A measurement of the distance of the tip of the specimen from the vertical arm of the right angle is made. The specimen is always aligned so that the maximum distance from the vertical arm can be measured. This measurement is then corrected by subtracting one-half of the basal width which then gives the observation in units from the longitudinal axis of the specimen. This value is further corrected by dividing the observed length into a standard (4.0 cm) and multiplying the result of step one by the result of step two [(observed measure—one-half of basal width) x (observed length—standard length)]. The latter correction is necessary because of a positive correlation between the length of the specimen and the distance away from the arm of a right angle regardless of the angle of basal orientation. Table I presents the angles represented by the various indexes of the angle of basal orientation.

Table I

Observed Index (In Centimeters)	Angle Indicated
.00 -.06 cm.	91 degrees
.065-.13 cm.	92 degrees
.135-.18 cm.	93 degrees
.185-.25 cm.	94 degrees
.255-.32 cm.	95 degrees
.325-.39 cm.	96 degrees
.395-.46 cm.	97 degrees
.465-.53 cm.	98 degrees
.535-.61 cm.	99 degrees
.615-.69 cm.	100 degrees
.695-.76 cm.	101 degrees
.765-.84 cm.	102 degrees
.845-.92 cm.	103 degrees
.925-.99 cm.	104 degrees
.995-1.07 cm.	105 degrees
1.075-1.15 cm.	106 degrees

DISCUSSION

It has been found that the utilization of the attribute list proposed here has served to standardize terminology not only with respect to the analysis and description of chipped stone projectile points but the attribute classes have been subsequently reapplied in speaking about copper forms, chipped stone artifacts of other forms and ground stone material. Aside from the obvious advantages accruing from a standardized set of descriptive terms the attribute list lends itself for use with and was designed in terms of a punch-card system for recording data. The use of edge punch cards for recording data has a number of advantages, (1) once the code is worked out data can be recorded much faster than with systems utilizing tables, and other means, (2) data once on punch cards can be organized in innumerable ways without repetition in transcription, (3) the cards lend themselves to a very efficient filing system in which data for comparative purposes can be amassed. In addition to the data which is punched on a card other information can be put on the face of the card, that is, a photograph of the specimen, bibliographic references, pertinent information concerning associated materials, age of the specimen, and the metrical attributes. This is all recorded in addition to the punched-in information coded according to the attribute list presented here. Over six hundred such cards are now in the files of the Museum of Anthropology at The University of Michigan representing materials which have been found in tight cultural association, dated specimens, and examples of defined types. Such a file allows quick, efficient, and meaningful comparisons to be made between materials that are actually housed in institutions of at least eight states.

Aside from the advantages mentioned, the use of a formal attribute list forces the analyst to be consistent in making comparisons and aids in making systematic observations.

The attribute list presented here is not considered as a finished, and therefore, a static tool. It is flexible and can be modified to serve a number of needs. There is no claim that the list is complete nor adequate for describing all the culturally significant attributes of all notched projectile point forms. What is claimed, however, is that it represents an objective, methodologically useful, and comprehensive tool for the analysis of projectile points.

www.ingramcontent.com/pod-product-compliance
Lightning Source LLC
LaVergne TN
LVHW050021250826
846302LV00008B/43